Home Advantage:
Social Class and Parental Intervention
in Elementary Education

Education Policy Perspectives

General Editor: **Professor Ivor Goodson,** Faculty of Education,
University of Western Ontario, London,
Canada N6G 1G7

Education policy analysis has long been a neglected area in the United Kingdom and, to some extent, in the USA and Australia. The result has been a profound gap between the study of education and the formulation of education policy. For practitioners such a lack of analysis of the new policy initiatives has worrying implications particularly at such a time of policy flux and change. Education policy has, in recent years, been a matter for intense political debate — the political and public interest in the working of the system has come at the same time as the consensus on education policy has been broken by the advent of the 'New Right'. As never before the political parties and pressure groups differ in their articulated policies and prescriptions for the education sector. Critical thinking about these developments is clearly necessary.

This series aims to fill the academic gap, to reflect the politicalization of education, and to provide the practitioners with the analysis for informed implementation of policies that they will need. It will offer studies in broad areas of policy studies. Beside the general section it will offer a particular focus in the following areas: School organization and improvement (David Reynolds, *University College, Cardiff, UK*): Social analysis (Professor Philip Wexler, *University of Rochester, USA*); Policy studies and evaluation (Professor Ernest House, *University of Colorado-Boulder, USA*).

Social Analysis Series
Editor: Professor Philip Wexler, University of Rochester, USA

A new genre of work has begun to appear that embodies a critical social vantage point. This work is both empirical and practical in style and purpose. The study of discourse is central in this new genre of critical social analysis, and there is also a return to careful, original historical work and to detailed qualitative research that is theoretically motivated. The Social Analysis series represents diversity in empirical topics, styles of work and practical interests. The disappearing 'social' is reasserted in these modern, empirical and theoretical studies.

Symbolizing Society:
Stories, Rites and Structure in a Catholic High School
Nancy Lesko

Home Advantage:
Social Class and Parental Intervention in Elementary Education
Annette Lareau

Home Advantage:
Social Class and Parental Intervention in Elementary Education

Annette Lareau

 The Falmer Press
(A Member of the Taylor & Francis Group)
London · New York · Philadelphia

UK   The Falmer Press, Falmer House, Barcombe, Lewes, East Sussex, BN8 5DL

USA   The Falmer Press, Taylor & Francis Inc., 242 Cherry Street, Philadelphia, PA 19106–1906

First published in 1989

British Library Cataloguing in Publication Data
Lareau, Annette
    Home advantage: social class and parental intervention in
elementary education.
    1. Great Britain. Education. Sociological perspectives
    I. Title
    370.19'09

ISBN 1-85000-312-2
ISBN 1-85000-317-3 (pbk.)

Library of Congress Cataloging in Publication Data
Lareau, Annette.
    Home advantage: social class and parental intervention in
elementary education/Annette Lareau.
    p.   cm. — (Education policy perspectives. Social analysis
series)
    Bibliography: p.
    Includes index.
    ISBN 1-85000-312-2. — ISBN 1-85000-317-3 (pbk.)
    1. Home and school — United States.   2. Social classes —
United States.   3. Education — United States — Parent
participation.   4. Education, Elementary — Research — United
States. I. Title. II. Series.
LC225.3.L37 1989
370. 19—dc20

Typeset by Imago Publishing Ltd.
Printed and bound in Great Britain by

Contents

3-26-90 ED/AL

For my parents,
Joe and Anne Lareau,
and for
Trishie Houck

Acknowledgements

Given the large amount of time writers spend alone at their craft, some might be tempted to conclude that the process of creating a book is fundamentally an individual experience. It is not. In researching and writing this manuscript I have benefited greatly from the assistance and wisdom of others.

This book began as a doctoral dissertation in the Department of Sociology at the University of California, Berkeley. I am very grateful to Troy Duster for all of his assistance. Arlie Hochschild and Charles Benson also were especially helpful. While at Berkeley I struggled with the problem of moving from a description of social events to an analysis and interpretation of these events. As I detail in the methodological appendix, this process of developing a conceptual analysis was neither linear nor smooth. I remain indebted to Michael Burawoy for his help in this area, especially his persistence in posing the question 'So what?' Others were also helpful, most notably John Ogbu, Karen Garrett, and Keith Osajima.

After leaving Berkeley, I was supported by a NIMH Post-Doctoral Fellowship in the Research and Training Program in Organizations and Mental Health, Stanford University, directed by W. Richard Scott. I am particularly grateful to Milbrey McLaughlin for giving me a clearer sense of what qualitative research is — and is not — and a new understanding of data analysis in qualitative work.

I probably would have never written this book if it hadn't been for Philip Wexler. He offered me the opportunity and, more importantly, he provided sage advice throughout. After beginning the project I undertook a new analysis of the data and completely rewrote the manuscript. This took time; despite my slow pace, he was always supportive. I am indebted to him also for his encouragement to study the linkages between social institutions.

Aaron Cicourel played an important role throughout the project. From the beginning his criticisms improved the work. I have found him to be a source of invaluable suggestions. I am indebted also to him and to Hugh Mehan for arranging office space during the summer of 1987 at the Department of

Sociology, University of California, San Diego, and for making me feel welcome during my stay.

At Southern Illinois University at Carbondale my department chair, Lon Shelby, supported the research in many ways, including arranging for the transcription of interview tapes. I appreciate Ruth Smith's coordination of this, as well as the work of Tamara Davis, Sara Eynon, Becky Frerker, Ruth Perk, and Deanna Yocum. Laura Cates has been an enormous help; her meticulous word processing is especially appreciated.

The book benefited from the advice of colleagues. Nicole Biggart, George McClure, Hugh Mehan, Cathy Vigran, and Julia Wrigley made detailed comments on the entire manuscript. Pierre Bourdieu graciously commented on an earlier version of this project. Samuel Kaplan has been a valuable source of criticism as we have argued about the contribution cultural capital can make to sociology. I owe a special debt to Katherine Mooney. Her fastidious editing of the draft manuscript greatly improved the book. For comments on portions of the manuscript I am grateful to Deirdre Boden, Marlis Buchmann, Thomas Burger, Michael Burawoy, David Fetterman, Michéle Lamont, Mary Metz, Kathryn Ward, and Amy Wharton. Of course I remain solely responsible for any errors or omissions.

Finally, I am very grateful to the parents, children, and school staff members at 'Colton' and 'Prescott' schools. They invited me into their classrooms and homes and with patience and good cheer answered my seemingly endless questions. Many of them took a special interest in the project; they included me in school events and shared materials that they thought would be of interest. Although to protect their confidentiality I cannot thank them by name, I remain deeply appreciative of their help.

1 Social Class and Parent Involvement in Schooling

In his autobiography *Making It*, Norman Podhoretz describes the journey he made in his life — 'one of the longest journeys in the world' — from the Bronx to Manhattan. Prodded by his high school teacher to apply for admission to college, Podhoretz, the son of working-class parents, won a scholarship to Columbia and ultimately became renowned as the editor of a national magazine. But success had its price. As he became more comfortable in the world of Columbia his Brownsville life began to appear shabby. As Podhoretz says:

> I knew that the neighborhood voices were beginning to sound coarse and raucous; I knew that our apartment was beginning to look tasteless and tawdry; I knew that the girls [I was] in quest of . . . were beginning to strike me as too elaborately made up, too shrill in their laughter, too crude in their dress (Podhoretz 1967:51).

Podhoretz's journey was shaped by his high school teacher, who had systematically tried to break him of many of the behaviors he had learned in his working-class home. Using stinging criticism of his satin jacket, his table manners, his language, and his demeanor, she sought to teach him the mannerisms of 'cultivated people', in the hope that these alterations would ease his entrance into the upper-middle-class world that she so desperately wanted for him.

In the end, Podhoretz left behind his working-class roots and joined what he called 'a foreign country':

> The country is sometimes called the upper-middle-class; and indeed I am a member of that class, less by virtue of my income than by virtue of the way my speech is accented, the way I dress, the way I furnish my home, the way I entertain and am entertained, the way I educate my children — the way, quite simply, I look and I live.

This view, that class membership has a powerful influence on family life and on children's lives outside the home, is not shared by some sociologists. Swayed by the ideology of classlessness in American society, the reluctance of Americans to define themselves as working-class or upper-class, and the lack of dramatic class divisions in political debates, some sociologists have argued that attention to social class membership does not significantly enhance our explanatory powers.[1]

Others have conceded that social class may influence dynamics within the home, but they maintain that social institutions outside the home are indifferent to class membership. In the area of schooling for example, some note the persistent failure of sociologists to find powerful evidence of class discrimination in school practices, after taking into consideration children's ability. Indeed status attainment studies have concluded that the impact of socio-economic status is on the values and educational aspirations which children bring to the educational process. These in turn influence educational achievement. Researchers have insisted that, with minor exceptions, focusing on social class (independent of aspirations or children's ability) does not significantly add to our understanding of the dynamics within the classroom or the school. They consider children's ability, aspirations, and social-psychological profile to be more revealing areas of investigation.[2]

In this book, I challenge the position that social class is of only modest and indirect significance in shaping children's lives in schools. I argue that social class (independent of ability) does affect schooling. Teachers ask for parent involvement; social class shapes the resources which parents have at their disposal to comply with teachers' requests for assistance.[3]

Indeed this book suggests that researchers have made a fundamental mistake in their conceptualization of the problem: they have limited their focus to experiences within a given social institution — looking at family life *or* school life. Parents do not automatically give up trying to control their children's lives when their children walk out of the front door, so what researchers need to examine are inter-institutional linkages. While working-class men have little autonomy on the job, at the end of the shift, their work is over. Upper-middle-class men, however, frequently carry their work into their family's life, as they travel overnight, work at home on weekends, and entertain co-workers and business associates as part of the standards for occupational advancement. Social class differences in family involvement in schooling appear to mirror these patterns in the amount of separation between work and home in working-class and upper-middle-class families. In *Middletown*, the Lynds (1929) spoke of the 'long arm of the job' in shaping family life. This research suggests that this 'long arm' may be longer than previously thought, extending beyond the home to influence dynamics in other social institutions.

Social Class and Parent Involvement in Schooling

Considerable attention has been devoted to parent involvement in schooling at the elementary level.[4] Researchers usually define parent involvement as preparing children for school (for example, teaching children the alphabet; talking and reading to children to promote language development), attending school events (for example, parent-teacher conferences), and fulfilling any requests teachers make of parents (for example, to play word games with their children at home). Others include in the definition providing children a place to do homework and ensuring the completion of homework (Epstein 1987; Epstein and Becker 1982; Hoover-Dempsey *et al.* 1987; and Van Galen 1987). Researchers argue that this kind of parent involvement improves school performance, as measured in reading scores or standardized test scores (Epstein 1988; Stevenson and Baker 1987; Henderson 1981).[5]

Although parent involvement is positively linked to school success, many parents are not as involved in schooling as teachers would like. This lack of involvement is not random: social class has a powerful influence on parent involvement patterns. For example, between forty to sixty per cent of working-class and lower-class parents fail to attend parent-teacher conferences. For middle-class parents these figures are nearly halved, i.e., about twenty to thirty per cent (Lightfoot 1978; Ogbu 1974; McPherson 1972; Van Galen 1987). In the areas of promoting verbal development, reading to children, taking children to the library, attending school events, enrolling children in summer school, and making complaints to the principal, middle-class parents consistently take a more active role in schooling than do their working-class and lower-class counterparts (Baker and Stevenson 1986; Heath 1983; Heyns 1978; Medrich *et al.* 1980; Stevenson and Baker 1987; Wilcox 1978).[6]

Many teachers work to increase parent involvement in schooling. Surveys of teachers show that most want parent involvement and ask for it, particularly in the early years of schooling (Gallup 1985). A few teachers are 'teacher leaders' and are particularly vigorous in requesting parent support (Becker and Epstein 1982), but almost all teachers in elementary school encourage parent involvement and many are discouraged by what they consider insufficient parent participation. In fact, in polls of teachers the lack of parent involvement is consistently named as one of the most important problems facing the public schools. And about one sixth of former teachers polled reported that they left the profession because of lack of community and parent support (Harris 1985a; 1985b).

Researchers have joined teachers in the efforts to develop and share strategies for increasing parent involvement. Indeed the policy implications of parent involvement in schooling have now come to dominate the research agenda. Using his research on high schools, James Coleman (Coleman 1987; Coleman and Hoffer 1987) has argued that parent involvement in the community reduces drop-out rates and improves school performance. He urges other schools to try to emulate this successful use of what he calls 'social capital'. Epstein (1986; 1987) has also called for increased parent involvement in schooling. Other social scientists, in providing models of home–school relations, have advocated strategies for raising the level of parents' involvement (Walberg 1986; Rich 1986; Clark 1983).

In championing the virtues of parent involvement in schooling, and promoting techniques for increasing it, researchers have neglected the more basic question of why social class so affects parent involvement. Every important social science study of family–school relations in the last two decades has noted class differences in parent–school relations, but none has systematically examined why they persist. Rather these works have focused on effective strategies for increasing parent involvement (Litwack and Meyer 1974; Leichter 1974; Epstein and Becker 1982; Clark 1983).[7] In a few instances researchers have studied the enduring tensions between the particularistic concerns of parents and the universalistic concerns of teachers (Lightfoot 1978; McPherson 1972).

As a result the current research approach to parent involvement in schooling is skewed. There is very good evidence that the character of child rearing has changed radically through history. There is also very good evidence that the curriculum, classroom goals, and organization and structure of schooling have also changed radically. This means that historically and cross-culturally a wide variety of home–school relationships are possible. Rather than continuing to take one type of home–school relationship as an ideal, sociologists should acknowledge and investigate this variety. To do so would entail a careful examination of social class differences in family–school relationships; such investigations would not immediately dismiss one set of behaviors as undesirable and seek to convert a wide range of behaviors by families into a uniform (and historically specific) style of interaction.

Biography and Social Structure

Some of the weaknesses in the research on family–school relationships are linked to unique problems in the study of education. Other problems, however, reflect enduring weaknesses in sociological models of the influence of social stratification on individual biographies. In documenting how social class influences social life, researchers often have presented correlations between social class and life experiences (Bielby 1981; Sewell and Hauser 1980). This provides statistical probabilities, the aggregated likelihood of social class influencing educational and occupational mobility. But statistical models contain many 'empty places' with no indication of how particular individuals will fill these places (Cicourel and Mehan 1985). Nor is it clear under what circumstances social class provides children with a powerful advantage, and under what circumstances the advantage is trivial or non-existent.

In addition many conceptual models focus on the influence of values on behavior. They suggest, explicitly and implicitly, that social class has a powerful influence on life chances because it influences the values that parents hold and pass on to their children. This assumption is overly narrow because it fails to recognize that, in addition to values, social class provides individuals with resources which they can effectively marshall in the social sorting process (Bourdieu 1977; 1984; Collins 1979; Swidler 1986).

In recent years a growing number of scholars have looked at the cultural patterns associated with social class and have tried to analyze how these patterns provide advantages in social institutions. French sociologist Pierre Bourdieu

(1977a; 1977b; 1984; 1987), for example, has argued that social class alters the cultural resources — including language and knowledge of art, music, and other cultural experiences — that individuals have access to in their home environment. He suggests that family life provides resources ('capital') which yield important social profits (Bourdieu 1977a; 1984).[8] Similarly Ann Swidler has conceptualized culture as a:

> ... tool-kit of symbols, rituals, and world-views, which people may use in varying configurations to solve different kinds of problems (Swidler, 1986, p. 273).

In focusing on the strategies individuals employ to improve their social positions, these social scientists offer a portrait of the individualized actor as engaged in creating his/her biography within specific social structural constraints.

Empirical work using Bourdieu's concept of cultural capital has begun to appear (Blau 1986; Cookson and Persell 1985; DiMaggio 1982; DiMaggio and Mohr 1985; Teachman 1987; De Graaf 1986; Useem and Karabel 1986). This research suggests that exposure to high status cultural resources is associated with educational success. Introducing cultural resources into the models usually, but not always, improves upon existing models of the linkage between social class and educational and social outcomes (DiMaggio and Mohr 1985; Robinson and Garnier 1985; Teachman 1987).

While important, this research has often failed to exploit the full potential of the concept of cultural capital because it focuses on individuals, showing, for example, the association between cultural consumption and educational performance. Individualistic analyses fail to demonstrate the standards of social institutions which, according to the concept, are infused with the family life and experiences of the privileged social classes. Nor does it show how an individual's class position provides advantages (i.e., resources) that help him/her comply with the standards of the institution. It is clear that taking art lessons and going to museums influences grades and college aspirations; it is less clear why it provides this advantage. Although the concept of cultural capital has the potential to show how social class differences in family life can help or hinder individuals in their efforts to meet the standards of school and go on to gain acceptance in college, empirical research has not demonstrated this potential.

Moreover, although acknowledging that social institutions do not operate in a vacuum, most researchers ignore the linkages among social institutions. Structural-functionalism provides a coherent theoretical model of these inter-institutional linkages, but more recent sociological research has failed — conceptually and empirically — to pursue these issues. Instead researchers have focused on dynamics within social institutions, or they have provided very general assertions about the 'congruence' or 'correspondence' between social institutions. For example, Alexander and colleagues correctly point out that researchers have had trouble looking at the influences of parents and teachers on one another (Alexander *et al.* 1987a). Their own research examines the standards of 'deportment', notably the degree to which parents and teachers share child rearing values (and the impact of this on school performance). While useful, their research does not take up the degree to which parents (or teachers) try to bring themselves into alignment with the standards of another institution. Nor does it investigate whether parents try to alter the school experience of children. Similarly, Bowles and Gintis (1976) articulated a 'correspondence theory' suggesting that classroom dynamics vary according to class differences in authority patterns, but presumed, rather than demonstrated, social class differences in the interactions between parents and teachers over the curriculum.[9]

Thus the conceptualization of the variation in linkages among social institutions — in the intensity, depth, and quality of these linkages — has been weak. These analyses fail to capture the notion of a family — school *linkage* with — to use an analogy–a small, rarely used pathway, in one community or a large, well-traveled, pathway in another. Researchers need to study the size, nature, and purpose of these home–school 'roads', as well as the number of travelers using them. Having the company of many others may shape the nature of the journey; by focusing primarily on individual travelers researchers have missed these possibilities.

Values, Discrimination, and Cultural Capital

Why does social class have such an important influence on parent involvement in schooling? At issue here is not the absolute level of parent involvement, but rather the gap between the relatively high level of involvement of middle-class and upper-middle-class parents and the relatively low level of involvement of working-class and lower-class parents. Three major intellectual positions have emerged.

Parents' values are a frequent, although often implicit explanation of why social class influences parent involvement in schooling. For example, in a study of teachers that revealed that parents' social class influenced their attendance at conferences and their willingness to work in the classroom, the authors considered a number of explanations:

> Higher SES [socio-economic status] parents, realizing the importance of education *and* feeling confident of their right to be involved in the school, may take a more active role than their lower SES counterparts in supporting school programs (Hoover–Dempsey, *et al.* 1987, emphasis in the original).

In suggesting that parents of high socio-economic position 'realize the importance of education', the authors are implying that parents of lower socio-economic status do not 'realize the importance of education'. This comes quite close to the notion of values, which is often defined as a 'standard of desirability', (Kohn 1977) but it is not an explicit theory of values.

The 'Wisconsin Model' (Sewell and Hauser 1980) is more explicit. The researchers argue that socio-economic status influences parents' values; these, in turn, influence children's educational aspirations. According to the model, social class influences children's performance by shaping children's educational goals and motivations. Earlier work, using the 'culture of poverty' perspective, attributed the lower levels of parent involvement in schooling to the lower value which parents placed on education (Deutsch 1967a; 1967b; Reissman 1962; Strodbeck 1958; 1965).

Other studies have traced unequal levels of parent involvement back to the educational institutions themselves. Some researchers accuse schools of institutional discrimination, claiming that they make middle-class families feel more welcome than working-class or lower-class families (Lightfoot 1978; Ogbu 1974). Connell and colleagues, for example, argue that while ruling-class families treat teachers as workers, working-class parents are 'frozen out' of schools (Connell *et al.* 1982).[10] There are few thorough studies of the interactions between parents and teachers, but the studies suggest a relatively high level of uniformity among teachers in their reports of requests for parent involvement. In addition teachers report making more — not fewer — requests for parent involvement to working-class and lower-class parents than they do to middle- and upper-middle-class parents (Epstein 1986; Hoover-Dempsey 1987). This relatively high quantity of interaction does not, of course, address the quality of interaction. It is possible that teachers (who are by definition middle-class) may be less comfortable, less friendly, and less talkative with lower-class and working-class clients.

Other researchers have looked at the impact of parent involvement on organizational dynamics (Corwin and Wagenaar 1976; Epstein 1987). Epstein, for example, has shown that within schools some teachers are 'leaders' in recruiting parent involvement (Epstein and Becker 1982; Becker and Epstein 1982). These teachers are more successful in getting parents to become involved, regardless of social class, and are also less likely than other teachers to use social class as an explanation for why parents are not involved. Instead they attribute parent involvement patterns to the strategies they did, or did not, use throughout that particular academic year.[11]

Thus organizational variations at the school site can influence teachers' and students' school experiences. Overall, however there is considerable uniformity in the requests teachers (particularly teachers in first grade) make for parent involvement, while there is substantial variation by social class in parents' responses. Even when they are interacting with the same teacher at the same school, working-class parents are less likely to attend school events than are middle-class parents (McPherson 1972). Looking at organizational dynamics can add to our understanding of this difference, but such an approach is clearly inadequate as a model of why class differences in parent involvement persist.

A third perspective for understanding varying levels of parent involvement in schooling draws on Bourdieu's work and his concept of cultural capital. Bourdieu (1977a; 1977b; Bourdieu and Passeron 1977) argues that schools draw unevenly on the social and cultural resources in the society. For example, schools use particular linguistic structures, authority patterns, and types of curricula; children of higher socio-economic standing enter school already familiar with these social arrangements. Bourdieu maintains that the cultural experiences in the home differentially facilitate children's adjustment to school and academic achievement. This transforms elements of family life, or cultural resources, into what he calls cultural capital.

This perspective emphasizes the importance of the structure of the school and of family life and the dispositions of individuals (what Bourdieu calls 'habitus') in understanding the different levels of parent participation in schooling. The standards of the school are not neutral; their requests for parent involvement may be laden with the cultural experiences of intellectual and economic elites. Bourdieu does not examine the question of parent involvement in schooling, but his analysis points to the importance of class and class cultures in facilitating or impeding parents' negotiation of the process of schooling.

Social Class and Family–School Relationships

This book explores how and why social class influences parent involvement in schooling. The research looks at a specific form of parent involvement: parents' role in their children's education, particularly classroom activities.[12] The book analyzes family–school relationships in a predominantly white, working-class elementary school and in a predominantly white upper-middle-class elementary school. It describes family–school relationships in one first grade class in each school; and, within the two schools, the analysis focuses on twelve families over the course of their children's first and second grade school years.

The research reveals that family–school relationships very between the working-class and upper-middle-class communities. Relations between working-class families and the school are characterized by *separation*. Because these parents believe that teachers are responsible for education, they seek little information about either the curriculum or the educational process, and their criticisms of the school center almost entirely on non-academic matters. Most working-class parents never intervene in their children's school program; their children receive a generic education. Although these parents read to their children, teach them new words, and review their papers, such activities are sporadic rather than enduring and are substantially less than what the teachers would like. Efforts to monitor their children's school activities are undertaken almost exclusively by mothers.

By contrast, upper-middle-class parents forge relationships characterized by scrutiny and *interconnectedness* between family life and school life. These parents believe that education is a shared responsibility between teachers and parents, they have extensive information about their children's schooling, and they are very critical of the school, including the professional performance of their children's teacher(s). Most, but not all, upper-middle-class parents read to their children and reinforce the curriculum at home. Many parents, particularly parents of low achievers, attempt to customize their children's schooling by requesting particular teachers, asking that their children be enrolled in school programs, and complaining to the principal about the teacher. Some parents also try to compensate for weaknesses in the school program by carrying out some of the classroom curriculum at home, hiring tutors, and having their children evaluated by educational consultants. Although mothers do most of the work in supervising children's education, fathers attend symbolic school events and take an active role in making important school-related decisions. Teachers are impressed by this participation on the part of fathers and see it as a sign that families value education highly.

The case studies of these families and schools, while small in scope, provide considerable evidence that the prevailing conceptual approaches are seriously incomplete. The research suggests that scholars of family–school relationships, in focusing primarily on parents' roles in preparing children for school and complying with teachers' requests for help, have cast their net too narrowly. The findings presented here show that upper-middle-class parents also attempt to shape their children's school site experience. Upper-middle-class parents, particularly those whose offspring are low achievers, try to take a leadership role in their children's schooling. They do not depend on the school for authorization, nor do they automatically defer to a teacher's professional expertise. As a result, the purpose and meaning of parents' activities differ between the two communities studied. There are much tighter linkages between upper-middle-class parents and the school than between working-class parents and the school because upper-middle-class parents closely supervise and frequently intervene in their children's schooling.

The study also suggests the importance of rethinking conceptual models of why social class influences school experience. In contrast to the assumptions associated with prevailing models, parents in both communities in this study shared a desire for their children to succeed in school. All of the parents valued educational success in first and second grade. In addition, the teachers took similar, and at times identical, steps to get parents involved in schooling.

The communities differed, however, in the skills and resources parents had at their disposal for upgrading their children's performance in school. By definition, upper-middle-class parents had more education, status, and income than working-class parents. This increased their competence for helping their children in school, as well as boosted their confidence that they were capable of helping. Working-class parents lacked both the skills and the confidence to help their children in school.

In addition upper-middle-class parents had relatives, friends, and neighbors who were educators. Upper-middle-class mothers also had close ties with other mothers whose children attended the school. As a result, upper-middle-class parents had much more information about the educational process in general and about the specifics of their children's school-site experience than did working-class parents. Upper-middle-class parents drew on this information as they attempted to gain advantages for their children at the school site. Class differences in gender roles also have an effect here; working-class families traditionally have much more segregated gender roles than do upper-middle-class families. This is reflected in parents' roles in schooling.

Thus the defining features of class position (e.g., education, occupational status) and the patterns of family life historically linked to class position (e.g., child rearing methods, kinship ties, gender roles) have unintended consequences for family–school relationships. In turning over responsibility for education to teachers, working-class parents thwart the expressed wishes of their children's teachers. Ironically, although working-class parents are much more respectful of teachers' professional status and expertise, it is upper-middle-class parents who fulfill teacher's expectations of the ways and the extent to which parents should be involved in schooling.

Parents' actions have direct consequences. This study documents how upper-middle-class children's school programs were influenced by parents' requests for teachers; by requests for placement in specialized programs; and by parents' interventions in classroom programs such as spelling and maths. Different styles of home–school relations influence how much exposure children have to academic material. They can also shape promotion and retention decisions in cases where upper-middle-class families take a more assertive role than their working-class counterparts. In a few instances teachers' expectations for academic performance appear to have been determined/influenced by the actions of parents.

The interventions by upper-middle-class parents appear to yield significant educational advantages, particularly for low-achievers, some of whose reading skills improved markedly over two years. Nevertheless, the pattern of intense parent involvement has a dark side: some of the children in this study showed signs of stress in schooling in first grade. Parent involvement also influences parent–teacher interactions, particularly when parents critically evaluate *teachers'* professional performance.

These findings suggest that the concept of cultural capital improves upon existing explanations of why working-class parents are less involved in school than upper-middle-class parents. Social class provides parents with social resources which they 'invest' to yield social profits. Class differences in parent involvement in schooling are rooted in more than the values parents place on educational success or the strategies schools adopt for recruiting parent involvement.

This exploration of family–school relationships also reveals that current formulations of the concept of cultural capital need modification. Persons with similar cultural resources did not equally 'invest' these resources to gain advantages for their children at school. Contrary to the assumptions of current research that uses a cultural capital approach, possession of high status cultural resources does not automatically yield a social profit; rather, these cultural resources must be effectively 'activated' by the individual. Most work on cultural capital has focused on 'high culture' but in the settings examined here, cultural resources not generally considered as cultural capital (e.g., vocabulary, parents' confidence in their abilities to help their children in school) yield a profit for parents of first grade children. These advantages, however, are revealed only when the more familiar approach of examining individual actor's behaviors within educational institutions is supplemented with a careful investigation of teachers' standards.

Most significantly, the research has implications for current models of social stratification and the linkages among social institutions. Most studies look at the impact of social class within social institutions, including family life, work, mental health organizations, or the criminal justice system. A few studies have shown how experiences in one institution can penetrate the other, as occurs when complexity of work and level of supervision influences child rearing values (Kohn and Schooler 1983).[13] Researchers need to do a better job of studying the ways in which families can — and do — bring themselves into alignment with the standards of 'gatekeeping institutions' responsible for social selection. There are indications that the long arm of the job reaches inside the home and beyond, shaping parents' management of their children's lives outside the home.

Organization of the Book

This book begins with a brief description of the school sites. Mostly, however, Chapter Two focuses on the requests which teachers in the two schools made. Chapter Three describes the pattern of separation between home and school which characterized the working-class community of Colton (fictitious name). Chapter Four portrays the pattern of interconnectedness between home and school in the upper-middle-class community of Prescott (also a fictitious name). As with many other areas of family life there was not one parent–teacher relationship but two: mothers and fathers had distinctly different experiences. Chapter Five describes these gender differences in parents' involvement in their children's school lives.

The question of why such dramatic differences in family–school relationships existed in the two communities is taken up in Chapter Six. The influence of values, institutional discrimination, and class resources is examined and I argue that social class had a significant effect in shaping family involvement in school. Chapter Seven shows that the impact of family–school relationships on children's school careers was not trivial. Parents' actions led to 'generic' and 'customized' educational careers, and the pattern of interconnectedness yielded educational profits for some children. These benefits were not without costs, however, and Chapter Eight takes up the dark side of family–school relationships. The research challenges the current view that, independent of ability, social class does not have a significant influence on school experiences, a matter discussed in Chapter Nine. I suggest that the 'long arm of the job' is even longer than previously discussed, shaping parents' roles in managing their children's lives outside the home. I conclude by outlining a direction for understanding the interaction between the class structure and organizations in shaping children's life chances.

The appendix provides a detailed discussion of the research methodology as well as the strengths and weaknesses of the data set. As I explain in more detail there, the research is based on six months of participant–observation in two first grade classrooms. In addition the mothers of twelve children (a boy and a girl from the high, medium, and low reading group in each classroom) were selected for interviews in their homes in the summer after first grade.[14] The following year, at the end of the second grade, these same mothers were interviewed again; and separately I also interviewed most of the fathers. The first and second grade teachers, the principals, and other school personnel were also interviewed. To prevent the confounding factor of race all of the children in the sample are white. In each school three of the mothers worked outside the home, either part-time or full-time. One child from each school was from a single-parent family. Almost all of the interviews (except with the principals) took place in teachers' and parents' homes. Each interview averaged about two hours and each was tape-recorded.

This research design has the advantages and the liabilities of other qualitative studies. It was designed to probe beneath the statistics of social class and parent involvement in order to understand better the social context and the meaning of those behaviors. The use of intense personal interviews to collect data makes it possible to examine issues that would have been precluded using methods such as survey research. With such a small, non-random sample, however, the research is necessarily exploratory. It does not attempt to test hypotheses. Instead it seeks to improve the sophistication and accuracy of conceptual models. It is a contribution to the ongoing debates among researchers about the influence of family background on parent involvement and, more generally, about the impact of social class on children's life chances in American society today.

Notes

1. See Nisbet (1959) for the classic statement of this position. Blumberg (1982) and Vanneman (1987) provide more recent overviews of the research on social class in America.
2. For a useful summary of the 'Wisconsin model' of status attainment research, see Sewell and Hauser (1980). Campbell (1983), Kerckhoff (1976), and Knottnerus (1987) also provide overviews of this research tradition.
3. Other studies also show, often in passing, upper-middle-class parents carefully monitor their children's classroom activities, while working-class parents show signs of hesitancy and passivity in interacting with the school (Wilcox 1978; 1982; Joffee 1977; Ogbu 1974; Rist 1978; Gracey 1972; Van Galen 1987; Metz 1986; Griffith and Smith forthcoming; Smith and Griffith forthcoming).
4. The literature on this topic, particularly by educators whose work's aimed at improving home–school communication, is voluminous. For representative examples, see Atkin *et al.* (1988), Bronfenbrenner (1979; 1982); Epstein (1986; 1987); Davies (1981); Fillion (1987); Gotts and Purnell (1986); Griffore and Boger (1986); Henderson (1981); Hymes

(1953); Leichter (1974; 1979); Morrison (1978); Rich (1987a; 1987b); Slaughter (1977); and Swap (1987).

5. Because parents and teachers have overlapping spheres of control (Epstein 1987; Lightfoot 1978; Lortie 1977; Waller 1932) in their interactions with a child, clashes sometimes occur. Researchers have understood these conflicts as stemming from parents, with a particularistic interest in their child, disagreeing with the teacher's need to treat children in a universalistic fashion (Parsons 1961). The problems of 'boundaries and bridges', or territoriality, have absorbed the attention of researchers. Many studies look at these boundary disputes and the attitudes of teachers and parents towards one another (Corwin and Wagenaar 1976; Henderson 1981; Herman and Yeh 1983; Hoover-Dempsey *et al.* 1987; Lightfoot 1978; Power 1985; Vernberg and Medway 1981). Researchers have not, however, clearly investigated the impact of social class on these territorial disputes and the way in which social class alters the content and the style of these conflicts.

6. This relationship between social class and parent involvement is not influenced by mothers' labor force participation. Children's age and gender do play a role — mothers are more involved when they have younger children and when the child is male (Stevenson and Baker 1987; Epstein 1987; Hoover-Dempsey, *et al.* 1987).

7. For educators, whose primary goal is to increase school performance, this focus on strategies for raising parent involvement is a reasonable position. Educators look at parent involvement as a weapon in their arsenal to increase learning. They are understandably interested in research which focuses on communication skills, site programs, and strategies for increasing parent participation. But sociologists have a different role. Educators are trying to change social behavior; sociologists are trying to understand it. As part of this investigation sociologists have a duty to examine a wide array of social variables — including those that cannot be easily changed through school programs and policies.

8. For analyses of Bourdieu's work see DiMaggio (1979), Schwartz (1977), Brubaker (1985), Collins (1981), Lamont and Lareau (1988), and Sainsaulieu (1981). Buchmann (1989) provides a lucid summary of Bourdieu's work.

9. For confirmations and extensions of Bowles and Gintis's work see Olneck and Bills (1980); Oakes (1982); and Howell and McBroom (1982). More general discussions of the issues of cultural reproduction and classroom curricula include Apple (1979); Apple and Weis (1985); Anyon (1981; 1985); Finley (1984); Gaskell (1985); Oakes (1985); and Wexler (1982). Debates regarding the cultural reproduction model and resistance theory can be found in Giroux (1983); Fritzell (1987); Harker (1984); and Walker (1985).

10. Connell and colleagues, in their study of Australian schools, also suggest that the different class location of parents influences their relationships with schools. Ruling-class parents treat teachers as 'workers' and enroll their children in private schools; working-class parents send their children to state regulated schools where they, and their children, feel as if they are in alien territory (Connell *et al.* 1982).

11. Researchers have also examined the impact of organizational factors on other, related, parts of the educational process. Alexander and colleagues found an interaction between teachers' status origins, their expectations for children, and children's school success. Teachers with low status origins did not have self-fulfilling prophecies while teachers of high status origins appeared to have negative expectations for low status children (Alexander *et al.* 1987).

12. Researchers have also discussed parent involvement in school politics, including desegregation, school closures, curriculum decisions, and — occasionally — personnel decisions (Metz 1986; Coons and Sugarman 1978; Levy *et al.* 1975; Haveman 1977; Katz 1968). Parents' political involvement in schooling, although an important area of inquiry, is generally excluded from this study of parent involvement. Neither does the work systematically examine the impact of family–school relationships on children's psychological development. For discussions in this area see Entwisle and Hayduk (1978); Entwisle *et al.* (1978), Epstein (forthcoming), Dornbusch *et al.* (1987) and Epstein (in press).

13. As the book *Work and Personality* makes clear, the work by Melvin Kohn has been carried out with a variety of colleagues in the United States including Carmi Schooler, Joanne Miller, Karen Miller, Carrie Schoenbach, Ronald Schoenberg, and Leonard Pearlin. Kohn began by looking at the impact of class-related job conditions on values, especially values regarding child rearing (Kohn 1959; 1963; 1977; 1983a; Kohn and Schooler 1983a; Pearlin and Kohn 1966) and alienation (Kohn 1983b). Kohn and Schooler extended it to look at the impact of dimensions of work, notably the substantive complexity of work, on an aspect of personality functioning, ideation flexibility (Kohn and Schooler 1983b; 1983c; 1983d; 1983e). The research has been applied to women as well as men (Miller *et al.* 1983), and the findings have been supported in cross-national data (Kohn *et al.* 1986; Kohn and Schooler 1983f). In addition the impact of dimensions of work on personality has been supported as the job tasks have been shifted to housework (Schooler *et al.* 1983) and school work (Miller *et al.* 1986). For extensions and debate of Kohn and colleagues' work see Gecas and Nye (1974), Hynes (1985), Wright and Wright (1976), and Kohn (1976).

14. Two Colton families moved away during the summer after first grade before I had a chance to interview them. Since the study followed children over time, I was interested in including children I had observed in first as well as second grade. In the end, as I explain in more detail in the appendix, I replaced these children with girls of comparable race, family structure, and reading group membership about whom I had taken notes during my observation. Unfortunately, selection of these new subjects upset the gender balance. While in the upper-middle-class school of Prescott the study was of six families (i.e., three boys and three girls), the final breakdown at Colton was two boys (in the high and low reading group) and four girls.

2 What Do Teachers Want From Parents?

Recent surveys of teachers, of publications by national teachers' organizations, and of policy studies, make plain what teachers want from parents: a 'partnership'. According to these studies teachers do not want parents to turn over to them the whole responsibility for educating the child. Instead they want parents to play an active role in the schooling process. Surveys suggest that a majority of teachers — particularly in the early grades — seek parent involvement in schooling.[1] Teachers report making uniform requests for parent involvement in schooling, but social class influences parents' response. Upper-middle-class parents are much more likely to become directly involved in their children's schooling than are working-class parents (Hoover-Dempsey *et al.* 1987; Herman and Yeh 1983; Becker and Epstein 1982).

Some scholars have suggested that teachers treat working-class and lower-class families differently from upper-middle-class ones. There are studies showing, for example, that class influences how counselors guide high school students in their choices regarding college (Cicourel and Kitsuse 1963) and in placement in kindergarten groups (Rist 1970). Others have pointed to correlations between social class and educational track placement and have argued that the content of the material and quality of teacher–student interactions varies by class as well (Anyon 1980, 1981; Oakes 1982, 1985; Bowles and Gintis 1976; Mickelson 1987; Aggleton and Whitty 1985). Other studies have suggested that teachers and principals may also treat parents from different social classes differently (Lightfoot 1978; McPherson 1972).

This chapter evaluates the possibility that teachers make substantially different requests of working-class and upper-middle-class parents by examining what the first and second grade teachers at each school sought from parents in their interactions during Back-to-School Night, parent-teacher conferences, telephone calls, Open House, and short visits after school.

Colton School

Colton school is located in a modest community in the San Francisco Bay Area of Northern California. The community sprawls across a flat terrain near a

Table 1   *The Occupational Distribution of Parents at Colton*

Parental Occupation	Colton School
Professionals, executives, managers	1%
Semi-professionals, sales, clerical workers and technicians	11%
Skilled and semi-skilled workers	51%
Unskilled workers (and welfare)	23%
Unknown	20%

Note: The data for Colton School are from 'California Assessment Program, 1981–82'
California State Department of Education, Sacramento, California, 1983.

major highway; at the school the hum of high-speed traffic is always audible. As you take the highway exit to Colton you pass a Shell Gas Station and a convenience store with gas pumps; both service travelers as well as local residents. The town is spread out; there is an older, deteriorating, city center, downtown section consisting of a single main street lined with bars, a key shop, and a restaurant. Most residents do their shopping at one of the newer malls located near the highways. Residents also drive a few miles to K-Mart, Lucky's grocery store, and Long's Drug store for their regular shopping. The only stores in town that look busy are the twenty-four hour convenience stores, of which there are several.

The town's new housing development features two and three bedroom suburban homes. Across the freeway are other, slightly older housing developments with large homes built up the sides of the hills. Most of the houses in the community, however, are much smaller than those in the new developments and were built in the 1930s and 1940s. There are many large apartment complexes. Typically these are three-story buildings which form a rectangle around an inner courtyard. There are also several mobile home parks.

Most of the parents of Colton students are employed in semi-skilled or unskilled occupations (see Table 1). School personnel report that most of the parents have a high school education, many are high school dropouts. Houses and apartment rents are low by Bay Area standards: they average one half to one third the cost of homes in the Prescott school community (Table 2). Here and there are well-maintained houses and yards, but on many streets the yards and bushes are overgrown and weeds have gained the upperhand. Old cars — some missing wheels and windows — are parked in front of several homes. Colton parents complain about drag racing on their neighborhood streets, crime, and drug use among teenagers. .

Colton school has a front entrance with a circle drive. The American flag flies at the front of the school. There is a little yellow sign labeled 'Office' with an arrow pointing straight ahead, down a concrete pathway with an overhang; another sign asks visitors to 'check in' at the office. The office typically is busy and noisy with children, teachers, and administrators walking through it, telephones ringing, and multiple conversations underway simultaneously. The

Table 2   *Selected Housing Characteristics of Communities Surrounding Colton and Prescott Schools*

	School Communities Surrounding	
Housing Characteristics	Colton	Prescott
Ownership Pattern		
Homeowners	71%	90%
Renters	29%	11%
Cost of Housing		
Median rents	$175	$425
Median housing value	$55,000	$190,000

Note: The data are from the 1980 Census.

school's two secretaries sit at adjoining desks, facing the office doors. On top of the desks, in the middle, are two boxes filled with cards listing the names, addresses, and home telephone numbers for all of the children's parents or guardians. The principal's office door, with a glass window labeled 'Principal', is to the left. Both secretaries are young (about 24 and 25 years old); they generally dress casually in pants and tops and wear heavy make-up. The office is dominated by a large calendar detailing the school's events for the entire year. Around the calendar hang pictures of the Easter Hat Parade and the Christmas program.

The school was built in the fifties. The classrooms are set in rows, with grassy areas and outdoor hallways separating each row. There is a large auditorium near the entrance to the school which doubles as a cafeteria: hot lunches are available. The school has 450 children in kindergarten, first and second grade. When children enter the third grade they move to another school not far from Colton. Slightly over one half of the children are white, one third are Hispanic, and the remainder are black or Asian, especially Vietnamese immigrants. About one half of the children qualify for free lunches under federal guidelines. Teachers estimate that over one half of the children are from single-parent homes. The school has a high mobility rate: according to the vice-principal, one quarter of the children 'turn over' every school year.

Mrs Thompson's Classroom

Mrs Thompson's first grade classroom is located in the second hallway. Mrs Thompson, a thin white woman in her early forties, is an enthusiastic teacher with a quiet voice and a frequent smile for the children in her class. She often dresses in black polyester pants, sandals, and a short sleeve sweater. She and her husband, who is a professional photographer, have three grown daughters. One daughter got married during the school year, and Mrs Thompson brought in wedding favors (almonds tied in blue net with a little blue satin rose) for each of the children. Mrs Thompson has been a teacher for over fifteen years, but the year I observed was only her second at Colton. She transferred to Colton from another school because of declining enrollments. Her aide, Mrs Hawthorne, is a woman in her late forties with teenage children. She has a much sterner manner with the children. Both Mrs Thompson and Mrs Hawthorne commute to Colton from upper-middle-class communities about a thirty-minute drive away.

Mrs Thompson's classroom is large and airy, with rows of windows along one entire wall. A row of closets, a counter and a sink line the back wall. A comfortable distance from these stands Mrs Thompson's desk, easels and paints, and a low table. The children's desks are next, placed in groups of six, facing each other. There are five groups of desks and they take up about three-quarters of the space in the classroom. Blackboards run along the front and side of the classroom. In the remaining area there is a piano, a reading corner and a floor area where the children sit during group activities.

The classroom is decorated by various art projects and stories written by the children. Flower pictures are on one side of the blackboard, squiggle drawings on another, paintings of dinosaurs are on the back wall. Across the top of the blackboard are the letters of the alphabet, paired with pictures of animals whose names begin with the appropriate letters. High on the walls are long charts recording the birthdays of children in the class and the times when they have lost a tooth.

There are thirty-four children in Mrs Thompson's class. Most are six years old but some are seven and eight years, usually because they have repeated a grade. Over one third of the class has repeated either kindergarten or first grade, and three more children are due to repeat first grade next year. One half of the children are white, and one third are Hispanic. Two of the children are black one child is Asian.

Most of the children come to school with clean faces and brushed hair. When the girls wear dresses, particularly the Hispanic girls, these tend to be very frilly. The children's jackets are usually nylon or polyester; many are dirty and old. Two or three of the children usually wear clothes that appear new and freshly ironed, but many dress in old, frayed and well-worn clothing. New clothes appear to come from stores such as Sears, Penney's, or K-Mart. When children do wear new clothes it is an event. They make spontaneous comments to one another about these new items and consider them worthy of mention during the class's 'sharing time'. The children do not go on expensive vacations during the school year; few have been to Disneyland.

Colton Teachers' Requests

First and second grade teachers at Colton asked for help from parents in the form of three 'Rs'. They wanted parents to *read* to their children, to *reinforce* the classroom material, and to *respond* to teachers' requests for assistance.

When asked what she saw as the proper role of parents in school, Mrs Thompson responded:

> The main thing that we tell them we want done at home is to read. That
> is the biggest thing they can do for their children is to read to them and,
> in turn, have the children read back.[2]

Although teachers' personalities, classroom styles, and warmth towards parents varied, they uniformly emphasized the importance of reading at home. For example, Mrs Thompson nodded more, smiled more, and talked longer with parents than did the second grade teacher, Mrs Sampson. Mrs Sampson had a more awkward manner with parents: she often looked at the floor or the wall rather than maintaining eye contact during her conversations with them. There were sometimes short silences in her discussions with parents before she would ask another question. Similarly, in conferences another second grade teacher, Mrs Percell, had a quieter, shyer manner, while the special education teacher, Mrs Jones, gave lengthy answers to parents' questions. During parent–teacher conferences all of these teachers recommended to parents at least once that they read to their children. Mrs Sampson and Mrs Thompson repeatedly encouraged parents to read to their children before bedtime, suggested that mothers have the children read to them, and asked the mothers to take children to the public library to check out books.

The teachers also gave advice to parents on how to handle tensions that might arise when children were reading to parents at home. For example, during the spring conference Sammy's mother, Mrs Klatch, said that problems over reading were developing between her husband and her son. Sammy's mother was not a strong reader:

> I had a reading problem myself and I have to admit that I still don't read
> very good myself.

Nevertheless she tried to read to Sammy at home. When they read Mrs Klatch insisted that he rewrite the words he didn't know:

> We would sit and watch the soaps together and then we would read.
> Those words he don't know I make him sound out.

Her husband found it frustrating that Sammy did not know certain words:

> His dad got very upset with him and started yelling. I told him that it
> don't do any good to yell at him. Like wait, 'w-a-i-t'.

Mrs Sampson told the mother that 'wait' was a 'hard word' and suggested that the mother not insist that Sammy sound out a word he didn't know:

> I don't do a lot of sounding out of words or family of words. I would
> prefer that you go over the words he does know ahead of time and then,
> if he doesn't know the words, just tell him it.

She also encouraged the mother to keep reading to her son and to have him read to his younger sister as well as to his parents.

In addition to the emphasis on reading in parent–teacher conversations, there were formal classroom and school programs aimed at increasing reading at home. For instance, Mrs Thompson maintained a small library in her classroom. At the end of the day she encouraged children to check out books from this collection to take home. She started school every morning with a twenty-minute silent reading period. Frequently children would not finish their books in this period, so both Mrs Thompson and Mrs Hawthorne would often suggest to the children that they take the book they had been reading home that night and 'read it to their mother'. Mrs Thompson kept track of how many books children had checked out, and she would sometimes report that number to their parents in conferences.

There was also a school program aimed at increasing reading. The Read-at-Home Program awarded children a free book for every eight hours of reading done at home. Children were able to choose a new book from a selection in the library. The school provided forms which children took home for their parents to sign, testifying that their children either had read a book themselves or had had a book read to them by someone at home. All of the classrooms had a chart, prominently displayed, with the number of fifteen-minute periods each participating child had completed. At the end of the school year there was a tally: the classroom that had completed the most hours of reading won a prize.

Reinforcing the Curriculum

In addition to reading to children at home, Colton teachers asked parents to play educational games with their children and to practice the curriculum, especially spelling. As Mrs Thompson said:

> The procedure that we have is that we send the spelling words home at the first of the week and [parents] know to expect them. [The words] are given four times during the week ... We try to teach them to them at school. [We tell parents] we would appreciate them calling the words out to the child at home and helping them learn.

Mrs Sampson followed a similar procedure in the classroom and in her conferences with parents. Mrs Sampson encouraged parents to work with their children regularly on the words, but only for a short period of time. As she explained to the mother of a low-achieving boy:

> If he brings words home he needs to study them. My suggestion would be ten to fifteen minutes so [he] doesn't get tired.

For low-achieving children, teachers were particularly emphatic about the importance of reinforcing educational activities. For example, in her spring conference Mrs Thompson encouraged Mrs Morries to enroll her son Tommy in summer school and persisted despite the mother's reluctance:

MRS THOMPSON: He now is [in] Find [a particular reader] which is a good place for him to be. He passed the test for 'Enjoy Again'. I think he's generally doing OK — just keep him reading. There is a summer school class, I don't know if you're interested or not.

MRS MORRIS: I usually don't send him to summer school.

MRS THOMPSON: Would you like to see it [the brochure]? It might keep him up so he doesn't slip back. [Without waiting for a response, she gets up and goes to her desk.] I wanted to show it to you.

MRS MORRIS: Isn't it more or less like last year?

MRS THOMPSON: They only come for one hour. It does cost $20. It would be at the school, but it would mean providing transportation. [Pause] It wouldn't hurt him.

MRS MORRIS: We're gone so much. We're gone for two weeks in the beginning of summer and two weeks in August.

MRS THOMPSON: It isn't necessary. Just so he doesn't lose everything during the summer. If you would just keep him reading. He could go to the library over the summer and that would help him. He hasn't been bringing any books home. Let's see if he's checked any out recently.

During this twenty-minute conference Mrs Thompson suggested at least five times that Tommy's mother keep her son reading during the summer.

In interviews Colton mothers confirmed that they had been asked to help. Mrs Morris said:

> They definitely want you to help. They give you suggestions on to do to help.

Mr Trenton, the father of a high-achieving boy, concurred:

> Whenever you go to the teacher–parent conferences, the teachers up there tell you what you should be working with your children with. They would come up with different ways. They suggested flashcards for Johnny. Well, he didn't like flashcards. It got boring for him. And Missy loves flashcards. So he would keep going over them with her. They [the teachers] suggested getting play money–learning to add that way. Different little magazines you can buy with quizzes. You know, they [the teachers] had suggestions. Some of them worked. Some of them didn't work.

As with reading there was also a school program aimed at increasing parents' efforts to reinforce the curriculum. Colton school offered a parents' workshop four times a year during the first year of my study. The workshop, which was held in the afternoon and evening, provided parents with grade-specific packets with educational games, puzzles, and activities in them. The packets were free; parents were asked to return the materials when they were done. The program, which was run by the reading resource teacher, also gave tips on how to improve school performance. The workshop leaders spoke of the importance of parents talking to children, asking children questions, and reading to children, as well as playing the educational games passed out in the workshop sessions.[3]

Responding to Teachers' Requests

In addition to working with children at home on reading and educational games, Colton teachers wanted parents to come to school. They invited parents to school during the day for an individual twenty-minute conference in November and in April. Parents were also encouraged to attend 'Back-to-School Night' where teachers discussed their goals for the year. In the spring, parents and children were invited in the evening for an 'Open House' where families could review some of the work that the children had done during the year. All of these invitations were dittoed notices sent home with the children after school. Teachers told children to remind their parents about Open House and, in some instances, about conferences. As Mrs Sampson said:

> The families that seem to be most supportive come to school on Back-to-School Night. They keep their conference appointments or they let you know that they can't keep them. If you send work home that needs to come back, it comes back.

The conferences were scheduled after school, usually between 2.30 and 4.00 pm. Following the school's system, teachers sent home a slip of paper with an appointment time on it. The teachers presumed that parents would attend unless they contacted the school to cancel or reschedule. Teachers worked longer hours on conference days. In the teachers' room and in the hallways teachers frequently, and at times bitterly, complained when they had waited after school for parents who neither kept their appointments nor called to say they would not be coming.

Teachers varied, however, in how much this 'no-show' behavior angered them and what follow-up steps they took. Most teachers simply let the matter drop and sent a notice at the next conference time. A few teachers would contact the parent again. Mrs Thompson would visit the home after school and have the conference there if she felt the child really needed help. For example, Laura's mother did not drive the family truck and she missed Laura's conferences in first grade (although not in second grade). Mrs Thompson was very concerned about Laura's performance and visited the home in April to ask that the parents work with Laura, particularly on reading. In June, at the end of the year, Mrs Thompson visited the home again and, because Laura had not made sufficient progress, secured the mother's permission for a retention.

In addition to attending school events, teachers requested that parents contact them if there was a problem regarding schooling. As Mrs Sampson explained:

> I have asked them if they are unhappy about something to let me know. Some parents are very good about that. They will come and say, 'So and so is bothering my daughter.' I had a Spanish-speaking mother in here towards the end of school. The mother couldn't speak to me, but she had a mother that could speak to me come to the door [and complain that someone was bothering her child]. I thanked them and said that I would move the child and I did. But things that I am not aware of they can make you more aware of.

In her interview Mrs Thompson reported that during Back-to-School Night she encouraged parents to visit the classroom and to volunteer in the classroom throughout the school year:

> I like parents coming in and I like them to just come in to observe . . . It gives them a better understanding of what we cope with at school and what the child is doing.

Mrs Thompson attributed her interest in having parents in the classroom to her own experience as a mother where she felt 'intrusive' when her child was having problems in school:

> My child, she was very sweet, and not a problem. I would go to conferences and they would say she was a sweet child and so forth, but she was not doing well in school. She needed help. I should have gone into the school. I felt intrusive. That's why I like parents to come in

She felt that visiting the classroom helped parents learn about the relative standing of their children in the class:

> It helps [parents] to see the child and be realistic about where their child is—what they are doing and what their capabilities are.

While teachers wanted parents to come to school and respond to teachers' requests, they also wanted parents to be unconditionally positive about the teacher in their interactions with their children. They wanted parents to 'back up' the teacher in front of the children, particularly in the area of discipline. Mrs Thompson outlined the ideal scenario:

> . . . parents would tell their children that the school was right. They wouldn't be critical of the school in front of the children.

Mrs Sampson also stressed the importance of parents not 'bad mouthing' teachers at home:

... not bad mouthing what you don't like at school in front of the child. I wasn't always happy with things but I tried not to speak about them right in front of that particular child. I feel that if you talk about that in front of the children, that is going to influence how they act at school!

In conversations among themselves teachers sometimes would complain about parents neglecting children, but there was less of a consensus of what teachers' proper role should be in these cases. Some teachers were assertive. Mrs Thompson, for example, bought an alarm clock for a child who was chronically late for school and took it to his home; quizzed a girl about her hygienic habits at home and ultimately sent her to the nurse because of bad body odor; and considered turning a girl's mother into Child Protective Services because the child was frequently late or absent, often dirty, spoke of 'partying' at home, and was not allowed into a particular room in her own home (the latter raised the issue of drugs, in Mrs Thompson's mind). Mrs Sampson, however, adopted a less interventionist approach to activities at home. She neither liked to quiz children about home activities nor become involved:

I try not to be too nosey about personal things that go on outside of school. Once in a while I will ask them something . . . It really isn't my business what went on at home except it might affect what is going on in the classroom . . . I would rather let the office do that type of work if they have to.

There are, then, areas of parent–teacher interactions where the boundaries are unclear and where the limits of parents' 'territoriality' are ill-defined (Lightfoot 1978). Teachers' requests for parent involvement in classroom activities is not, however, one of these. All of the Colton teachers and administrators I spoke with viewed educating children as a process which extended beyond the walls of the classroom. They saw parents as having a responsibility to help in the educational process, particularly by reading to their children at home and by supporting the actions of teachers at school. Colton teachers appeared neither ambivalent nor haphazard in making their requests that parents help in schooling.

Prescott School

Prescott school is located on a hill in the middle of a residential district. The view from the school includes trees, small hills, and residences. It is quiet. Many children walk to school; the district does not provide transportation for the children. Other children are driven by their parents, often in car pools. Accessing the school involves driving through a prosperous downtown section where shoe stores, a candy store, two clothing boutiques, a gourmet coffee store, a flower

Table 3   *The Occupational Distribution of Parents at Prescott*

Parental Occupation	Prescott School
Professionals, executives, managers	60%
Semi-professionals, sales, clerical workers and technicians	30%
Skilled and semi-skilled workers	9%
Unskilled workers (and welfare)	1%

Note: The data are based on the principal's estimation of the school population.

stand, a produce shop, a book store, restaurants, an ice cream parlor, and other small shops vie for the patronage of well-heeled shoppers.

The area surrounding Prescott is hilly; many of the streets have large, expensive homes on the hillside. The streets are narrow and wind around the hills. Some of the homes have views of the surrounding hills and valleys. Not far from the school is a large, clean, and well maintained park. In another, smaller shopping district are more gourmet shops and a bank. The area is almost entirely single-family dwellings; apartments are rare. The homes are often two-storied and have three and four bedrooms. Some have gardeners, and all but one of the families I visited had a house-cleaner who came weekly. Although families lock their houses and are concerned about burglaries, the crime rate is far lower than at Colton.

The parents of Prescott children are primarily professionals, including doctors, lawyers, engineers, and corporate managers (Table 3). Teachers report that most of the fathers have a Bachelor degree and many have advanced degrees. Possibly as high as twenty-five per cent of mothers, aunts, and grandmothers of the children are current or former teachers.

It is a short walk to the school from the narrow street. The American flag flies above the blacktop. The school was originally one large building with an enclosed hallway and classrooms on either side of the hall. Because of increases in enrollment, portable classrooms now contain the kindergarten, one first grade, the library, a reading specialist room and a day care center. Inside the main building is the office. The school secretary sits in the outer office. She is in her late forties and is usually dressed formally (i.e., a blazer, a polyester blouse, and a plaid wool skirt). Her office is small and overcrowded with mailboxes for all of the teachers and posters for school events on the wall. Through an open door is the principal's office, which has a large wooden desk and pictures on the wall. The main office is usually quiet, although children bring messages and attendance records back and forth during the day.

Prescott school is smaller than Colton. It enrolls only 250 kindergarten through fifth grade students.[4] Over ninety per cent of the school is white; the remaining students are Asian or black. This distribution mirrors the composition of the surrounding community. The school does not offer a school lunch program and less than five per cent of the children would qualify for one. The school does have a monthly 'hot dog day' sponsored by the Parents' Club as well as 'popsicle days'. Usually, however, children bring bag lunches and eat outside on benches. When the weather is poor the children eat lunch in their classrooms.

Mrs Walters' Classroom

Mrs Walters teaches first grade in classroom number four. She has been an elementary school teacher for twenty-two years, but has only taught for four years at Prescott. She is a white woman of forty-five, who has a quiet, warm manner with the children. She is married to a corporate executive and they have a boy in junior high school. Her aide, Mrs O'Donnell, is a bubbly, cheerful woman in her early forties.

Mrs Walters' classroom is a free-standing portable with carpet on most of the floor and four windows along one wall. The back of the classroom contains a loft — that Mrs Walters built herself — which contains numerous pillows and books. Next to the loft, there is a fish tank, a television, and a linoleum area with a sink and easels for art work.

In the center of the classroom are the children's desks, placed together in groups of six, with one group of nine. There are four groups in all. On the top of each desk is a large cardboard strip on which the child's first and last name is printed in big, block letters.

The front wall of the classroom is covered by three blackboards. Along the top of the blackboard is a number line, counting the number of days the children have been enrolled in school, and cards with the letters of the alphabet. On the side wall is a calendar and a chart marking the birthdays of children in the room. A huge tooth, on which the names of the children who have lost a tooth during the year are recorded, and miscellaneous art work cover the other walls. All major items in the classroom are labeled (e.g., mirror, closet, wall).

There are twenty-eight children in Mrs Walters' classroom, all of whom are white, except for three girls who are Asian. The children's ages range from six to eight. One quarter of the children in the class have repeated either kindergarten or first grade or are scheduled to repeat first grade next year. Typically, children wear new-looking clothes, in some cases probably purchased at Sears or Penney's, in other cases at stores such as Macy's. Boys usually wear jeans and plaid or printed shirts. Flannel shirts are common in winter and short-sleeve shirts (often with the alligator symbol) are common in spring. Periodically, boys wear T-shirts with the name of another place on the front, including Hawaii, Disneyland and New York City. Most of the girls wear pants, jumpsuits or jumpers. The dresses that the girls wear are often a cotton print, lacy dresses are rare. Many of the girls' clothes are fashionable, carry designer labels, and are expensive.

Children are often taken on vacations to distant places. Many of the children have been to Hawaii; almost all have been to Disneyland. During the winter, many children go to ski resorts regularly. Many of the children have lessons after school, particularly for sports. Swim team and soccer team practices involve a number of boys and girls in the class.

Prescott Teachers' Requests

As at Colton, Prescott teachers emphasized the three 'Rs' of parent involvement: reading, reinforcing the curriculum, and responding to teachers' requests. But Prescott teachers added a fourth 'R': *respecting* the advice and actions of the teacher. Unlike their counterparts at Colton, Prescott teachers often struggled to control parents' behavior and worked to discourage parents' actions that they found to be unhelpful.

In their work with parents, Prescott teachers in first and second grade emphasized the importance of reading. When I interviewed Mrs Walters, she noted that during the Back-to-School Night program in September she spoke to the parents at length about reading:

> I think bedtime reading is a really special time. I think it gives parents a kind of time to really get a sense of what they [their children] are doing. Some people feel like first grade maybe is getting too old for story time and put it aside, [thinking] that's something for little kids. So I talk [to parents] about doing that.

As part of building reading and verbal skills, Mrs Walters said she encouraged parents to talk about the content of the story with their children in a 'low-key' way:

> I talk to them about ... questioning their kids. You know, you can have the kids retell the story from the night before. You can do all those kinds of reading skills just in a very low-key conversational way. And parents can have a sense of what their kid remembers.

Again, this emphasis on reading occurred despite differences in teaching style. Mrs Walters had a soft and gentle manner with the children and parents, she accepted classroom noise and allowed children to move about, she believed in 'hands-on' education where children manipulated objects rather than simply working with pencil and paper, and she was not popular with parents. Mrs Hoffman, the second grade teacher, is an older woman with a stern manner, who insisted on quiet and order in her classroom, was not impressed by 'hands-on' education, and was extremely popular with parents (although some confessed to being intimidated by her). Yet both Mrs Hoffman and Mrs Walters stressed the importance of reading.

Moreover, in a Back-to-School Night meeting that included parents of children in all grades at the school, the Principal, Mrs Harpst, asked the parents to continue reading to their children and to consider it a form of the *parents'* homework to read to their children. Mrs Harpst told the parents that she had just become a grandmother for the first time. One of her first gifts to her grandchild was the book *The Read-Aloud Handbook* (Trelease 1982) which contains lists of books for parents to read to their children. She encouraged parents to purchase this book or talk to classroom teachers about possible books to read to their children.

Although teachers stressed the importance of reading, Prescott school did not have a formally organized, school-wide program comparable to Colton's Read-at-Home Program. Unlike Colton, however, the school library was open during the summer and staffed by parent volunteers. This allowed children to check out books throughout the year.

In addition to reading, Prescott teachers encouraged parents to reinforce the curriculum at home. Mrs Walters felt that reviewing papers that children brought home from school was an important and fruitful way for parents to help children review their work:

> I think it is really important that parents do look at papers. [At Back-to-School Night] I talk about that. You know, hanging the papers up. It is a really good review kind of process for the kids, to tell their parents about what they've done—as opposed to saying, 'What did you do in school today?' Kids never know; they just don't know what they have done.

In most cases, Mrs Walters preferred parents to review papers and simply read to children rather than try to teach new information:

> I stress reading to them rather than trying to teach them math facts.

To the dismay of some parents, Mrs Walters did not believe in homework in first grade. She resisted and, for the most part, denied parents' requests to send work home with the children on weekends. Rather than emphasizing the importance of parents reinforcing the curriculum, Mrs Walters worked to limit parents' efforts to helping their children with reading rather than other forms of teaching.

Similarly, Mrs Hoffman saw parents' primary role in preparing children for school as consisting of getting their children to school on time, well rested, and with a good background in reading. If children did not finish their work during the allotted classroom time, then she sent the work home where the parent could help the child:

> Parents can help by seeing that the child gets enough rest, instilling health habits, [and] reading to the child . . . I view my role to set up an educational program for the child. I encourage the parent to help the child if the child needs help. I encourage the parent to stay away if they are putting on the pressure.

Mrs Hoffman disliked parents 'playing teacher'. When I asked her for her thoughts on parent involvement, she said:

Sometimes it can be very helpful. Sometimes it is too much pressure and the child will learn things wrong. It is better to pick a subject that we don't stress at school. They can play teacher that way. Leave the basics alone, unless the child really asks for it, which they usually don't. Unless we ask them to work with them. They can take them to museums, to plays, to science [exhibits].

Prescott teachers asked parents to come to school for a series of events similar to those at Colton, including two parent–teacher conferences, Back-to-School Night, Open House, and a holiday program. In addition the school had a formally organized volunteer program. As part of this program, teachers asked parents to volunteer in the kindergarten through third grade classrooms. Parents were asked to volunteer in a class one hour, twice per month. In Mrs Walters' class, parents supervised children in the self-paced, 'hands-on' math program. In other classes, including Mrs Hoffman's, parents corrected papers and answered children's questions. The program was coordinated by parent–volunteers who set up the schedule, found substitute volunteers, and organized an introductory session at the beginning of the school year.

As at Colton, Prescott teachers encouraged parents to share their questions and concerns with teachers. As the principal explained:

Communication is always two-way. I think that teachers have to do a very careful job of explaining to parents what their program is and how it affects their child. But they also need to be very good listeners and see where it is that parents have fears and what are the concerns the parents have.

Managing parents: Prescott teachers

Prescott teachers asked for parent involvement in schooling, but they wanted parents to respect and defer to their professional expertise. Prescott parents did not always do so, and teachers both complained about this and took steps to manage and contain parents' actions.

Teachers clearly did not appreciate it when parents tried to take the upper hand. Mrs Hoffman, for example, complained about parents passing judgment on the quality of teachers' performance and sharing that with teachers. She complained about 'gossipy mothers' who, for instance, evaluated the performance of a new teacher:

One mother was just yesterday talking to me. The mother was saying it was nice that there was an equal number of girls and boys in this [fourth grade] class. And the mother says, 'You know the mothers think she is doing a good job.' [Reaction of bewilderment and anger] I didn't ask for that!

Mrs Hoffman also complained about the 'pesky parent' type, which she defined as one who:

> . . . calls about nonsensical things. Gail didn't get her weekly newsletter. Gail left her coat. Have a conference on the first day. Now how can you have a conference on the first day of school?

Mrs Hoffman felt that parents could wield influence and power in the district. Knowing that Mrs Walters was disliked by many parents, she said:

> I wouldn't put it past some of those parents putting a lot of pressure on so Anne would have to go to another school . . . Parents can cause a lot of trouble.

Mrs Hoffman cited instances where parents' concerns led to the reassignment of teachers. She objected to this:

> One of the teachers in the high school was gay and he took a six month leave of absence. Parents were so upset that he was [re-]assigned to the audiovisual equipment. They put pressure on. He retired early. It was degrading.

Although aware of parents' power, she did not have those kinds of problems. Parents did not complain about her to the principal nor did they intervene and try to alter her school program. For example, annoyed at the common belief that smart children had reading in the afternoon ('late birds') and slow children had reading before school ('early birds'), Mrs Hoffman reversed the schedule and was pleased that none of the parents complained:

> So last year I switched everyone around. And the parents didn't say boo. I heard there was a coffee and Suzanne Harpst, [the Principal] overheard one mother say, 'What is this about changing all the kids?' A second Mom said, 'I don't know.' The third Mom said, 'Well, if Mrs Hoffman did it she had a good reason' and to just relax.

She felt that 'maybe my reputation is such that parents don't question me'.[5] Mrs Hoffman took steps to make sure parents were well-informed:

> You cover yourself when you can show parents what you have done. They like that. I don't blame them. I would like it too.

She objected to the 'hands-on' math program in Mrs Walters' class because it did not leave teachers with anything to show parents:

> You leave yourself open to criticism that you are not teaching them anything. When a child comes into my class they do five to six pages a day. We do every page, it is corrected and everything. I can show the parents.

Miss Chaplan took over Mrs Walters' class six weeks before the end of the school year, when Mrs Walters left to have an operation. At twenty-four years old, Miss Chaplan was markedly younger than her colleagues. She also reported adopting strategies to manage parents. She said when parents came in to talk to her:

I put on a professional air and increased the number of large words in my vocabulary [laughs, embarrassed]. It is a game. But especially because I am young. I am almost twenty-five, but when they come in the classroom they *look* [demonstrates, eyes get big].

Other teachers, especially Mrs Walters and a third grade teacher, Mrs Dillon, did have problems with parents. Parents complained about both of these teachers in interviews, and some parents felt that the time children spent in these teachers' classrooms was a 'lost year'.

Influenced by Piaget, Mrs Walters felt children should learn material when they were developmentally ready to do so. She also felt that parents were placing too much pressure on their children and decreasing the pleasure of the learning process. In her talk at Back-to-School Night Mrs Walters took steps to assuage parents' concerns, as she recounted to me in an interview:

There are a lot of people [for whom] ... my math time was a worrisome thing. Especially with the television and magazines stressing the idea of basics. So you have to talk to parents and make sure they understand that you really are teaching the basics. It's just that you're trying to be more humane about it.

Mrs Walters also asked parents to volunteer in her classroom and was happy to have special conferences with mothers after they finished volunteering. She did not, however, agree with parents requests even when they expressed their concerns to her. She refused, for example, to send home extra math packets on the weekend as homework. Although aware that parents were very concerned about academics, she did not display children's academic work during Open House because she didn't want parents to compare their child's work with that of another child.

When she felt parents were trying to 'put her in her place' she struggled to maintain control. Salutations could be symbolic of this struggle. At Prescott the norm was for parents to address teachers using both names; but one day in the classroom, after school when we were talking about names Mrs Walters told me that she had once received:

a note from a parent which was addressed to her with her first name and signed only with the parent's first name. So when she responded, she signed only her first name. Then she got a response which was typed and very formal and used both names. So, she said, 'It can be a power thing. Now I always sign both of my names. The attitude in this district is that you are servants, public servants... When there is a problem then sometimes they put you in your place'.[6]

Every year at least two or three sets of parents, and sometimes many more, complained to the principal about Mrs Walters. When parents complained Mrs Harpst referred the parents back to the teacher for discussion. Teachers, and many parents, knew that Mrs Harpst believed that parents should 'talk to the teachers' about their concerns. For her part, the principal felt that some of Mrs

Walters' transition periods when children had finished one lesson and were moving into the next one were in need of improvement and she (Mrs Harpst) 'worked with her on that'. Privately, the principal described Mrs Walters as 'a good, solid, average teacher in a cast of stars'. Publicly she was unsupportive of parents' efforts to alter Mrs Walters' program or to remove her from the classroom. At the same time, Mrs Harpst worked, with limited success, to make parents feel as if their complaints were being heard and their concerns understood, even though she refused to compel Mrs Walters to change her classroom program.

Other forms of parent intervention

Research on parent involvement in schooling has examined it primarily from teachers' perspectives (Epstein and Becker 1982; Lightfoot 1978; Van Galen 1987). As a result, most studies focus on what teachers define as the key elements of parent involvement. The focus is on parents' help in preparing children for school and reinforcing the curriculum at home.

This perspective is too narrow. It fails to take into account other ways in which parents are involved in schooling that were evident in classroom observations. For example, teachers wanted parents to bring their children to school on time, clean, fed, clothed, well-rested, and ready to conform to school rules. Parents also had to make sure that their children had lunch or lunch money; that various papers had been signed (e.g., field-trip permission slips); that, periodically, their children had something to show the class during 'Show and Tell'; and that their children were supplied with empty orange juice cans, popsicle sticks, yarn, and other miscellaneous equipment for class projects when the teaches requested such items. All of the teachers presumed that parents would do these things. When asked about parents' role in schooling, teachers rarely mentioned these factors. Only Mrs Hoffman noted the importance of parents making sure their children had enough rest. Parents' responsibilities that fell outside the four 'Rs' were never discussed in interviews, as teachers focused, instead, on the parents' role in educational activities.[7]

Yet fulfilling these other obligations was not a trivial matter, either in the amount of work they required of parents or the impact failure to discharge these duties could have on classroom dynamics. If children went to bed late on a school night it could and did affect the teacher's life, as this example of a high-achiever at Prescott makes clear:

> Carol was working quietly on an art project with two other girls when all of a sudden her face screwed up, turned bright red, and she burst into tears. The other girls looked up in amazement, and then got up from their desks and ran over and got Mrs Walters. The teacher's aide came over and after a brief discussion, put her arm around Carol and took her out of the room to the office.

Carol's father came to pick her up and he said that the family had gone out the night before and that Carol had gone to sleep very late. He attributed her behavior to her simply being over tired.

Educators at both schools also *allowed* forms of parent involvement that they did not request. Teachers varied in how enthusiastically they tolerated parents' unsolicited interventions, but in both schools, educators made efforts to honor parents' requests. For example, both schools allowed parents to make requests for specific teachers for the following year. At Colton it was a very rare event for parents to do so, and teachers appeared to react positively when a special request was made. Although teachers told parents they could not guarantee that the child would get that teacher, they said they would do their best to see that this happened. At Prescott, parents' requests for teachers were allowed but strongly discouraged. As Miss Chaplan said:

> Suzanne [Harpst] really tries to keep a lid on those because otherwise you are opening up a can of worms. The school needs to set limits with parents . . . to set controls. You can't have parents shopping for teachers and for the school.

Mrs Walters also said that requests for teachers were discouraged:

> The rule is that it has to be in writing . . . And it has to be a real reason, not just that you prefer so and so because you heard about her. It has to be a request for valid reasons.

Mrs Walters felt there were some valid reasons:

> There are some children that would be just too timid to be in Sandi's [Hoffman] room. It wouldn't be good for them.

Parents knew that it was very difficult to get requests through. Some parents would express their 'concerns' to teachers in the conference without making a formal request. Despite the rule, Mrs Walters averaged five formal requests per year (out of a classroom of twenty-eight students). She said that she 'tried' to honor the requests and 'on most occasions' was able to do so.

Parents — particularly at Prescott — also requested that their children be placed in the gifted program. Teachers at both schools allowed parents to request that their children be tested for learning disabilities (a very expensive procedure — and one often refused at Prescott), or that they be placed in a special learning program (e.g., speech therapy, occupational therapy), the reading resource program, or special education. Parents were not always successful in gaining entry to the program of their choice, but some parents did gain entry for children whom the classroom teacher had not recommended.

Some parents at both schools would request special conferences during the school year with the classroom teacher. Teachers almost always accommodated these requests. If parents were unhappy they could and did complain to the principal. Again the principals virtually always agreed to meet with parents.

Some parents tried — at times successfully — to circumvent school rules. For example, Prescott teachers complained about parents who tried to pressure teachers into placing their children into the gifted program although they did not formally qualify. Parents' efforts sometimes paid off, as Mrs Walters' description of a 'typical' parent makes clear:

> The man was a Fathers' Club president and the mother volunteered in the classroom and their daughter was under pressure from them all the way through school. They wanted her in the gifted program and she didn't test high enough. They took her out and had her tested privately. The school district won't accept that. Finally, the district said okay, she can be a guest in the program.

Teachers and principals did not ask parents to intervene in these ways nor did they always appreciate their actions. Nevertheless they tolerated and sometimes encouraged parents' interventions in the school site even when these deviated from school or district rules.

Standards in Schools

Some have argued (Cohen 1978) that educational systems have been significantly standardized during this century. Although funding and administration of schools remains a local or state rather than a federal matter, the federal government has taken an increasingly visible role in the last decades (Haveman 1977). In addition, the growth of national teachers' unions, textbook companies, educational research firms, an nationally accredited teacher education programs have influenced the dynamics in local schools.

The case for parent involvement in schooling has been supported at the national level in reports of 'What Works' by the Department of Education (1986), by the National Education Association, and by educational researchers. Supermarket bags proclaim that 'Parents are Teachers Too'. The idea that parents can and should be involved in their children's education, particularly in the early years, has attained the level of an institutionalized *standard*. It is espoused by a wide variety of social institutions and there is very little opposition to the idea.

At both Colton and Prescott schools teachers and administrators asked for parents' help with the three 'Rs': reading, reinforcing classroom work, and responding to teachers' requests. They made these requests for involvement repeatedly, although parents of low-achievers were asked more frequently than other parents (Becker and Epstein 1982; Hoover–Dempsey *et al.* 1987). There was no evidence that Prescott teachers solicited parents' involvement more vigorously than did Colton teachers. If anything, Colton had more organized and visible school programs to encourage parents' involvement than those in place at Prescott.

Still, the formal requests by teachers and school programs for parents' assistance did not cover the full range of parent interventions tolerated by the school. Schools have scarce organizational resources. Principals cannot easily transfer or fire school personnel. Administrators cannot afford to encourage parent requests. If a substantial number of parents sought to avoid a particular teacher (as they would have at Prescott), principals would be placed in an untenable position. Meeting parents' requests would lead to violation of class size rules, imbalanced classes by achievement level, or teachers with smaller teaching loads than others. Similarly, allowing children who did not qualify for special programs to attend them would also create pressure on organizational resources. At the very least, it would raise class sizes to counter-productive levels and alter the goals of the programs.

These constraints are important, for they underlie teachers' obvious reluctance to tell parents the full range of organizational alternatives that are *theoretically* (but not practically) available to them. Teachers at both sites did evenly enforce the formal standards of the school and the profession. They told all parents to read to their children and to attend school events. In addition to these formal standards there were informal possibilities for intervention in schooling. Parents did not, at least in these two schools, learn about these possibilities from teachers.

Not a Partnership

Teachers wanted parent involvement, but their actions strongly challenge the dominant view that teachers want a 'partnership' with parents (Seeley 1982; 1984; Gray 1984). By definition, a partnership implies a relationship between equals where power and control is evenly distributed. Teachers did not, as Prescott teachers' efforts to rebuff parents make clear, want to be equals with parents. Instead, they wanted parents to defer to them and to their decisions in the classroom.

Rather than a partnership, a more accurate term for what teachers wanted is a 'professional–client' relationship, where — at least in first and second grade — both parents and children are seen as clients. In this relationship, teachers view education as a round-the-clock experience in which parents can, and should, play a role in supplementing the classroom experience by preparing children for school, reinforcing the curriculum, and showing support (often symbolic) by attending school events. Teachers saw an interdependency between home and school, not a separation.

What teachers wanted to control is the *amount* of interconnectedness between home and school. They welcomed only particular types of parent involvement in schooling — involvement they defined as supportive and fruitful. Although they wanted parents to respond to their requests for help, they did not want parents at the school monitoring their decisions and trying to influence children's school experience. They resisted and rebuffed these attempts. Although viewed as 'semi-professionals' (Etzioni 1969, Goode 1969) by many Prescott parents teachers wanted parents to defer to their professional expertise.

Notes

1. Teachers' views here are part of a national consensus among educators — at least in general terms — about the proper role of parents in schooling. The publications of leading teacher associations, parents' groups, surveys of teachers and parents, educational policy reports, and statements of 'What Works' by the United States Department of Education share a similar message (National Education Association 1972; Comer 1980; Henderson 1981; Harris 1985a; Gallup 1985; National Commission on Excellence in Education 1983; United States Department of Education 1986). These groups are seeking a family–school relationship where parents bear responsibility for education by actively preparing children for school, reinforcing classroom material in a helpful and supportive fashion, monitoring children's educational progress and raising their concerns about their children's performance with school officials.

    In short, the current dominant view is that families and schools are 'partners' in the educational process. Parents have a right, responsibility, and obligation to be actively involved in their children's education. These groups can, and do, differ in how they interpret these goals. There are vigorous debates, for example, on the subject of parents' control of the school and the ability of parents to fire teachers. But in terms of children's individualized classroom program there is less debate. The dominant view today is that 'concerned' parents will see an interconnection between home and school and play an active role in their children's schooling.

2. Throughout the book, quotations are generally from tape-recorded interviews with parents and teachers. There are two types of markings within quotes. First, quotations have underlining, parentheses, and other forms of punctuation to provide a clearer portrait of the respondents' comments, particularly the stress that respondents' placed on particular words in their statements. (There are no instances when I have added underlining to quotations for additional emphasis.) Second, when necessary I have provided comments or clarification of the respondents' statements. These additions to the quotes are always set off by brackets (i.e., [ ]).

    On occasion I quote from field notes rather than from interviews. In most instances I mention directly that I am quoting from my field notes. In a few instances I simply report my observations of parents' and teachers' behavior at school. These examples, of course, are from my field notes rather than interviews. The methodological appendix provides more detailed information on the procedures used in interviewing and participant observation.

3. The vice-principal also held a weekly parent education/support group for single parents at the school in the first year of this study.

4. It would have been better, of course, if the schools had matching grade levels and school populations. The differences between the two schools raise the possibility that variations in parent participation may be linked to school characteristics. In particular, it may be easier for Prescott parents to collect detailed information about teachers given the smaller number of teachers. Parents also might feel more comfortable becoming involved in a smaller school rather than a larger one.

    There are signs, however, that school size may have a weak influence. First, a larger school increases the number of parents one can potentially know, even casually. Second, if school structure influences parent participation, it should have increased Colton School's parent involvement relative to Prescott. In both districts, parent participation was stressed much more heavily by the primary grade teachers than upper grade teachers (the fourth and fifth grade teachers did not use parent volunteers in the classroom). (See Becker and Epstein 1982 for a similar pattern.) Thus, all of the teachers in Colton were requesting intense levels of parent involvement, while at Prescott only the primary grade teachers were seeking this form of parent involvement. In addition both schools had very stable staffs which increased the likelihood of teachers developing reputations in the community.

Nevertheless school size may interact with social class and parent participation. A research methodology which included a large number of schools would be required in order to address this issue systematically.

5. Parents also did not report voicing complaints to Mrs Hoffman. One mother did confess that her duaghter — who was at the top of the class — came home and cried when she found out she was assigned to early reading. The mother and the father were worried too, until they discovered that 'another bright little girl' had been moved as well.

6. At Prescott all of the parents I observed used surnames in their interactions with teachers. In interviews, however, several parents referred to teachers using only their first name or both names (i.e., 'Suzanne Harpst'). By contrast, parents at Colton only used formal means of address in their interactions with teachers and their comments about teachers in interviews. I never heard a Colton parent use any teacher's first name.

7. The schools appeared to have comparable resources. For example, teachers in both schools had a classroom aide for one half of the school day, usually in the morning. Both schools had a reading resource teacher, school psychologist, school nurse, speech therapist, and special education teacher available for teachers and students. These educational consultants spent more hours at Colton than at Prescott. On the other hand, while Mrs Thompson, the first grade teacher at Colton, had a piano in the classroom, Prescott had a more elaborate music, art, and drama program than at Colton. Prescott teachers also had about $100 per year to purchase classroom supplies and the use of a xerox machine, luxuries not available at Colton. The physical plants were both older and well-maintained; Colton was painted during the study and Prescott had regular 'maintenance' days.

What did vary, however, was the source of funding for the additional educational programs. Colton received federal funds for the large number of disadvantaged students; Prescott did not, At Colton these programs were heavily underwritten by federal funds and, to a lesser extent, district funds. Thus at Prescott, parent volunteers, parents' fundraising efforts, and district funds provided funds for programs and volunteer labor to maintain the building and the educational programs. (See Levy *et al.* 1975 for a discussion of social class and funds for schooling.)

3 Separation Between Family and School: Colton

Every morning the circle in front of Colton school was jammed with parents dropping off their children. At the end of the day parents returned to walk or drive their children home. But during the school day, it was unusual to see parents in the halls, in the classrooms, or in the main office at Colton. When parents were there, it was usually to drop off a forgotten lunch or to pick up a sick child. Since visitors were expected to check in at the main office, forgotten lunches, jackets, and medicine, as well as sick children, were generally routed through the central office building.

The appearance of a parent in the doorway while school was in session was considered an unusual event by both the children and the school staff. Children stopped what they were doing to watch the teacher talk to the parent. For their part the parents appeared anxious about interrupting the class and tentative in their actions. Parents either knocked on the classroom door (if it was closed) or hovered near the doorway before being recognized by the teacher. None simply walked in to speak to the teacher.

Over the six months I observed at Colton school I saw only four mothers of children in Mrs Thompson's class come in during the school day.[1] In one case, the mother was a voluntary assistant in the classroom. She spent an hour in the classroom taking a very unobtrusive role, but helping to pass out paper and give the children scissors. The other three mothers had come to school to drop off something for their children. For example, the class celebrated children's birthdays with a treat. Some mothers were apprehensive about letting a six-year-old carry a cake or a box of cookies on the bus: they preferred, instead, to bring the treat to class during the day.

Parents were invited to school to participate in a series of school events, including Back-to-School Night, a Christmas program, an Easter Hat Parade, Open House Night, a Book Fair, Grandparents Day, and fall and spring parent-teacher conference. As Table 4 indicates, attendance at these school events ranged from about one third of the parents (for Open House) to about two thirds of the parents (for parent–teacher conferences). Attendance at these events is overwhelmingly dominated by mothers; fathers are less active

Table 4 *Parent Participation in School Activities: Colton School*

School Activity	Number of Children's Parents Attending
Parent–teacher Conference	60%
Open House	35%
Volunteering in the Classroom	3%

n = 34

participants in school activities. (These gender differences are analyzed in Chapter Five.) Given teachers' hopes, the response to these events on the part of Colton parents was very disappointing. The 'neglect' by Colton parents of their children's education was considered to be a serious problem and surfaced frequently in the staff's comments and complaints. To gain more insight into why parents failed to respond to teachers' requests, I visited parents in their homes to talk to them about their perceptions of the family–school relationship.

The Morris Family

The Morrises live in a two story house in an older housing district in West Colton. The house is one of the bigger homes in the area. Most of the other homes are small and many have weeds growing in the front yards. When I visited there were two trucks and a small recreational vehicle parked in front of the house; there was a Toyota in the yard. Inside, everything was very clean and carefully arranged. The living room had a variegated orange carpet and an imitation leather couch facing a large television, which Mrs Morris was watching when I arrived. The dining area had a black table with four chairs and a basket of straw flowers on the table. A black cupboard with the china bells Mrs Morris collects was in the corner. There were framed color pictures of the two Morris children on the wall.

Mrs Morris is a tall, slender woman in her late twenties. She was dressed in jeans and a velour top, with heavy blue eye shadow and bright red spots of blusher on her cheeks. Her nervous smile revealed crooked teeth. After greeting me she turned off the television and offered me a cup of coffee. As she was fixing the coffee she confided, nervously, 'I have never done anything like this before.' I tried to reassure her, telling her that I was attempting to learn more about how families help their children in school. I emphasized that no one — including the teachers at Colton school — would hear what she told me that day. She seemed to relax a bit. She brought in the coffee from the kitchen in two mugs and lit a cigarette. I began the interview.

The Morrises have two children: Tina, a fourth grader, and Tommy, who had just finished first grade with Mrs Thompson. Mr Morris used to work with Mrs Morris's father in construction: during the last few years he has started his own business out of the home. Mrs Morris works part-time on the business, keeping the books. Two years ago she also worked part-time in the cafeteria at Colton school. The Morries have been married over ten years; Mrs Morris was eighteen when she got married. She is a high school graduate; her husband is a high school drop-out.

Mrs Morris described a clear division of responsibilities between herself and the teacher with respect to Tommy's schooling:

> To me, my part was here at home. I'm to teach him manners and to see that he did get to school and that he was happy. To try and show him different things. It was like I told my husband, there was nothing that I wanted the kids to miss out on. Now her part, the school's part — to me was that they were with him to teach him to learn. Hopefully someday he would be able to use all of that. That was what I thought was their part — to teach him to read, the writing, any kind of schooling.

When I asked if there were any areas that overlap, that were blurry, that teachers and parents worked together on, Mrs Morris replied:

> No, not really, unless he was not getting satisfied. Now he was getting frustrated at the beginning of the year because he didn't know how to do certain things that the rest of the class was doing. So we worked with him on that.

Hence, Mrs Morris perceived a separation between family life and school life. When Tommy entered first grade, she turned over responsibility for his education to the school. She did not expect home and school to overlap unless there were extenuating circumstances. She felt that she and her husband had been more heavily involved this past year, especially at the beginning of the year, than they might normally have been, because Tommy was having some trouble in school.

At the end of the school year, however, Mrs Morris was startled to learn that Mrs Thompson recommended that her son repeat first grade:

> I guess she had been trying to tell me that all along but it didn't sink in. But I went in for my last conference and she wrote it on his report card: it would be better for him to repeat first grade. Then, you know, I thought she was kind of suggesting it. Then she called for a special conference. And I wasn't going to. I don't know if she told you [blushes, slight nervous laughter] but I wasn't going to keep him back. Now they call him the baby of the class because he is so much younger than the other kids. And I had the same problem with my daughter. I didn't hold her back and she was a 'B' student. So I wasn't going to do it with Tommy.

In the special conference at the end of the year, Mrs Morris refused to sign the paper allowing retention. In Colton school district, retention is not permitted without the agreement of the parents. Mrs Morris did not want her son to repeat first grade, as Mrs Thompson explained:

She very much felt that we could help Tommy at home ... can't he go on. Can't he do it ... But I just strongly advised that it would be a shame for Tommy. I showed her the books that the other children were doing and I showed her where Tommy was. To put him in with the other children next year would be a wrong-doing for Tommy. She seemed to listen at school.

She didn't want it. She said 'we will help him at home. And I am sure he will catch up'. It was only at the last when she saw the work books that the other children had done, saw the books they were reading, that she realized that Tommy wasn't there.

After the conference Mrs Morris discussed the matter with her husband and her relatives. Her aunt (who is about her age) has a son who also was held back. Mrs Morris said the child was 'crushed' by the retention and his mother felt that 'it didn't do him any good.' Mrs Morris was worried about her son being teased and being considered an educational failure:

I asked her [the aunt] if he got teased and she said, 'No.' That was what got me because when we were in school, if you were held back, you *failed*. There wasn't anything else about it. You were dumb and you failed. But now, I don't think that they tease you and I guess that there were a number of kids who were held back each year.

She and her husband were also bewildered by Mrs Thompson's recommendation because they were under the impression that Tommy had been doing well in school. She described her husband's reaction to the teacher's recommendation:

At first he couldn't understand why she was holding him back. He brought home star papers. And if he was having problems I would have, or I think I would have, caught it. Because he never brought home a bad paper. So my husband didn't know what was going on.

Mrs Morris did know that her son was feeling frustrated in school and was not having an easy time. She felt that she and her husband had worked with him to help him and did not understand that the problem was more serious.

Mrs Morris was aware, however, that Tommy was maturing more slowly than his best friend Toby (who also was recommended for retention) and a cousin:

Then the maturity, I don't know how you say it, but even him and Toby, Toby was more mature. He thought different from Tommy. I have a nephew and they were nine months apart and they were totally opposite. The games they played and then Tommy had a speech problem and so we tried to baby him around. My nephew was nine months older to the day and he was much bigger. He had lost more teeth. I looked at things like that which probably didn't amount to nothing. The games they played and the way they could play it.

After Mrs Thompson recommended retention, Mrs Morris considered having Tommy go on to second grade and then holding him back at the end of the next year if he got behind. She knew that at the end of second grade, Colton students move on to a different elementary school. Mrs Morris thought that postponing the decision until the end of second grade would be easier for Tommy and would prevent him from being teased. Mrs Thompson, however, did not support this idea; she insisted that Tommy wouldn't be able to keep up with the work next year.

In the end, Mrs Morris returned to school and told Mrs Thompson that she and her husband would agree to having Tommy repeat first grade. During their efforts to reach a decision, she and her husband asked their son about the matter:

> I came home [from the special conference] and told my husband and we talked about it for a couple of days. And then we asked Tommy what he wanted. And Tommy was excited about it. His best friend [Toby] lived up the street and she was holding him back too and so it worked out good.

In repeating first grade, Tommy would have Mrs Thompson again. Mrs Morris reported that 'Tommy *really* liked her and I liked her.' She felt that Mrs Thompson 'really took the time to help him' and was sensitive to Tommy's frustration and 'kind of gave over to him sometimes' while at other times she helped him conquer problems and make progress with his work.

Repeating a grade becomes a public event. Mrs Morris reported that her husband's relatives (including an uncle and three cousins who lived next door to them) accepted the news that Tommy would repeat first grade. Mrs Morris's mother, however, was very upset by it.

> My mother hit the roof. In my days, if you were held back you failed. That was all there was to it. Well my mother couldn't understand. He wasn't behind from missing or any of that kind of thing. She took it pretty hard. My husband took it pretty hard. And then I explained it to him how things worked.

> Now his side of the family, I think just about everyone had been held back. So it was really no big deal on their side. My father was saying that my brother graduated at almost 17 years old. If he had it to do over then he would have held my brother back just as far as the age went. So my father took it pretty good but my mother just [felt] 'it was horrible'. I don't even think I told her until July.

Mrs Morris's mother, like Mrs Morris, viewed retention as occurring as a result of intellectual failure or failure to complete work.

> She just couldn't understand why he was held back. There was no medical problem. There wasn't . . . he wasn't a complete dummy . . . I was brought up that if you were held back, you failed. You didn't do your work. That was it. Finally I told her, the other kids were really

more advanced than he was, they were more higher as far as reading and that Tommy had a hard time.

Mrs Morris's mother was very upset and bewildered by the decision. It had not been a topic of conversation again, although Mrs Morris talked on the telephone to her mother at least once a week:

> She brought it up the once. And that was it. Then this year when he started back she asked how he was doing this year. My mother was kind of funny. She wouldn't talk about things like that. She wouldn't talk about bad things that she thought were horrible.

Mrs Morris attributed her mother's reaction to the high value which her family placed on education, particularly regular school attendance and graduation.

> I knew it was important. Now my mother was one of these, that she still is, all of us kids graduated regardless of what, we graduated. You went to school unless you were completely sick and had to go to the doctor. You went to school. Now my husband's side of the family, you went if you wanted, if you didn't you didn't. So I knew that it was no big deal to them. That the kids graduated was no big deal. Whereas on my side, if you didn't graduate it was terrible.

Within working-class families then there are variations in attitudes towards educational failure. In Mr Morris's family, there is an acceptance of retention as normal; among Mrs Morris's relatives, there is more embarrassment and a sense of failure over the retention.

Mrs Morris's belief in the separation of home and school was evident in other ways as well. Although she dropped Tommy off at school and picked him up every day, she had been in the classroom only a few times. Her meetings with Mrs Thompson occurred in formally scheduled conferences. She rarely met or conferred with Mrs Thompson at other points. When she did come to school she stayed in her car or waited until school was out before coming to the door of the classroom. She did not want, as she put it, to 'butt in.'

Mrs Morris had only very general information about Mrs Thompson and Tommy's schooling. She had not heard of Mrs Thompson's reputation (or the reputation of any other teachers) before the beginning of the school year. She could make only very general comments about Mrs Thompson's teaching style; she noted that Mrs Thompson was 'nice' and that 'she doesn't raise her voice.' From what Tommy told her, and from his papers, she knew a bit about the curriculum. She knew, for example, what words they were learning in school (e.g., broom) and that they were working on sounds, as well as learning to count by circling the number of chickens or cows.

In both the first and second year of the study, however, she did not know what reading group Tommy was in, could not provide details about his academic strengths and weaknesses and did not know that spelling words were given at a special time or that parents were asked to help their children with the words. Neither did she know the name of the reading specialist or the classroom aide, or that there had been a change in the principal at the school. In short, while she carefully monitored her child's experience in school, most of her information came from her child rather than from other adults.

Tommy Morris had a speech problem. In kindergarten and first grade he went to the speech teacher. At the end of first grade he had improved and the following year he did not continue speech therapy. Mrs Morris was concerned about this and thought he could benefit from more speech lessons. In our interviews she mentioned her concern. She did not, however, bring it to the attention of Mrs Thompson through a special conference. Nor did she directly raise it during the regularly scheduled parent–teacher conference (which I observed). Instead she simply asked if he was going to speech lessons and express-ed great relief when Mrs Thompson suggested signing him up for therapy again. In sum, she was very non-directive with the school; she left her son's schooling up to his teacher(s). Although there were times that she resisted teachers' recommendations (as with the retention) there were not signs of her taking a leadership role in directing teachers' actions and her children's academic program.

Her criticisms of the school centered almost entirely on non-academic issues. She was very upset about the 'bad language' and 'cuss words' in the school. She, along with many other parents, was irritated by the school's extremely short lunch period. She thought it was unfair that her fourth grade daughter's class did not have a Halloween party, and she had even called the principal about it. (He responded that each classroom had only two parties per year and that the timing of these events was up to the teacher.)

Moreover, in those interactions with the teachers at the school site which I observed, Mrs Morris often appeared tense and ill at ease. At Open House night she did not speak to the teacher's aide; she and her husband and children quietly wandered around the room. The parent-teacher conference consisted primarily of the teacher's comments; Mrs Morris asked a few questions but did not speak at length. In addition she looked uncomfortable, shifted in her chair, and appeared relieved when the conference was over.

Mrs Thompson's view

Mrs Thompson was pleased that Mrs Morris had agreed to the retention. She thought it was the best thing for Tommy. She was disappointed, however, by what she perceived to be the Morris's lack of interest in their son's schooling. She found that her efforts to encourage their involvement were not successful:

> I sent work home. I don't know if they worked with him or not. [So he didn't bring the work back?] No.

She reported that despite her efforts to encourage the children to read in first grade, Tommy did not take books home regularly and she did not get slips for the Read-at-Home Program. This frustrated her. Mrs Thompson thought that Mrs Morris was a capable mother, noting that she would take Tommy places. Nevertheless she did not believe that Tommy's mother was doing all she could do and should do to promote his educational success.

> The parents and their attitudes towards the school didn't help Tommy all that much. They didn't come to school to get work that much to work with Tommy though they knew he was behind. And I felt they were capable of doing it, even more so than Mrs Brown. I felt that Mrs Morris could have helped him more at home.

Mrs Thompson would have liked Tommy's parents to read to him and to request additional school work. She noted that Tommy's pride was hurt sometimes in the classroom; for example, this would occur when he had an 'easy' book to read and someone next to him had a more difficult one. He did not want to be reading the easy one. She also noted that Tommy did not tend to bring home his papers:

> He was one who would leave his papers in his cubby and he would leave his papers in his desk (a very sloppy desk). He would just leave them there and until finally they would be thrown out at school. If he was proud of a paper I guess he took it home. And he took some of them home but he wasn't one of the ones who was anxious to take them home.

Mrs Thompson was seeking much more interconnectedness between the Morris's home life and Tommy's school life than she got from Mr and Mrs Morris. She wanted the educational responsibility to be shared, and she wanted Tommy's education to be viewed as part of 'living' rather than simply limited to school hours.

In addition she suspected that the parents were not completely supportive of the school:

> I got a sense that they didn't build a confidence in Tommy that the school was doing their job as well as it should. It could be all wrong and I hope it was. I think I got it from little comments she would make. But a couple of comments that he made about his mother saying the teachers didn't know what to do with Toby and him. That they weren't learning.

> Shortly after I asked that he be retained [she made] some comment [that] was derogatory to the teachers. So they weren't feeling that comfortable with the decision or that confident that we really knew what we were talking about. I didn't mind confronting this and I would have liked her to come to school [to confront] that.

Despite the retention and the lack of parental involvement, Mrs Thompson was optimistic about Tommy's academic future. She believed he was capable of being a good student. She also believed his frustration and behavior problems would subside as he enjoyed more success. She felt he had a drive to learn — he particularly liked math. She saw him as a 'late bloomer' who would do well after repetition of first grade. She thought his home situation was an advantage:

> He had a home situation that was going to be fine for him. I felt that it was a substantial home ... from her ability to express herself, the mother and the sister would come in and the sister would seem to be confident, the way that the children were groomed. It seems as if they had a little more togetherness in the home.

Mrs Thompson would have preferred a more active role for the parents, but she did not expect that Tommy would continue to experience failure in school.

Conflicts over Parental Roles

Mrs Thompson and Mrs Morris had different ideas about the process of schooling and the proper role of parents in schooling. Mrs Morris viewed schooling as similar to work — something that took place between eight in the morning and three in the afternoon, at school. Mrs Morris placed responsibility for education with the teachers. By contrast Mrs Thompson saw education as taking place during all of each child's waking hours. She wanted the parents to work with her and to work with Tommy at home.

This conception of education as work which takes place during prescribed hours is perhaps best exemplified by Mrs Morris's treatment of the Read-at-Home Program. In the parent–teacher interview, Mrs Thompson repeated five times in twenty minutes the importance of Tommy's reading at home. She also checked with Mrs Morris to see if Tommy had checked out any books to read at home as part of the Read-at-Home Program. Mrs Morris knew of the Read-at-Home Program and liked it:

> I think it was good. Now my daughter used to do it and she would collect a lot of books from doing it. They looked forward to reading it. Tommy looked forward to reading it and took that time and turned it in. Because he had earned that book. You know it really made him feel good because he didn't have to pay for it. Or I didn't have to pay for it. I guess that they had a chart in the classroom. He looked on that chart and found where he was and everything. I think it was real good. I think a lot of kids around here liked it.

She also noted that her son was reading a lot more his second time through first grade than in the previous year:

> He had a real bad time with reading last year. He couldn't get the sounds down. He would get so frustrated and so mad. So my daughter would read to him unless we made him read. Whereas this year he reads.

He brought books home and then she checked out books from the library. They more or less, well he would read a story and then she would read a story. Then they ordered books. He got the reading time, the extra reading time for free books.

As a result he was now reading almost every night:

I put them to bed at nine and then by 9.30 or a quarter to ten they were asleep. So I usually gave him about a half an hour reading time on that. But they read almost every night.

Surprisingly, however, she only gave her son credit for the reading he did between Monday and Friday. She did not count reading on the weekends for the Read-at-Home Program:

I just did it during the week. He did read on the weekends but I felt that he shouldn't get time for that. I figured on the weekends it was his free time. If he wanted to read or if he didn't. But then during the week they did read and why not let him put his time in?

This rule that weekend time did not count was not part of teachers' views of the Read-at-Home Program. If anything, teachers considered any and all forms of reading as legitimate participation in the program, including a parent reading to the child or the child reading to the parent.

Mrs Morris approved of the program, particularly the economic savings of getting a free book. Yet in separating out weekday from weekend reading time Mrs Morris treated schooling as a job which her children did. This highlights her perception of home and school as separate spheres. She resisted integrating these spheres in spite of the teacher's suggestions.

Mrs Morris's resistance to adopting a more active role in schooling also was apparent during Tommy's second year in first grade. Mrs Morris came to school regularly to pick up her son at the end of the day. Mrs Thompson encouraged Mrs Morris to come into the classroom and sit next to Tommy while class was going on. Mrs Morris was astonished by this:

You know before when I was in school if your mother came you waited outside. But Mrs Thompson seemed to try to get you involved. Like, she made sure I came in. I guess because it tickled him. She made me sit next to him and look at what he had done and what all was going on in the class and that kind of thing. I liked Mrs Thompson; she was real good.

At the beginning of the year Mrs Morris did enter the class for a few minutes at the end of the day. By the middle of the year, however, she had reverted to her previous pattern of waiting for her son in the car.

Mrs Morris was aware of Mrs Thompson's wishes that she and her husband read to Tommy. Nevertheless, she did not take a leadership role in educational activities with her children. As a result, when these activities occurred at home it was because the children actively sought them, by bringing books home and suggesting that they read or play school.

The experience of the Morris family provides insight into the quality of family–school interactions, but leaves open the question of common experiences in family–school relationships in the community at large. Below I describe regular features of family–school relationships at Colton school which emerged from classroom observations in a six month period, interviews with teachers, and interviews with six families when their children were in first grade and again in second grade. While there were shared features of family–school interactions, there were also significant variations.

Elements of Family-School Relationships at Colton

The 'Proper Role' of Parents in Schooling

During the course of each interview, I asked Colton mothers and fathers to describe what they perceived to be their proper role in schooling. All the parents indicated that they wanted to be helpful and to work with the teacher. As Laura's mother put it:

> Working together, keeping in touch with the teacher and what is going on at school. Just showing her [Laura] what you can get out of life. Everything is a new experience. We do a lot of traveling and showing her. Not everything she learns comes out of school.

The parents' definition of how to help, however differed from the teachers'. In addition to Mrs Morris, other parents described a clear division of responsibility between the home and the school. Parents prepared children for school; teachers educated them. A Colton mother who was one of the most active parents in the class described her role in this way:

> I prepared them to go to school. That was my place. They had to learn maybe like you could say basic structure. Behavior. You know, you didn't throw things all over and you did what you were told and things like that. That was my job. And her [Mrs Thompson's] job was to really teach them. She had gone to school to learn the best way to teach reading, mathematics, science, things like that. I don't know that. So, she took the lead in that and I simply followed what she did.

This mother tried to support her son's schooling by reading to him at home and reviewing his math papers. The teachers considered this mother and her husband to be extremely supportive of schooling. Even with this family, however, there is a relatively clear division of labor between home and school: mothers and fathers teach children good manners and proper behavior and turn over responsibility for education to the school.

The teachers recognized this division although they did not support it. As Mrs Thompson explained:

> In general [the parents] expected the school to do most all of it. Most of the parents did expect the school to do the majority of the job. They didn't have as much confidence in their ability to help the children. They didn't want to interfere. I heard this over and over again. 'We don't want to teach our children incorrectly.' So they didn't have as much confidence.

This lack of confidence led parents to defer to the teacher's professional expertise. Mrs Thompson noted:

> Over and over I would get the comment that, 'You at school know what is best for my child. You know; I don't really know'. Lack of confidence in their ability to affect the child or the child's need. So that they would think, whatever you say was okay.

The lack of confidence was also apparent when parents and teachers conferred face to face. Colton parents appeared nervous and genuinely anxious in front of their children's teachers. Many shifted from one foot to another, had trouble maintaining eye contact, spoke very rapidly, and, in a few cases, stumbled over their words. In parent–teacher interactions after school, on field trips, and during Open House Nights, teachers spoke at greater length than parents, used longer sentences, and usually opened and closed the conversation. In parent–teacher conferences, parents primarily listened quietly to the teachers' comments and asked few questions. I did not observe nor was I told of an instance where parents asked penetrating or critical questions about the teachers' programs and their children's academic progress.

To be sure, a few parents appeared at ease with teachers. For example, on the last day of school one parent came by to thank Mrs Thompson for all that she had done for her son. The boy had had a difficult time as the parents had separated and divorced during the school year. The mother was very grateful to the teacher for the help she had given her son and thanked her sincerely. Mrs Thompson warmly congratulated the mother and father for handling a difficult situation so well. These moments, however, when a teacher and a parent achieved a warm rapport, appeared to be very rare at Colton.

In general teachers saw relatively little of parents. When they did meet their interactions were brief and professional. Some parents did have friendly relations with school staff members that included chatting about non-academic matters. These relationships were almost always with the janitor, the cafeteria workers, or the teachers' aides. Working-class parents' relationships with professionals were instrumental and focused; if more informal and social relationships did occur at school, they were with persons of similar class status.

According to Colton parents, their job was to get children to school prepared and ready to learn. The learning itself was up to the teachers. Parents varied, however, in how well they executed their half of this implicit bargain.

Rubin (1976) and others have divided working-class families into 'settled-livers' and 'hard-livers.' Settled-livers have clean and orderly lives, despite modest incomes and frequent periods of unemployment. Hard-livers are often plagued by problems of alcoholism, economic instability, and physical abuse; the lives of these latter families are much more chaotic.

Most of the children in Colton school appeared to be from settled-liver families. They arrived at school on time, looking clean and well cared for. These children were awakened by their parents in time to dress, eat breakfast, get to the bus stop, and catch the bus. The majority of Colton parents made sure that their children had lunch money, had any materials needed for class projects (e.g., milk cartons), and that papers sent home by the school requiring signature were signed and returned.

Some families, however, did not meet this standard. Mr Wagner, the principal, complained of four children with chronic absenteeism (e.g., thirty to fifty per cent of the time) and others with irregular attendance and serious problems of tardiness. As Mr Wagner said:

> [There were] those who didn't even go to the trouble of getting them up. [If a] kid didn't get to school it was not her [the mother's] fault, it was the kid's fault. He didn't set his alarm. He didn't get out of bed. We had a few like that.

In Mrs Thompson's class, one talkative little girl named Ann-Marie was an hour or more late to school about once a week. When she appeared her hair had not been brushed. Her clothing often looked as if she had chosen it without adult guidance — items of clothing did not match or were not warm enough (e.g., a sleeveless dress on a cold, rainy day). When she finally arrived at school, she would occasionally tell the teacher that she was late because they had 'partied' the night before. Both her first and second grade teachers were frustrated by Ann-Marie's frequent tardiness and absences. Mrs Thompson considered reporting Ann-Marie's mother to Child Protective Services for child neglect, but because she thought the evidence was insufficient she did not do so. Cases such as Ann-Marie's were a recurrent problem for teachers and administrators at Colton. Most parents did comply with their half of the educational bargain, as they understood it. Still, it did not match the teachers' definitions of what their role should be.

Information about Schooling

Colton parents were eager for their children to achieve success in school. They were pleased that the children brought home stars and 'smelly stickers' on their papers. In interviews all of the mothers and the fathers knew the name of their child's teacher. Based on their evaluation of the school papers that their children brought home, some of the parents had a general idea of what their children were learning in school. As one mother explained:

They counted how many chickens there were and circle[d] the numbers.

Most parents did not, however, have detailed information. Only one parent knew the name of the classroom aide. None knew that there had been a change in the principal between the first and second grade school year.

Parents of low-achievers knew that their children were going to the learning center and were working with specialists, but they did not know their children's in-school schedule or the exact nature of the educational problems:

She went [to the learning center] every day I think. No, well she had learning center or had [sighs] something new had just started or something new that she was going to. I can't remember what it was called. It was like another type . . . it was like a learning center but it was with a different teacher. She told me what it was called an I can't remember. Anyway, they told me that they would bring me all up to date on everything after Jill was tested and we all got together again.

Similarly, parents could describe their children's academic strengths and weaknesses in a general way. One mother, for example, accounted for her daughter's retention the previous year this way:

She didn't enjoy school too much last year because she wasn't up to par . . . up to grade. You know Mrs Thompson explained that to me. Mrs Thompson explained that Laura wasn't the only one. She was trying to keep six of them back because of their age. They just weren't old enough and mature enough. So that kind of helped me feel better and made Laura feel better.

Laura's mother could not provide a more detailed assessment of what it meant for Laura not to be 'up to par', but she did note that Laura needed to be given a 'push' sometimes in her school work. Jill's mother said that her daughter had a problem of immaturity and a problem with her attention span. Johnny's mother knew that he was doing well in school and knew the math problems and spelling words that he was being given. But most parents did not know which reading group their child was in, the position of their child within the classroom, the name of the boy or girl who was best in math, spelling, or art, or their children's test scores from the previous year. All of the parents knew and said that they liked Mrs Thompson, but they did not know the names of any other first or second grade teachers. They did not know the reputations of other teachers in the school.

The lack of information that Colton parents had about schooling was also apparent when their children entered school. Three mothers mentioned that although their children started school in early September, it was not until the first conference in November that they realized that they had not adequately prepared their children for school. One mother, a high school graduate, complained:

> They [her children] knew their ABCs, they knew their colors and could identify them, and they knew a square and a triangle and a circle and all of those sorts of things. But I hadn't sat them down and showed them enough. So they couldn't identify 1, 2, 3 or 4. They could show you this is four apples and this is three apples but they couldn't write the number. They couldn't identify the number on a piece of paper. You know, because I — I neglected it. So they had to learn that in school. But that wasn't any big thing. They caught it real quickly.

Another mother told a similar story. When asked if there were things that the school could have done differently, she replied:

> No, not really. I didn't have many gripes with the school. I did have a gripe though (pauses). Now, when he went into kindergarten he was already supposed to have known his numbers and his ABCs. To me, they didn't need to know that when they go to school. That was where they taught him. He was only four and one half when he started school. And he didn't know it and everyone else knew it and I didn't *think* to teach him that when he started school.

In the first conference in November, one mother learned of her son's lack of adequate preparation for school when the teacher asked her to work with him at home:

> I had my first conference and that was when she told me that everyone else knew it. So then my husband and I, well she gave me some cards ... and I started buying these books, these little workbook things, and he caught right on.

This problem of not knowing the school's expectations was not limited to low-achievers. Mr and Mrs Larson, for example, were surprised to find out that their children were more advanced than others in the school:

> We did work with her when she was quite young, only because we didn't know better. We just thought that was what you did with kids. You taught them their ABCs by the time they were three and they could learn to add by the time they went to kindergarten. That is just [what] we thought kids should do. We didn't know better.

As a result their children entered kindergarten knowing not only their ABCs but also how to write their name and count to 200. They were considered advanced by the Colton teachers.

Lacking information about the classroom program, Colton parents appeared to rely heavily on children's grades in first and second grade. Children regularly brought home papers they had completed in class with rubber stamps at the top of the page with brief evaluations, (i.e., good work, messy, neat) or stickers with facial expressions (i.e., a happy face) or smells (i.e., strawberries). In addition children received report cards four times per year with three possible letters (i.e., VG for very good, S for satisfactory, and N for needs to improve). Teachers often added pluses or minuses to the grades, especially to the S.

In interviews, parents saw grades as a primary indicator of children's performance. Tommy's mother, for example, felt her son's grades had improved when his papers came home with fewer stamps of 'Messy' and more stamps of 'Good Work'. Laura's mother was surprised that her daughter had so little reading or homework the year she repeated first grade, but concluded that since 'her grades were good' her progress was smooth. Teachers, however, rarely discussed children's grades and were preoccupied with their curricular goals (i.e., children's reading fluency or reading comprehension). The details of children's academic program were unfamiliar to Colton parents; instead they relied on the indicators that children were conforming to institutional standards.[2]

Lack of information about the curriculum appeared to be related both to parents' conception of their proper role in schooling and the lack of social networks among Colton parents. Parents' sources of information about schooling were their children, their relatives, and their children's contacts with teachers. None of the mothers knew the names of or had social ties with other mothers in their children's classroom. Many parents had information about schooling, but it was confined to topics such as the lunch program, the bus schedule, the yard duty teacher, and the safety of their children on the school site, rather than the content of learning.

Even parents whom teachers considered to be very active in supporting their children's schooling lacked information about academic matters. Very involved parents could not provide detailed assessments of their children's academic strengths and weaknesses, nor could they name the strengths and weaknesses of either the teachers or the school. Colton parents depended upon the school to educate their children: this created a fundamental separation between home and school.

Interventions in Schooling

All of the families reported that they helped their children in school. Parents read to their children, played educational games, made up math problems for them to do, and helped them with their spelling words. For example, parents had children count the silverware as they set the dinner table or played license plate games using the alphabet while on long trips.

It was difficult to determine how frequently these activities occurred. For example, one step-father said that he helped his step-daughter 'all the time' with her school work. But the examples he gave were from the previous year. The girl's mother said that she had learned from Mrs Thompson that spelling words were handed out on Mondays. Her daughter was repeating first grade, and she said that this second year she worked with her daughter on her words. The mother explained:

The first year I didn't know that they brought their spelling words home on Monday. She never did tell me she was having trouble with spelling. I asked Mrs Thompson. I said, 'You know she never seems to bring home any words.' Mrs Thompson said Laura brought the words home on Mondays. I said, 'Ah hah!' So I know that these spelling words were coming home. So she didn't get away with that anymore. She would hand them to me because there was no getting out of it.

Mrs Thompson, however, said that she did not see evidence of Laura's being read to at home, nor did she know her spelling words when she came to school. She thought that Laura was a 'pretty bright little girl' who was able to 'pick up' her spelling words during class lessons.

Mrs Thompson did say that some parents worked with their children at home, including Johnny's parents. Mr Trenton told of helping Johnny with his spelling:

And then [there] were words, certain words, that boy, no matter what, you couldn't get him to spell that word. He would spell it and then five minutes later he couldn't spell it. So what we did was take a piece of paper and I wrote the word on it and then I taped them everyplace. We had them taped in the bathroom and on the doors and on the refrigerator. They saw it all the time. And every time I would see Johnny or Missy I would say, 'How do you spell cat?' And pretty soon they got past it. Same way with Phil's colors. Everything was blue.

Mr and Mrs Trenton also reported that they made Johnny go over his math problems when he brought them home and do over the ones that he missed. They worked with Johnny on his penmanship, having him practice at home and encouraging him to do better. Mrs Thompson considered the Trenton family to be very involved in education but believed that this was very unusual. It is difficult to say how accurate her assessment is. The Trentons did emphasize that they worked with Johnny daily and provided details about the ways in which they did this. Other parents were more vague in their comments. Even these families, however, probably worked with their children in educational activities at least a dozen times during the academic year. For most families, it was not a daily occurrence.

One problem parents reported was that children sometimes resisted working at home. Parents mentioned that their children would squirm in their chairs, ask to get a glass of water, try to watch television, or ask permission to go outside to play. During the Colton school program to increase parental intervention in schooling one mother recounted:

Carrie listened to me all day long and she got tired of that. She should have been learning to tell time and so I sat her down and she said, 'Why should I learn it?'

I told her it was important, 'What if you want to go to your friend's house?' She was not interested at all. Then she went to school and learned it from Mrs Adams [her teacher] in one day! [Laughed, frustrated]

It is hard to estimate how much parents were working with children at home, but it was clear that parents made relatively few interventions or requests about their children's program on the school site. Only one or two parents in the entire school made special requests for teachers each year. Mr Wagner noted that in his previous school (in an affluent community), he received about twenty-five such requests each year. At Colton teacher requests were virtually unheard of, even among the most active parents. As Suzy's mother explained:

At Colton I had never come across anyone that said this person was not qualified to teach. So I felt as if they had qualified teachers and one was as good as the other.

None of the parents requested a special conference with the teachers during the school year, although Mrs Trenton was considering requesting a special conference for her younger daughter. Nor did the parents make formal requests for their children to be enrolled in special programs. Entrance to the gifted and talented program was determined by the teacher's recommendation. Suzy's parents, for example, received a letter indicating that she would be enrolled in the program.

Teachers and principals complained that it was hard to reach Colton parents sometimes:

It was much more difficult to get ahold of people here [than at my previous school]. There were some that did not have telephones and they were difficult to get ahold of. I found that to be a significant factor as opposed to the previous school I was at.

In the teachers' opinion, a majority of parents were not regularly involved in their children's schooling. A small minority, however, were active. Mr Wagner described this group:

However, there were others, who because they were in a low economic area they valued it [education] very high as they saw that was their passport to make a change. A few kids in that case really came through and did wonders. They [the parents] were here. They checked on their kids. They came to all of the report periods. They were involved sometimes in the PTA. They were more involved in the whole process of raising and educating kids.

Criticisms and Challenges of the School

Parents at Colton school were uncritical in their evaluation of teachers. The criticisms that parents had, and the challenges that they made to the school, were almost entirely about non-academic issues.

All of the families I interviewed reported that they and their children liked Mrs Thompson. Questions about her strengths and weaknesses as a teacher, however, drew puzzled looks and responses from parents. I had the following exchange with one of the most active parents in the class:

> Question: Every teacher has her strengths and her weaknesses. Can you tell me what you think are Mrs Thompson's strengths as a teacher and her weaknesses?

> Her weakness? I don't know weakness. I just thought she was really really a very good teacher. She had a lot of understanding. It seemed that she really loved children. Reading was important to her. I don't know. I didn't see any particular weakness in her. I really, really liked her. I thought she was really good. Johnny loved her. You know he still went back and saw her and this kind of thing. He has liked all of his teachers.

Other parents evaluated Mrs Thompson and other teachers in similarly general and positive terms:

> When I was in Jill's class, her regular class, there was really not much to observe. I mean they just went about what they were doing. The teacher was very nice. She didn't let the kids get away with a lot, which I think was good. Because, you know, the less time they played around in there the more they were going to learn.

Most of the parents were satisfied with the school's academic program. Only one parent, Mr Trenton, had a complaint:

> I thought that they should be learning more than what they were. I thought that in kindergarten was when they should have learned when to count their change. I just thought that they should be learning more than what they were. It has been a long time now. But when I lived back East, the second graders were into multiplication and division. But that was in a Catholic school. And it wasn't just a few special students who went to some brainy little room. It was the school. Second grade was when you learned multiplication and your division and things like that. They weren't reading books like, 'Jack went up the hill'. It was more advanced material than our children were reading.

While the academic program of their children was not a subject of criticism, parents did have things they were unhappy about in the school. The lunch program drew complaints from all of the parents. At Colton children had only fifteen minutes to eat lunch. As Mr Trenton explains:

> I had gone to the school, not so much about the education but there was a thing here where they gave the children fifteen minutes to come in the

> lunch room, sit down, get their food, eat it, and get out. Hell, even the
> Marines give you half an hour. When Johnny went to school he had
> fine table manners. I noticed here about six months ago he would sit
> down at the table and just wolf his dinner. He would hold his fork like
> this [demonstrates] and would just wolf it down. And I chewed him out
> for it and finally he told me that that is what they do at school. So when
> I found that out, I went down raising hell about that.

The principal maintained that he did not like the schedule either, but that he was
powerless to change it:

> He gave me a whole bunch of reasons which, I guess, were logical.
> They had buses that had to be there at a certain time and they only had
> so much time to feed the children and when you divided it up you come
> out with fifteen minutes. And all this you know. I just told him, I am
> going to tell my son to eat his lunch slowly and my daughter. If
> someone here didn't care for it, that was too bad. I was not raising
> animals because you didn't have time to do the job properly. So that
> was what the kids did.

Other parents also complained about their children being rushed through lunch
or not being able to eat lunch if they forgot to bring their money. Across the six
families, this problem with the lunch schedule prompted the only visit to the
principal by a parent (Mr Trenton) during the study.

In addition to the lunch schedule, parents disapproved of bad language at
the school site and the lack of a fence around the play yard. In the second year of
the study a strange man was observed on the school site and in the door of a
classroom while school was in session. Because of recent kidnappings of children
in other California communities this incident created alarm among many
families in the school. The school received numerous complaints from parents.
The principal reported that he 'had parents coming out of the woodwork over
this thing'. A special parents' meeting was called, and the parents' group began a
fund-raising drive to build a fence. For a few weeks some of the fathers patrolled
the school during the school day. Although this crisis subsided after a month or
so some parents were angry and felt that the school was minimizing or 'covering
up' the problem. While the administrators insisted that the problem was under
control and children were not at risk, some parents continued to worry about
the safety of their children at school.

The vigor with which parents criticized the lunch program and school
safety suggests that Colton parents had strong feelings about their children's
experiences at school. This makes parents' silence about the school's academic
program more striking. This uncritical attitude gave Colton teachers considerable autonomy in relation to parents. The teachers did not have to face the
personal challenges and criticisms that confronted their counterparts at Prescott
school. But Colton teachers, for the most part, did not appreciate this autonomy.
Instead, they were pre-occupied with the lack of involvement of parents in their

children's schooling. The benefits of this separation between home and school were not readily apparent to teachers.

Depending on Teachers

In turning over responsibility for education to the school, working-class parents were deferring to the notion of professional expertise. Unlike their more privileged counterparts, working-class parents granted teachers full professional status. They saw teachers as undergoing specialized training, having a 'backstage' of specialized information and knowledge, having a monopoly on the area of expertise, and capable of self-regulating the quality of work in the profession. From their position in the class structure, working-class parents looked up to teachers; teachers had higher social and educational status than the parents in the Colton community. Parents were less aware of educators' standards for parental involvement in schooling and, as I argue in Chapter Six, had fewer social resources to meet these standards.

The parents' approach resulted in their children experiencing a *single educational career*. Colton children's educational success was negotiated on the basis of the children's own ability, diligence, and overall performance in the classroom. Their academic experience at school was a matter between themselves and the teacher and, to a lesser extent, between themselves and other members of the class. The responsibility for education lay with the teacher; as a result, teachers generally had professional autonomy in academic matters. Parents might work to prepare children for school or reinforce classroom materials, but parents did not try to change children's school experiences.

Notes

1. The one exception was the day there was a field trip when five mothers helped with the excursion.
2. Kohn and Schooler (1983) report that working-class fathers place more value on indicators of conformity to external standards than do middle-class fathers. Middle-class fathers, for example, value their children understanding how and why things happen. Working-class parents, however, value their children getting good grades in school.

4   Interconnectedness Between Family and School: Prescott

Family–school relationships in Colton were characterized by separation. In the upper-middle-class community of Prescott, the pattern was different. Here parents were a visible presence on the school grounds. Parents of first grade children, particularly mothers, monitored their children's schooling, intervened in their children's classroom program, criticized the actions of teachers, and worked to supplement and reinforce the classroom experience. There was an *interconnectedness* between Prescott family life and school life not found in the working-class community. This interconnectedness was observable at the school site as well as in interviews with family members at home.

Prescott School: Parents' Presence

The narrow street in front of Prescott school was lined with cars each weekday morning as mothers dropped children off for their school day. This bustle of activity was repeated in the afternoon. Unlike at Colton, however, mothers were frequently seen at Prescott during the school day — walking back and forth in the corridors, coming into classrooms for a period, and visiting with other parents and school staff outside of the classroom. Parents were also frequent visitors inside the classroom. According to the first grade teacher, Mrs Walters, about forty per cent of the mothers visited the classroom at some point during the school year.

Why were mothers so often at school? The school volunteer program was the most common reason for their frequent appearance. Mrs Walters used volunteer mothers regularly. Each mother volunteered every other week; hence twelve parents were required to fill six time slots. The kindergartens and all of the other primary grade classrooms also had volunteers two or three times per week. As a result, from ten to twenty-five different mothers were coming to Prescott school to help in the classroom for an hour during a typical week. In addition mothers helped with the library, various school committees, and assorted school functions. On designated weekends, mothers and fathers helped with school clean up days. I visited Prescott school two to three times per week over a period of six months; I almost always saw at least one parent during my visits.

Mothers moved freely in and out of the classrooms. In Mrs Walters' classroom, for example, mothers did not hesitate outside the door, nor did they knock before entering the classroom when school was in session: they walked directly into the room. Often mothers walked around to the back of the classroom; other times they interrupted the teacher and classroom activities. The following excerpt from my field notes is illustrative:

> Mark's mother burst through the classroom doorway. She was out of breath and seemed slightly in a panic. She hurriedly explained to Mrs Walters that she had to take her father-in-law to the hospital and would try to be back at noon. She might be a little late; could Mark wait on the sidewalk? Mrs Walters said that would be fine. Mark's mother went over to the desk where Mark was playing a numbers game. She stroked his hair and his face as she told him that she was going to the hospital and would be back a little after twelve. Mrs Harris [a parent-volunteer], the children around Mark, and I were all listening and watching this interaction. Mark's mother said good-bye to Mark and left. The children resumed playing the numbers games.

Not only did mothers feel comfortable walking in and out of classrooms without a teacher's permission, they also played an important role in classroom activities. As part of the volunteer program, parents helped children during 'independent time' with the buckets of math manipulatives, wrote down stories that children dictated to them, and sometimes guided a group through a classroom activity. When parents were in the classroom they sometimes scolded children and took a leadership role in prodding children to work during 'independent time'.

In addition to helping shape the activities of the classroom as a whole, parents also monitored, supervised, and intervened in their own children's activities. Some mothers actively sought additional information about their children's academic performance during their visits to the classroom. Other mothers viewed their visits to school as an opportunity to have a mini-parent–teacher conference. In these brief meetings they would ask the teacher for suggestions for activities to do at home and offer the teacher their thoughts on their children's educational status.

For example, Mrs Harris, who volunteered regularly in the classroom, substituted for a friend one morning. She arrived at 11.00 am, and although volunteers normally stay at least an hour, Mrs Harris reported to me and to the teacher that she had to leave at 11.30 to go to a funeral. The class was doing math in 'independent time' and the children were working with objects called manipulatives. Individually or in small groups, children were adding beads, cubes, or squares to total the number '9' and then writing the number combinations on a ditto sheet. Five children (including Mrs Harris's son Allen) were making up a math test with Mrs O'Donnell, the teacher's aide, in the corner of the room. Mrs Harris used her time in the room to help the children — and also to collect more information about her son's school performance:

> Mrs Harris continued to circulate but rarely made comments or interacted with youngsters. She periodically glanced over her shoulder at her son, who was doing his test in the last sound booth. At one point Mrs Harris went up to the table with the math folders in them (no one was then at the table). She went through the folders until she found her son's math project folder. The folder contained a list of math projects completed. Mrs Harris pulled out Allen's folder, studied it for a few minutes, then folded it and put it back in the box.
>
> At 11.25 Mrs Harris headed for the door, but just before she got there, she saw that Allen had just finished his math test. She stopped, turned around, and hurried back. Mrs O'Donnell handed her the test without comment. Mrs Harris stood in the middle of the corner area and looked at the test for three or four minutes. After studying the test intently, she looked up, sighed, and made a face at Mrs O'Donnell, showing disappointment, resignation, and lack of surprise. Without a word, she handed the test back to Mrs O'Donnell, who then wished Mrs Harris a good day as she left the classroom.

Mrs Harris, along with other mothers, took the liberty of leafing through their children's folders in the classroom without the teacher's permission. She and other mothers carefully scrutinized their children's performance during their visits to the classroom.

Of course parents varied in their demeanor in the classroom. For example when boys started shoving each other, some mothers simply looked at the children disapprovingly — or waited (often in vain) for Mrs Walters to intercede. A few mothers, however, would grab the boys by the arm, speak sternly to them ('You boys stop that this minute') and chide the children to get back to their school work. Just as parents differed in their levels of control with their own children, they also were more or less controlling of children's behavior in the classroom. All of the parents, however, entered and exited the classroom without asking the teacher's permission, and most moved about independently within the classroom. As a result, some mothers who visited the classroom collected substantial amounts of information about the curriculum and about their children's academic standing.

In addition to classroom volunteering, parents were invited to a series of school events that were almost identical to the ones offered at Colton school, including Back-to-School Night, a Holiday Program, Open House, Grandparents' Day, and fall and spring parent–teacher conferences. As Table 5 reveals, parental attendance was very high at these events, over twice the rate at Colton. The school also had a Mothers' Club and a Fathers' Club. Prescott school, along with schools in other districts, had faced several years of fiscal constraint, particularly following the passage of a tax reform law, Proposition 13,

Table 5   *Parent Participation in School Activities: Prescott School*

School Activity	Number of Children's Parents Attending
Parent–teacher Conference	100%
Open House	96%
Volunteering in the Classroom	40%

n = 28

consequently the parents' clubs sponsored fund-raising activities. Together these associations raised about $12,000 a year, which was used to support a variety of routine educational activities at the school and on-site enrichment programs. The parents' clubs also sponsored several school events which parents were invited to, including a Father–Child dinner, a Pumpkin Patch sale, a coffee for mothers on the first day of school, and an adults only Mexican dinner in the spring. The teachers and the principal were pleased with the level of parent involvement in the school. Parents' attendance at these events was widely interpreted by school staff as an indication of the 'value' parents placed on education.

Parents too valued their involvement at the school, but for reasons that differed from the staff's. Interviews with parents in their homes revealed some of these differences. For example, teachers sought parent–volunteers to increase their (the teachers') resources and to improve the quality of education, and a few mothers did volunteer simply to help teachers out. Most mothers, however, used their appearances at the school site as a way of monitoring their children's schooling. Mothers felt that they learned a great deal from being at school and that their involvement at school helped them to work more effectively with their children and the teacher to improve educational achievement. This was particularly true among mothers of low-achieving children. One mother, a nurse, worked full-time in the Emergency Room at a local hospital. Her schedule frequently changed from day to evening shifts. Still, she always volunteered in the classroom:

> I always had Wednesdays off. I usually only worked in the class every other Wednesday. But I really felt that was the best way to know what was going on in the class. My main motive for doing that was not particularly to help the teachers. I think that was important. It was a really good way to find out where your child was in relation to other children and what they were working on.

The importance of 'knowing what was going on' was frequently mentioned by Prescott mothers in classroom visits and in interviews. In addition, the teachers, particularly Mrs Walters, were very aware that mothers were 'looking around' when in the classroom. All of the teachers complained about the amount of 'talking' Prescott mothers did about school. Clearly mothers gained information in their classroom visits which they then used to criticize teachers in private conversations with other parents, as well as in visits to the principal.

Interconnectedness Between Home and School

The classroom volunteer program was a critical linkage in family—school relationships at Prescott. Because so many parents volunteered in the classroom, mothers had other mothers to talk to about classroom dynamics. But the volunteer program was not the only aspect of the family—school relationship that tied parents into their children's schooling. Parents' own conception of their proper role in schooling, the information they had about their children's school experiences, their interventions in schooling, and their criticisms and challenges of the school, all promoted much tighter linkages between home and school than existed at Colton. The character of family—school relationships can be seen by carefully examining the experience of the Simpsons, a Prescott family with a high achieving son.

The Simpson Family

The Simpsons live on a hill in a two story house. When I visited, their yard was immaculate; two porcelain geese stood outside the door with bows around their necks. The house is spacious. The hallway opens into a formal dining room with a large wooden table with candles on it. The stairway leads to the bedrooms. To the right of the stairs is a large living room with a thick carpet, two flowered couches, a glass coffee table, and built-in bookshelves along one wall. French doors along another of the living room walls open onto a narrow deck. The windows reveal a partial view of the valley and surrounding hills. Mr and Mrs Simpson had lived in this house three and one half years, but they had lived in Prescott for fourteen years. The house was quiet except for the music from the living room stereo and the periodic chimes of a clock.

Mrs Simpson, a slightly plump woman about forty years old, greeted me dressed impeccably in a red and white silk blouse with a bow and dark slacks. She seemed relaxed and well-prepared for the interview, including having an extension cord for the tape recorder already on the table, as I noted in my field notes:

> Mrs Simpson was a very gracious woman who was obviously well-prepared for my visit. She had an extension cord in the living room, coffee made, which she served in teacups, and bakery tea cakes carefully arranged on a plate. Classical music was playing in the background. Mrs Simpson said, 'I had hoped that we would be able to sit outside on the deck but the weather clouded over'. As I got set up, she asked me a few questions about my graduate work at Berkeley and said that a daughter of some friends of theirs also was getting her Ph.D. at Berkeley.

Mrs Simpson is the daughter of a physician. She attended college but, after a car accident, got behind in her school work and never graduated. She does not work outside the home. Her husband earned his Bachelors from a state university in the South and then went to Harvard where he received an MBA. He works as a manager in a local corporation, a job that requires that he travel overnight about thirty per cent of the time. They have three children, Cathy (thirteen) and Sarah (twelve), and Donald, who is nearly eight.

When asked about her role in her son's schooling, Mrs Simpson asserted that she and the school shared responsibility for education, although she noted that Donald got more of what he needed from Prescott than from home:

> I saw the school as being a very strong instructional force, more so than we were here at home. I guess that I was comfortable with that, from what I had seen. It was a three to one ratio or something, where out of a possible four, he was getting three-quarters of what he needed from the school and then a quarter of it from here. Maybe it would be better if our influence were stronger, but I am afraid that in this day and age it is not really possible to do any more than that even if you wanted to.

Their activities at home included reading, enrichment activities, and general discussions about schooling:

> We did a lot of reading to them. We set an example, because we were both great readers. We exposed them to things that came along, you know, special events that we thought might be of interest to them without making it kind of pedantic or something that is an ordeal. We tried to be open to discussing things with them or asked them hopefully how their day went and hoped that they would open up and tell us how things were.

The Simpsons read to Donald about five times a week, usually for about twenty minutes at a time; they took turns at this. Donald's older sisters also read to him. Both parents tried to encourage Donald's interest in drawing, and his father brought home paper from the office for him.

In addition, Mrs Simpson went to school twice a month to work in the classroom:

> I volunteered in his classroom, which I had always done and that way I was open to seeing what was being taught and I knew what he was covering at the moment. So if he had any questions or if I could bring up anything that maybe I noticed in school and saw what he had to say about it — [it] was kind of valuable. If he was having a problem I would be eager to help him. But he seemed to be doing okay.

Donald liked his mother to visit school:

> They really like you being there. He was very happy when I was at school. I think they liked the parents to be part of what was going on. If I said that I was working today he would say, 'Oh good!'

On the basis of her visits to the classroom, Mrs Simpson formulated ideas about ways to coordinate home learning activities with the school curriculum. For example, in second grade they had dictation in spelling. After visiting the class she suggested to Donald:

> Someday, just for fun, how about if I dictate and I give you some new words that you have never heard before and see if you think that you can spell them right?

In this way Mrs Simpson worked to reinforce and supplement the curriculum goals of the classroom. In addition Donald was enrolled in supplementary enrichment activities, including art lessons, French lessons, soccer, and Indian Guides. His mother also expected that he would begin to study a musical instrument in third or fourth grade.

Not only did Mrs Simpson invent educational games, but Mr Simpson tried to select educational presents to bring home to his children when he returned from business trips:

> I tried to find some little thing for them in a store or an airport or hotel shop or somewhere when I was out. I would prefer it to be something educational like a book, or a coloring book, a pen . . . I found a book on how to become a cartoonist in an airport book shop. I bought him that to build on his interest in drawing.

When out shopping with his son (about two times per month) he encouraged Donald to make educational choices as well:

> If I am out with him in a store or some place and he just wanted a silly furry animal or some other thing like that, I would try to push him toward something that was more constructive, such as a drawing book or a story book.

With their efforts to make *learning fun* and to make *fun a form of learning*, Mr and Mrs Simpson attempted to tighten the linkages between home and school. They encouraged Donald to read and they sought out activities, including word games, that would improve his educational performance. Education was integrated into home life and, to a lesser extent, home life became part of school. In short there was an interconnectedness between schooling and family life.

Both Mr and Mrs Simpson acknowledged that Mrs Simpson was more active in her children's schooling than was Mr Simpson. Most of what Mr Simpson knew about school-related matters he learned from his wife and from his brief visits to the school for ritualized events (e.g., Open House night). Mr Simpson did not have accurate information about the day-to-day workings of the academic program or the 'cast of characters' in his son's classroom. By contrast Mrs Simpson had detailed information about Donald's school experience. She knew the names of the teachers, the aides, the principal, and other school personnel at Prescott. She knew details about her son's academic performance. She was also well informed about the academic hierarchy in the classroom. She was easily able to name the children who were doing well in the class, as well as those who were having trouble. She came by some of this information through conversations with her son:

> Just out of my own curiosity, I would ask, 'How is so and so doing? Who is in your math group?' or 'Who is in your reading group?' Then, of course, I did have a number of friends [who were parents of children] in his age range. So occasionally we would talk about things. I knew the children who were having some problems or who had to go to the reading resource teacher.

Other information came from the parents in Mrs Simpson's friendship networks. Mrs Simpson knew almost all of the parents of the children in her son's class, and she reported being good friends with about five of these parents. As information resources these individuals played an important role, mediating Mrs Simpson's assessment of her son's schooling. In particular she evaluated her son's academic performance in the light of the performance of other children that she knew. For example, at the end of second grade she was very pleased with his school year. When asked how his school year had gone she replied:

> It has gone really, extremely well. Better even than my expectations. Donald has been really happy and he has done fine and he has really bloomed and thrived and had a good time in Mrs Hoffman's class. His one weak point, although it wasn't too severe, but he was not as strong in math as he was in verbal skills. But seemingly his math was coming along real well. His writing skills and comprehension had increased over the last year. So he was definitely on or above grade level which I was happy for. He was reading really well. He was generally just using his mind independently and was happy. He was very happy with the class.

But part of her happiness was linked to her knowledge that for many children in the class it had not been a good year:

> There were several kids in the class that . . . really had a bad year. Some of them had gone from just loving school to just dreading [it] and crying in the morning when it was time to go. . . . She was an excellent teacher and she had brought out a lot of good qualities even in the kids who protested. But her methods were a little bit stricter and she was not permissive and really soft . . . a number of them in Donald's class last year had Mrs Walters who had a different approach entirely. I guess they got used to that attitude and found that Mrs Hoffman really means business and they found that hard to take. So consequently I was doubly happy because, as I said, it wasn't that everybody had that good a year.

Mrs Simpson's fairly detailed information about the experiences of other children in Donald's class provided a social context within which she evaluated her child's experience. This knowledge of others' experiences also provided her with information about effective and ineffective strategies for intervening in schooling.

Although interested in Donald's progress, Mr Simpson was considerably less active than his wife in his son's schooling. Maintaining that he did not have time to be more active, he saw his role as one of guidance and encouragement:

> I would like to have done more in schools here but I didn't have the time to do that during the day. So I saw my role as encouraging them. Number one: think in terms of what you can get out of school. What is it doing for you? Don't take the usual attitude of just complaining about school; that school is bad. It is not bad. I have far more years than you have and I am telling you it is a good experience.

For Mr Simpson, the son of a barber, education has been a pathway for upward mobility and he repeatedly stressed to his children the importance of a good education. He expressed hope that his children would find interesting careers, and he believed that educational success was critical to job satisfaction:

> I think that the main thing was trying to find something that really turned you on, that made it fun to get up in the morning and go to work. One of our older kids was not a good student. I tried to push her by saying, 'You are going to wind up spending your life doing a very menial task'.

As part of his efforts to encourage Donald's school success, Mr Simpson looked at his son's papers at night; occasionally discussed these papers with Donald; and attended school events. He also read to his son frequently. The two had an evening ritual that involved Donald reading a page and then his father reading a page. Mrs Simpson laughingly noted that her husband sometimes fell asleep while Donald was reading, leading Donald to take the book, saying, 'That's okay, I'll finish it'.

In acknowledging that his wife did more with the school than he did, he noted he did not share her 'rapport' with the teachers:

> I saw her doing a lot more because she was able to work at the school. She knew, had a relationship with, the teachers by being at school either by helping out, food service, or attending meetings or things like that. She was more familiar with what goes on.

Coincidentally, Mr Simpson had worked with the husband of Robin Emerson, one of the kindergarten teachers; the two couples socialized periodically. Every year, even when they no longer had a child in kindergarten, Mr and Mrs Simpson stopped in to say hello to Mrs Emerson during Open House. Mr Simpson reported:

> I went down there every year to see Robin and give her a hug and say that I am going to have another kid just so I can send it to her class. But I would never have thought of doing that with Mrs Taylor.

Although he lacked his wife's rapport with the teachers and her daily involvement in Donald's schooling in the primary grades, Mr Simpson saw himself as playing a larger role in certain areas, including math and science:

> Susan [Mrs Simpson] was a liberal arts major and was uncomfortable with math and science and I had a fair amount of that. So they turned to me for that.

As a result, while his wife took almost complete responsibility for schooling at younger grade levels, he took a larger role as the children got older. Although he invested fewer hours in interacting with his children, he was an important source of authority:

> As they got older then I think that I came into play more because then they got into things like science or math and they called me for help. She was of course here when they came home from school so she played more of a role in determining what they were going to do. Were they going to go out and goof off for the afternoon or were they going to do their homework or were they going to do some chores. And then I came in at night and sometimes I found that somebody had goofed off and hadn't done their homework and then she was annoyed about it and I would get into [it at] that point.

Although Donald and one of his sisters were doing very well in school, the eldest child had been getting Ds and Fs in her junior high school classes. As a result, her parents forbade her to watch television during the school semester, unless she received at least a C in all subjects. Mr Simpson said that although his eldest daughter was honorable in other matters she frequently broke this rule. Two or three times a week she would be caught watching TV. This led to 'fierce battles' over television. In addition this daughter had 'constant excuses' for not doing her school work (e.g., she needed to wash her hair, play with the dog, etc.) Her low grades were considered to be an important problem in the household, and they introduced regular tensions into the Simpson's family life.

Unlike many Prescott parents, Mr and Mrs Simpson were very supportive of the teachers and the principal at Prescott. Of the Prescott parents interviewed they were the least critical of the school. Mr Simpson acknowledged that they were very supportive of the school, particularly in their interactions with their children:

> I thought, and sometimes I had felt guilty about this, that we had been more supportive of the teacher in almost all cases than we had been of the child.

Neither Mr or Mrs Simpson had visited the principal with a complaint about their children's schooling nor had they requested special conferences with Donald's teachers.

Still, Mrs Simpson had informal criticisms of the teachers. For example, she was critical of Mrs Walters' teaching style and noted that many parents felt that it was not rigorous enough:

> It was fine for a child that was doing all right and it was very good for a child who was overly sensitive to have her for a teacher, because I thought that she really approached them and made them feel comfortable. I did feel, however, and I may have been a little bit biased because of comments that I had heard from other people, there were a lot of areas that perhaps were not covered completely or as fully as they might have liked academically. I thought that a few of them felt that she didn't get as much work out of the children as they were capable of doing.

When asked if she felt that the children were not challenged enough academically, she sighed and then said:

> Oh, possibly, but then again, I guess I felt that it wasn't a serious offense in first grade. Not that they play in first grade but that they covered some basic things and seemed to do that all right.

It was her son's strong school performance, rather than an admiration of Mrs Walters, that influenced her here:

> I would have been more disturbed if he hadn't been doing well. If it had been my eldest child I would have been more disturbed because she had a similar experience in third grade. In many respects it was almost a lost year for her and she got into fourth grade and didn't know all of her math facts. In Donald's case, it was okay. He came though and plus had the art which was an extra, but it was really individual.

Hence, at least for the Simpsons, the level and intensity of parents' involvement in schooling depended, in part, on their child's school performance. Parent involvement was more intense with low-achieving youngsters.

School-related decisions that frequently elicited a strong response from other Prescott parents did not necessarily disturb the Simpsons. For example, they knew that in third grade Donald might get Mrs Dillon, a teacher with a bad reputation among parents. Mrs Simpson felt that her son did not need a structured teaching environment as much as other children might and could 'survive' the year. She had no plans to protest the decision or to let Donald know her feelings about the matter:

> As a matter of fact, the next year there was a possibility Donald could have gotten a teacher who had a reputation of being almost like Mrs Walters in that she was very, [easy-going] almost on the lax side. But I certainly didn't want to say anything to Donald, [like] 'Gee, I hope you don't get Mrs So and So'. Because the chances were great that maybe he would.

> Plus, I guess I felt that he was strong enough that he could probably have survived the year. Not that I was being that self-sacrificing, but I

mean I didn't think that I would go and say, 'I do not want my child to have that particular teacher'. Whereas somebody else might have a better right to because they might need a lot more structure. But he was pretty self-motivated, and I thought he could probably get through the year and still gain something from the experience. Whereas somebody else [who] might have needed a lot more structure, or a lot more information, might have really floundered and would really not have been well placed in that classroom.

Mrs Simpson knew, however, that it was difficult, if not impossible, to request successfully a different teacher at Prescott:

Well, they *really* frowned on that. Years ago it was the kind of thing where they didn't encourage it but they would listen to you and sometimes you would get your way. But as of, I guess the last three or four years, they had really been pretty adamant about please do not request teacher changes. And I knew of maybe one or two cases of where somebody had gotten a change through. But it was pretty unusual.

Mrs Simpson was well informed about successful and unsuccessful strategies for interacting with the school. She drew on those informational resources in evaluating her options with her own son.

The Teachers' Perspective

From the teachers' side, both Donald's first and second grade teachers reported having enjoyed him as a student. He was well-behaved and one of the best students at each grade level. He was also well known in the class for being good at art. Mrs Walters and Mrs Hoffman found Mrs Simpson to be supportive of schooling. For example, Mrs Hoffman noted that she did not use her time as a classroom volunteer to scrutinize carefully her son's performance, nor did she stay after class for a mini-conference. Mrs Hoffman felt that the mother's behavior in the classroom was an indication that Donald's mother 'trusted' her:

Donald did very well. He wrote beautiful stories. I am not sure if she read to him. She came to class and worked. She was never concerned with him at all. She trusted me and she was satisfied with Donald's progress. If he had a problem, he could ask his older sisters.

When at the school site, Mr and Mrs Simpson appeared relaxed and jovial. At Open House Night in first grade, Mr and Mrs Simpson, the two older girls, Cathy and Sarah, and Donald visited the classroom. There they talked at length with the teacher's aide, with other parents in the classroom, and with Mrs Walters. Mrs O'Donnell (the teacher's aide) had sons in junior high school, and she spoke to Cathy and Sarah for a few minutes about their classes. The girls were poised; they answered Mrs O'Donnell's questions in clear voices, maintained eye contact, and did not stumble over their words. There was a discussion of how lucky Donald was to have two older sisters to help him and how Sarah, especially, 'dotes' on Donald. When Mrs O'Donnell, praised Donald for his art work, the parents' response was light-hearted:

> Mrs Simpson laughed and said, 'You can't give the credit to us. We certainly don't do anything to promote it.' Mr Simpson chimed in, laughing also, saying 'We tell him to pick up his papers so we don't trip over them'.

Mr and Mrs Simpson were joking when they said they didn't nurture their son's drawing since, as noted earlier, they regularly supplied him with paper, bought him books on drawing, and enrolled him in art classes.[1] As with other Prescott parents, they appeared at ease in the classroom and in their discussions with school personnel.

Clearly, Mr and Mrs Simpson worked to promote school success, and their youngest child did very well in school. A high-achieving and well-mannered student, Donald was at the top of his class. The fact that Donald was 'doing okay' led Mrs Simpson to be more passive than she might have been if he were having trouble in schooling. She had other resources that she could have used to provide extra help for him in school (e.g., request specific teachers, work with him more at home, hire tutors), but she didn't use them.

Even with their youngest child there were important linkages between home and school. The parents presumed that they were responsible in critical ways for their son's education. They worked to fulfill that responsibility by reading at home, reinforcing learning in routine family activities, and exposing their son to enriching experiences. When possible, Mrs Simpson sought to replicate and reinforce the classroom curriculum. She and her husband carried out activities at home that were similar to those at school and supplemented, through private lessons, the classroom curriculum.

Elements of Family-School Relationships at Prescott

Conception of Parents' Proper Role in Schooling

Colton mothers maintained that it was their job to prepare children for school and the school's job to teach them. Prescott mothers had a different view. They saw themselves as playing an active role in their children's education. As one mother said:

> Well, I felt [I was] more than just a mother making lunches and sending my child off to school. I think that was probably how I was raised. I felt much more than that. First of all, I was at school a lot more. And I also felt that if David and I didn't keep on top of their education

and if we couldn't supplement it at home, then we were going to be out
in left field and who knows where our children would be.

Mothers and fathers suggested, as Donald's mother had, that the responsibility
for education was shared between the home and school. Parents taught children
new information, supplemented schooling, and monitored their children's
academic progress.

One way that parents were an instructional force was by helping their
children see the practical applications of learning. The mother of one first grader
explained:

> Out responsibility was to give a backdrop for that educational
> experience that they had at school. Why was it useful to know all of that
> stuff. And to make it kind of fun. The other day [Carol and I] were
> making cookies. It was a chance to practice the numbers she had been
> learning in arithmetic. It was fun, and it helped to see how useful her
> knowledge is.

Carol's mother, Mrs Smith, attempted to reinforce knowledge in many ways in
her children's lives. For example, the family was planning a trip to Hawaii over
spring vacation. During a visit I made to the house, she showed me the lists that
the girls had drawn up of the new clothes they needed for the trip. The lists had
the large uneven handwriting of the girls. In constructing these lists Mrs Smith
had helped Carol and her younger sister spell new words. The girls took the lists
with them in the car on the day that they went shopping. Educational activities
were integrated with routine aspects of life.

This generalized effort by parents to reinforce learning at school was both
more specific and more intense during the summer:

> Over the summer, we were very conscious of teaching them things. I
> was more conscious of telling them the names of things at the grocery
> store or asking them questions as we traveled. Reading signs, doing
> those sorts of informal educative things. Why did this car start up at the
> intersection instead of the other car? We took all these passive things
> that we didn't even think about in our daily life and made them more
> intentional and conscious.

Not only did parents try to supplement schooling during the summer, they also
integrated educational goals into virtually all aspects of home life. In leisure time
activities, cooking, cleaning, and shopping, parents promoted educational
activities. Among Prescott parents it was considered the parents', particularly
mothers', job to help make education a daily, year-round experience.

Prescott parents viewed education as a division of labor between home and
school. All of them mentioned that, because they had not been trained as
teachers, they did not know the proper age at which to introduce specific
curriculum to their children. Teachers also knew strategies for making learning
more appealing. As one mother conceded:

> We did depend on the teacher to keep a steady, consistent source of new material. I really wouldn't have known what to teach her and how to make it appetizing.

As part of this division of labor parents envisioned their role as overseeing their children's education. They critically evaluated the academic training their children received at Prescott. If the school did not provide enough opportunities to learn in a given area, parents worked to compensate for that lack by enrolling their children in community programs:

> My feeling was if a child didn't get something in school, you supplemented it. We had a great recreation department that had wonderful classes in music, art, gymnastics, and everything else. If a child particularly liked one area and didn't get enough about it at school, you just supplemented it. It was like everything else.

In interviews parents expressed the view that it was their right and responsibility to share in the education of their children. They saw themselves as dividing that responsibility with teachers, but retaining the right to supplement, oversee, and monitor their child's school experience. Implicitly and explicitly, parents presented themselves as equals to the teachers.

This sense of confidence about their role in their children's schooling was also apparent in the quality of interaction between parents and teachers at the school site. Prescott parents appeared to be relaxed in front of teachers. Mothers and fathers easily maintained eye contact, did not blush or stutter, and did not appear visibly nervous. Many parents, particularly fathers, joked with the teachers in their conversations, which were longer than at Colton school and were more likely to include social conversation (e.g., the weather, community events, vacations). Teachers also reported that Prescott parents challenged them in conversations, criticized their teaching methods, complained to the principal, and took the attitude that they were 'not taking no for an answer.'

Prescott parents varied in the degree to which they supplemented, intervened in, and critically evaluated their children's schooling. Yet in their comments and actions, Prescott parents, including all of the families in the study, expressed their belief that their duty as parents included the responsibility to promote and scrutinize actively their children's education at home as well as in school. As these parents saw it there was an interconnectedness between home and school.

Information about Schooling

In addition to having different conceptions of their proper role in education, Prescott parents had more information about the schooling process than did parents at Colton. All of the mothers in the classroom were friendly with other mothers of children in the classroom. Three of the mothers knew over twenty of the mothers in the class; the other three mothers knew at least some of the parents. The mothers in the study talked on the telephone with other mothers in the class regularly. Indeed, mothers and teachers in this study estimated that most Prescott mothers talked on the telephone two to three times per week with other mothers in the school. Sometimes mothers had long conversations about school, sometimes school was mentioned only briefly in the context of another conversation. But virtually all Prescott mothers had social ties with other mothers in the school.

Through these networks passed information about schooling. For example, before the school year began mothers heard about the reputation of Mrs Walters from other mothers in the district. As Emily's mother noted:

> Basically her reputation was that she was a very nice lady but that she was very non-academic. That she would just not push the children. If your child was bright and a lot of children went into first grade reading or just on the verge of reading . . . then you could make it through. Then it was okay. But if your child needed special help, you were not going to really get the academics.

Mrs Hoffman also had a reputation with the mothers as well as with the children. Allen's mother put it this way:

> Sandi's [i.e., Mrs Hoffman's] reputation preceded her as a gruff, stern, unfriendly, uncaring teacher. Children had been known to run out of her classroom in tears. But they loved her. And I was absolutely intimidated. Allen said to me, 'Mom, I am really worried about having her for a teacher'. I said, 'Allen you don't have to worry. All she wants you to do is work hard'.

Several parents privately referred to Mrs Hoffman as a 'Hitler' in interviews. Still, according to parents, Mrs Hoffman was considered to be a very good teacher, and 'you [could] hear a pin drop' in her classroom.

Teachers were aware that they had reputations among parents. Anne Walters made the following comment:

> Each of us definitely had reputations. Now I wasn't, I was personally not really sure about mine . . . Now Nancy [Dillon], our third grade teacher, who was a very talented teacher, did a fantastic science program, happened to be an artist. And somehow she'd been hooked on the thing, 'Well she can't teach but I guess she is alright at art'.

When asked about her reputation with the parents, Sandi Hoffman said:

> I am probably seen as being very hard. Straighten up all of the boys. They also say, if you don't get it in first, wait until Hoffman.

Not only did Prescott mothers have information about teachers' reputations in the classroom, they also had details about their children's performances. When asked if she had any sense of where her son was academically, one mother replied:

I do. I know exactly where he is, in fact. He is in the last quarter of the second grade on the reading level. On math, he is on beginning third grade level. He was just evaluated by the special education teacher.

Similarly, parents of low-achievers knew the formal terms to describe their children's problems. One mother described her seven-year-old child's reading problem:

Some of the reading is developmental. Emily has good language strengths. She has the language strengths of a nine-year-old. Yet she has the auditory perception of a five-year-old. Somewhere we have to get these two more in line.

Jonathan's mother could also provide a detailed assessment of her son's academic problems:

His attention span is poor. He has auditory reception problems, which I guess means what he is hearing he didn't quite understand sometimes. He needs real specific directions. I noticed a lot of times in class when I was there and the teacher would give the children instructions he would be confused because he couldn't seem to remember a list of things to do. I thought that was a big problem.

Prescott mothers' knowledge included details of the performance of other children in the classroom. When asked if she knew the names of children who were doing well in school, one mother said:

Donald Simpson, did you know him? He was real bright, I thought he was real bright. I thought Art Kaplan read real well, he was a little hyper but he read well. Whe else? Nathan Briton, I thought he was a bright boy — I was not sure — I heard he was always getting in trouble in class, but I thought he was real bright.

Most of the mothers also knew details of the curriculum, including that children had math packets, spelling packets, a writing booklet, and a 'hands-on' math time with manipulatives for counting.

Criticisms at Prescott

At Prescott as at Colton, parents had complaints about their children's experiences at school. Teachers and parents noted occasional problems in non-academic areas. For example, during 'sharing time' in April Jonathan brought in the snake skin that his pet snake had recently shed. While we were cleaning up after school Mrs Walters and I discussed the snake skin. She noted that Jonathan was allergic to animals with fur and that earlier in the year he had a reaction to the mouse which Mrs Walters kept in the classroom. Mrs Walters said that Jonathan's mother, Mrs Roy, was incensed over this classroom pet because her son came home sick every day. She complained directly to Mrs Walters and asked that the mouse be removed. Mrs Walters responded that she had to find the mouse first [it was lost in the classroom]. This made Jonathan's mother 'livid'. Mrs Walters thought it was too bad that the mouse had to go since Jonathan really liked it. Mrs Walters was pleased that Jonathan had been given a snake. It was, she commented, 'the perfect per for him'.

In my interview with Mrs Roy that summer she also referred to this incident. She was still angry about it:

> He was a very allergic child. He had asthma and he had allergies. She had an animal in that room. It took me over a month for her to get that out of there. I was picking him up from school [and] all of the time he would have hives, he would be wheezing, his nose would be full of snot. That really made me angry. Finally, she got rid of it.

Jonathan's mother had considered going to the principal to lodge a formal complaint, but Mrs Walters finally found the mouse and removed it from the classroom.

Most of the complaints from the parents, however, including those of Jonathan's mother, focused on academic matters, including the professional capabilities and performance of school personnel. For example, many parents were deeply unhappy with Mrs Walters' performance. Mrs Roy, for example, was much happier with Mrs Hoffman:

> I was very disappointed in his first grade class. In first grade there just didn't seem to be much of an expectation for him to succeed and he didn't really succeed. It wasn't expected. He fooled around quite a lot. This year, Mrs. Hoffman is really structured. She has high expectations, but not excessively so. He did quite well. Much better than I thought he would do and much better than she herself thought he would do.

Most mothers felt that Mrs Walters was a 'nice lady' and that the children were happy in her class. Unlike at Colton, however, that was not sufficient. Parents were disturbed by the manner in which Mrs Walters conducted her class. Emily's mother, for example, had been very unhappy with the lack of academic rigor in the classroom and was irritated that her son had been placed in Mrs Walters' class for the following year. As she explained:

> She was nice to the children. I thought that she genuinely liked them. She had a very soft approach. Personally, I think that would be better in kindergarten than in first grade. But maybe not. The children liked her. Ross has her now and loves her. Emily had a very nice experience.

Despite her children's apparent enjoyment of their teacher, this mother found Mrs Walters' performance deficient:

> I think the thing that I resented most of all was that she didn't really stay on top of Emily in terms of reading. She totally misplaced her in her

reading group. Which really put Emily behind, terribly . . . Professionally, I thought that she really blew it.

Parents felt Mrs Walters' expectations were too low, the discipline was lax, the class was too noisy, and the children were not required to work consistently or finish their projects.

One indication of parents' concern was that the mother putting the volunteer schedule together did not have any problem filling the slots for Mrs Walters' class, although she had some trouble recruiting enough parents in other classes. This 'overabundance' of parents was linked to the rumors about Mrs Walters' capabilities as a teacher. Parents wanted to be in the classroom to make their own judgments.

Parents differed in the level of their anger and/or distress, and in the likelihood of their sharing their complaints with school personnel. For example, some parents were very supportive of teachers and deplored the pressure which many Prescott parents placed on the teachers. As Gail's mother said:

> I was very empathetic with teachers. I just felt so — I had the feeling that it was a rough role. The parents in this community were pretty [hesitates], well, they wanted a lot for their child. And a lot of them expected the education to be like private school education where children get all this personal attention from the teacher. Let's face it, the parents here, most of them were pretty successful. And I wanted success for my child, but I didn't want to put on the pressure of professional success. But I thought a lot of parents came from backgrounds where they had had it pushed on them.

Gail's mother, along with other parents, including Donald's, shared only their positive feelings with teachers; they did not air any complaints they had about their children's experience.

Nevertheless all of the Prescott mothers and many Prescott fathers did have criticisms about the academic program at Prescott — they simply used different strategies for managing these criticisms. Some of the criticisms were minor (e.g., children shouldn't be allowed to read comic books as part of their reading time in class) and some were serious (e.g., Anne Walters is a bad teacher and should be fired). Unlike Colton parents whose complaints encompassed only non-academic issues, Prescott parents had strong feelings about the quality of the academic program. Some parents felt free to share those complaints with Prescott school personnel.

Interventions in Schooling at Prescott

Prescott parents reported numerous educational rituals in their family life. The most common of these was reading to children in the evening, usually before bedtime. All six families I interviewed said that they read aloud to their children regularly. The parents reported that they tried to read to their children every day; in some families this goal was achieved four to five times per week. Across all of the families, however, children always were read to at least three times per week, for about fifteen to twenty minutes at a time. Some of the children also read silently to themselves, particularly in the second grade year, when their reading skills had improved.

Not all Prescott families in the school read to their children. Although there was no Read-at-Home Program to provide a more accurate count, Mrs Hoffman estimated that one half of her second grade children were read to regularly or had a silent reading time monitored by their parents. Some parents almost never read to their children. One mother of a low-achiever admitted — with a laugh — during Open House night in first grade:

> I can't think of the last time I read to her. You know when you have four kids it gets hard. When the first one does something you get all excited and it is new. You read to them and play soccer with them and everything. And when the second one does it, it is interesting but — but when you get to the fourth child. Why Penny was on the soccer team and my husband and I had to drag ourselves to her games.

Clearly all Prescott parents were not reading to their children regularly but there are many indications that most Prescott children were being read to more often than children at Colton school.

Besides regularly reading to their children, Prescott parents made an effort to integrate educational goals into family life including, teaching children new words when driving by billboards, having children practice penmanship and vocabulary by writing out shopping lists, practicing mathematics during baking projects, and practicing vocabulary during breakfast time. Parents also took an active role in monitoring, supervising, and intervening in their children's schooling by:

* requesting a specific classroom teacher for the following year
* requesting extra conferences with the teacher
* requesting that their child be placed in a certain school program (e.g., gifted program, speech therapy, learning resource center)
* requesting that the teacher send home a duplicate set of textbooks to work with at home
* requesting that their child be allowed to work on the curriculum (e.g., math packets) while at home
* asking for additional information to confirm the accuracy of the teacher's judgment (e.g., in reading group placement)
* complaining to the teacher about the classroom program
* complaining to the principal about the teacher's performance
* having their child's academic standing evaluated independently (e.g., tested by a psychologist)
* having their child tutored during the school year and the summer

★ rejecting the recommendation of the school to have their child repeat a grade and suggesting to the school that they place the child in a split grade combination classroom instead

Many parents also worked to review and reinforce the material presented in the classroom. One mother, for example, said that every two weeks or so she would 'drag out' her son's papers and go over them with him. This activity (which her son vigorously resisted) would usually take place on weekends. It was part of her effort to reinforce his education and build good study habits.

Not all parents engaged in these activities all of the time. Requesting a special conference and complaining to the teacher about the classroom program were probably the most common occurrences by parents with children in the first grade classroom. Many parents also spoke with the principal; Mrs Harpst estimated that she spent one fifth of her time talking to parents. There were variations in the level and frequency of parents' activities, as well. Parents were more involved when they thought the teacher was weak than when they thought the teacher was very good. Parents of low performing students were also more heavily involved than parents of high performing ones.

Parents' actions sometimes had a significant impact on children's school careers, particularly the amount of the curriculum to which they were exposed and the intensity and the duration of their exposure to academic material. (See Chapter Seven for further details.) Even if they did not always have a positive impact on the outcome, parents' actions altered the process of schooling. Parents did not defer to teachers' professional expertise; they preferred to keep abreast of their children's schooling. They also routinely challenged the professional expertise of teachers and principals, although they often did so politely.

Moreover parents tried to retain control of their children's school careers. Their actions included carefully assessing their children's performance, their children's academic standing in the class, and the amount of material to which their children were being exposed. Parents actively supplemented the school curriculum and worked to tie their educational games at home into the structure of classroom activities. Thus there was an interconnectedness between home and school at Prescott that had no counterpart at Colton. Parents' actions influenced their children's schooling and children's school experiences influenced family life.

Education as a Shared Enterprise

Other studies have also found similar class differences in how and how much parents 'help' at home. But the actions of Prescott parents went substantially beyond those usually described in the literature on family–school relationships. Parents, especially mothers, were not simply focused on activities they could do at home. Instead they were trying to influence their children's *school site* experience. Mothers requested teachers whom they thought would work particularly well with their children, they employed strategies to avoid being assigned a 'bad' teacher, they requested that their children be enrolled in special programs, and, in some instances, they even taught their children the curriculum at home. Mothers of low-achievers were particularly likely to carry out these interventions in school-site experiences. Parents sought to individualize their children's schooling in significant ways.

Most of the existing research has focused on the activities which parents carry out with their children, rather than looking at the meaning or intention behind those activities (Henderson 1981; Becker and Epstein 1982). Many researchers suggest that parents help children at home because the parents are trying to support the activities of the teacher and improve their children's performance. Certainly some Prescott parents helped their children because the teacher had recommended that they do so. But some Prescott parents explicitly tried to *compensate* for weaknesses in the school-site program. These parents had critically evaluated a teacher's professional performance and found it wanting. In these instances parents' efforts at home reflected their negative assessment of actions at school. They tried to take a leadership role in their children's education.

Prescott parents' proclivity for intervening in their children's school site experience and compensating at home for omissions in the school's program meant that many Prescott children had a *two person single career* in education. Both the mother and the child were involved in the child's school career, although the parent's role was often facilitating rather than direct action. Unlike at Colton where children forged their way through the institution based on their own ability, diligence, and temperament, Prescott children were guided and supervised by their parents in elementary school.

Notes

1. As Julia Wrigley pointed out to me, this 'joke' may be part of an ideology where upper-middle-class parents hide their work in developing children's skills. Instead they present their children as naturally gifted.

5   Mothers and Fathers:
Gender Differences in Parent Involvement in
Schooling

Social definitions of motherhood and childhood have changed radically over the last two centuries (Aries 1962; Demos 1970; Stone 1977; Zelizer 1985; Dye and Smith 1986). There have been regular changes in child rearing styles, particularly among upper-middle-class parents in the United States (Alwin forthcoming; Bronfenbrenner 1966). A century ago many upper-middle-class mothers rigidly followed a schedule in infant care, feeding their babies by the clock. Experts insisted that feeding on demand could harm infants' physical and psychological development. Today the notion of feeding infants on a rigid schedule has been largely abandoned in favor of a more flexible feeding and playing schedule. There have been dramatic changes also in experts' advice regarding other aspects of parenting (e.g., toilet training, masturbation, punishments) (Wrigley 1989). These changes have altered the behavior of many mothers over the course of the past several decades. Upper-middle-class mothers appear to be more dependent upon the advice of professionals than are their working-class counterparts (Bronfenbrenner 1966).

Mothering and fathering roles have shifted, reflecting women's increased labor force participation (Blau 1984; Mason and Lu 1988). There have been more changes in attitude than in work, but women continue to do most household duties and to act as the primary caretakers of children (Berk 1985; Coverman 1985; Coverman and Sheley 1986; Rossi 1984). Still, upper-middle-class men now often express a belief that they *should* help with the housework. Contemporary fathers also report that they would like to be more intimately involved in child rearing than their fathers were (England and Farkas 1986; Stein 1984).

Most research on American family life has neglected a critical change in parenting roles in the last three decades. In addition to their traditional nurturing obligations, parents are now responsible for promoting *cognitive development*.[1] This change has had a particularly strong effect on upper-middle-class mothers. In earlier decades mothers were expected to help stimulate children's physiological and psychological growth. As nurturers, mothers had a special obligation to promote their children's happiness, giving them love and affection that would enable them to thrive. Today, as some authors point out (Arnot 1984; Griffith and Smith forthcoming; Smith and Griffith forthcoming), mothers are increasingly held responsible for their children's intellectual growth. Professionals stress the importance of parents providing children with a stimulating environment that fosters intellectual development. For pre-school children this involves promoting language and verbal development. For school-aged children, it includes overseeing and encouraging educational achievement and, in some instances, volunteering in school programs. This movement from physiological and psychological arenas to cognitive development significantly increases the duties and obligations of a parent. It is a trend that deserves the careful attention of social scientists.

Little is known about the impact of these new role obligations on parents' lives. This chapter provides preliminary evidence that mothers' educational obligations, particularly in upper-middle-class families, are a significant part of their child rearing responsibilities. I also suggest that the responsibilities for promoting cognitive development fall primarily to mothers. While fathers express interest in the process and often have considerable authority, they are generally not involved in the daily routines of their children's lives. This pattern, of course, mirrors mothers' and fathers' roles in housework and other aspects of children's daily lives. In addition mothers' and fathers' roles differ by social class. Upper-middle-class mothers are the most intensely involved in their children's schooling; working-class fathers are the least so.

Class and Gender in Parent Involvement in Schooling

There is considerable evidence that mothers and fathers have radically different experiences in family life. Bernard (1982) argued that there are two marriages: a 'his' marriage and a 'her' marriage. It also appears that there are two types of parent–school relationships: 'his' and 'hers'. Thus a discussion of parent involvement in schooling requires separate analyses of mothers' and fathers' roles.

In the working-class families at Colton school there was a clear division of labor by gender. Overseeing the children's school experience was seen primarily as 'her' job. This was most clear in parent–teacher conferences; almost all were attended exclusively by mothers. For example, Laura's step-father a high school drop-out, did shift work at a local plant and was usually home in the afternoon. When parent–teacher conferences were held he drove his wife to the school, (she did not know how to drive) but he never went into the classroom to talk to the teacher. He waited in the car. Colton mothers and fathers reported that mothers were more involved in the schooling process; they woke the children in the morning, got them to the bus stop on time, and monitored their day-to-day emotional states and experiences at school. For example, as one mother said, although her children brought papers home from school almost every day their father only looked at their schoolwork periodically:

> It was not every day. It was more if they wanted to show him something particular or else if I wanted to show him something. He didn't go through it every day.

The definition of parent involvement in schooling as women's work was also apparent in the language parents used: mothers almost always said 'I' rather than 'we' when discussing their perceptions of their children's school experience. Fathers were an important source of authority. If mothers felt that the children were not 'minding' them, they would arrange for the father to become involved. Children would tell their fathers about their school day, particularly at dinner time. Fathers occasionally read to their children or helped them with their spelling words. Fathers also attended Open House nights at school; mothers and children saw this as a special event. One mother, Mrs Morris, told Mrs Thompson that she was angry with her son Tommy because he had not cleaned up his desk 'for his father' for Open House night. Throughout they year fathers talked with their wives about important changes in their children's schooling, including promotion and retention decisions. They had little detailed information, however, about their children's schooling (one father had trouble remembering what grade his child was in). Nor did fathers routinely monitor their children's schooling. Mothers, fathers, and children in the working-class families in Colton appeared to define parent involvement as mothers' involvement.

In upper-middle-class families it was also mothers, rather than fathers, who shouldered the burden of parent involvement in schooling. For example, Prescott mothers were the first to meet children when they came home from school, to look at their papers, and to talk to them about their day. Mothers sometimes read to children in the afternoon or in the morning, before school. They also determined in what spelling, reading, or math activities their children needed help; and they decided when supplementing their children's schooling with private tutors might be advisable. Finally, as volunteers and schedulers, they generally informed their husbands of key school dates, including parent–teacher conferences and Open House nights.

In the lower grades especially, Prescott fathers' role in the routine events of schooling was a more peripheral one. Fathers did spend time on their children's schooling, just as they spent some time on other aspects of child rearing. Some fathers read to their children every night for about twenty minutes. More often fathers read to their children at bedtime two or three times a week and talked to their children about their papers once a week. They also discussed their children's school day with them at dinner and visited the school periodically. Involvement by fathers in schooling was often organized, coordinated, and monitored by mothers. It was mothers, rather than fathers, who took the lead in deciding how much school work would be done at home; in hiring tutors; in scheduling special conferences with the teachers; and in monitoring improvements in the classroom performance of low-achievers. As part of that process mothers asked fathers to help them.[2]

For example, Jonathan Roy was in special education and his mother and father worked with him at home regularly. As a nurse his mother sometimes worked swing shift at the hospital and was gone in the early evening. By volunteering in the classroom and having a series of mini-conferences with the teacher Mrs Roy accurately anticipated when Jonathan would be bringing work home. His father, on the other hand, admitted that he had no idea when to expect homework:

> . . . [his] mother seemed to know prior to his getting homework what he was going to get. She seemed to, I don't know how. But maybe she had an idea of what was going on in class, with his spelling and the spelling lists. She knew that he had one a week. She knew the schedule of the homework. She was able to keep up on that.

Jonathan's mother worked with him when she was home in the afternoon. But two or three times a week Jonathan's father would work with him at home, reading to him, helping him with his math, spelling or other school work. Still it was 'the wife' who decided what work needed to be done and told Jonathan's father what areas to work on with Jonathan. Mr Roy explained what he and his son did with spelling words:

> Well you got the list every week. The only time I did it is when his mother told me he had to do his homework. She worked. Then [I tried to do it and help him with it.] He did sentences, but only within the structure of the homework. He had to use a certain word in every sentence. Having him do it, not telling him how. Which I did a lot [laughs]; you know, it is hard not to. You know, give them ideas.

In addition to keeping track of the curriculum at school Jonathan's mother also scheduled all of his lessons. As his father acknowledged:

> She had control as far as knowing what he was doing or where he was at in school. She seemed to have a fairly good idea of where he was in regards to the class. She tried to improve his ability. It didn't always work. See, she scheduled everything. The piano lessons, the karate lessons, swim team, the soccer practice. She looked it up. She found the schedule.

In summarizing his role in schooling, Jonathan's father said he was 'supportive but not what you would call active.' Instead his wife took an active role in overseeing and supplementing their son's schooling.

Other Prescott families described similar patterns. Fathers attended school conferences, Open House nights, reviewed papers, and read to children at night. But it was mothers who 'kept on top' of the children's schooling, who knew the names of children's friends in the class, who were at school during the day, and who monitored the day-to-day changes in their children's school lives. Other research findings suggest a similar pattern of mothers spending more hours supervising children's lives than fathers (Berk 1985; Coverman 1985; Coverman and Sheley 1986).

The coordination and supervision of their children's educational activities often demanded a major portion of mothers' waking hours. This was particularly the case for upper-middle-class mothers whose children were doing poorly in school. One mother reported that she was 'consumed' by the process during her daughter's first grade year. During the spring she spent some time almost every day calling tutors, arranging testing, visiting the school, and talking with family and friends about her daughter's poor school performance. She reported that for a period of six months she and her husband talked about her daughter's school problems on a daily basis.

Other mothers' lives were also significantly influenced by their role as guardian and booster of their children's cognitive development. As part of their family life mothers spent time reading to their children and driving them to lessons; time talking to adult friends about the quality of their children's educational program at school; and time consulting with teachers and other professionals. They also spent time volunteering in the classroom twice a month, and many mothers were active in the Mothers Club, particularly in the annual fund-raising event. Some mothers spent over ten hours per week in school site activities at different times of the year, in addition to their educational activities with family members.

As with studies of housework, mothers' labor force participation appeared to reduce, but not eliminate, the number of hours they devoted to promoting children's cognitive development (Benin and Agostinelli 1988; Coverman and Sheley 1986). For example, one single mother worked full-time outside the home. Because of this she was unable to volunteer in the classroom. She did, however, alter her work schedule to be able to attend parent–teacher conferences, Halloween parade, and Holiday program. In the evening, she read to her daughter, took her to the library, and encouraged her daughter to spend time reading to younger children in the neighborhood. Thus her labor force participation reduced — somewhat — the amount of time she spent on educational activities. Other mothers showed a similar pattern. Working outside the home reduced the hours they devoted to classroom volunteering and school fund-raising, but it had a less dramatic influence on time spent reading to children or promoting their verbal development.

Mothers' labor force participation did not appear to shift dramatically the burden of educational related chores to father. As with other areas of housework and child rearing, mothers appeared to bear the responsibility for the overseeing of their children's schooling. Fathers 'helped' mothers from time to time. For example, when one mischievous boy fell behind in his spelling lessons at school, his mother (who worked twenty hours per week) had him do his spelling lessons at home in the evening (at the same time that she worked on her bookkeeping). While his father was informed of this development it was his mother who made arrangements with the teacher to send home the spelling words, negotiated with her son regarding when he would do his homework, supervised him to ensure that it was done correctly, and reminded him to bring it back to school the next morning. His father gave him son words of encouragement (and criticism at times), reviewed his papers when they were sent home, and supported the endeavor. The only notable exception to this pattern of maternal activity an paternal passivity was math and science education where, because of mothers' alleged lack of knowledge, the responsibility for assistance was left to fathers.

Disruption and Protection from Disruption

One consequence of mothers' more intensive involvement in schooling is that it is mothers' lives, rather than fathers', that are disrupted when changes occur in the regular school schedule. Such disruptions are an inevitable — if unpredictable — part of children's school experiences. Children become sick at school, forget their lunch, need to be taken out of school for a medical appointment, or come home early because of a temporary change in the school schedule. Some of the parents surveyed reported that they found these disruptions irritating.

For example, once a month, Prescott school would have a shortened day to allow teachers to attend a workshop, have parent-teacher conferences, or prepare for an evening event. This infuriated Mr Harris — even though it was his wife, not he, who had to adjust to these schedule changes:

> He would get upset about the screwy schedules that they would have. I would say to him, 'I don't know why you get upset because you don't have to deal with it. I am the one who deals with it. I am the one with the revolving front door. I am the one who has to remember that they all go to school at 8.30 today and they are all coming home at 12.30 or whatever. So why are you getting upset about it?' Then he [would go] into a tirade about they had all of this time off . . .

Sometimes the children's reading group schedules were very inconvenient. While fathers were consulted about their children's reading placement it was mothers who were responsible for shepherding children back and forth to school. For example, a family with two girls, one in kindergarten and one in first grade, lived a ten minute drive from school, but it was too far for the girls to walk. Mrs Walters put the first grader in the later reading group which did not coincide with the kindergartener's schedule. This reading group assignment forced the girls' mother to make four round trips to school each day. Mrs Walters noted that it was the father who called her to talk about the inconvenience:

> The father called me and talked to me at the beginning of the year. I sent assignments home, their reading times, and I talked about the differences that I would be doing with the two groups. And they went for the option which was right for her really. But it was kind of hard for

her [the mother]. I mean think of your day being broken up by driving
. . . The mom was really sort of put out of her way for a whole lot of
time.

Mothers also bore the brunt of an inconvenient classroom volunteering
schedule, particularly if they had more than one child. Allen's mother finally
offered to coordinate the schedule for classroom volunteers after having her day
broken up in bits and pieces:

As the mother of more than one, I didn't want to be going back and
forth. I wanted to be able to say that Thursday morning between 9.30
until 1.30 I was going to be at school. In the past I personally had been
frustrated. Last year my volunteer days were the first and third
Tuesdays and the second and fourth Thursdays. It was very difficult. I
was meeting myself coming and going.

In not having to chauffeur their children to school, coordinate child care after
school, or volunteer in the classroom, fathers' lives were often exempt from the
disruptions caused by changes in children's schedules.

The division of responsibility between mothers and fathers in these Prescott
homes mirrors the research findings on the sexual division of labor in child
rearing and household duties. Upper-middle-class fathers expressed the belief
that they had a responsibility to share these roles but said that their work
obligations precluded them from spending more time on these tasks. For
example, all of the fathers interviewed said that, had they more time, they would
like to spend some of it in the classroom. One father stated:

I didn't have the time to actually participate in activities at school, to be
a parent volunteer or something like that.

Working with children generally, and in elementary schools in particular, is
a low-status task which, historically, has been allocated to women. The gender
segregated character of volunteering may contribute to the lack of fathers'
involvement in this area. When asked if he volunteered in the classroom Allen
Harris's father's first response was the same as the other fathers': 'I would have
liked to, but I didn't have the time.' He then paused for a moment and
added:

I never thought of it, but if it was something I wanted to do, like skiing,
I would find the time. It never crossed my mind. I guess I thought that it
was women's work. It was not manly — was that too much of a male
chauvinist thing to say? I would have rather do the soccer than sit
around with the little kids cutting out paper.

Mr Harris felt he could not justify the expense of hiring a substitute at his work
so that he could volunteer in the classroom. As he acknowledged, however, he
thought the work 'was not manly'. He justified the expense of finding a
substitute for other tasks, such as soccer practice with the boys.

In fact, parent involvement in schooling often includes tasks that are not gender neutral. The lack of upper-middle-class (and working-class) fathers' involvement is not simply a question of time. It is linked to their definition of their proper role. The existence of gender segregation is further supported by comments made by fathers who expect to become more involved as their children get older and have more courses in math and science.

In Prescott homes, as in most intact families, the fathers' role as economic provider was central; their child rearing activities were supplemental (Bernard 1989). Although many mothers were employed, they tended to have 'jobs' rather than 'careers' and thus viewed child rearing as a central part of their lives. These different relationships to the labor market and child rearing seemed to shape parents' roles in schooling and the kinds of interactions concerning schooling they had with their children. For example, all of the fathers reported emphasizing the significance of school success. They stressed to their children the importance of studying hard in school in order to get an interesting job.

> Emily said that she wanted to be a cheerleader someday. 'Well, Emily, [I would say] the cheerleaders have to get good grades. It is important that you give yourself a good foundation to be able to do those things'. ... I viewed my role as providing support to the children in explaining to them what the educational process was for. And why it was important.

Children are not always receptive to this form of encouragement. Donald's father notes, for example, that his children do not appreciate his sermons on the importance of schooling for later success:

> My kids didn't like to be told that it was a good experience. This is an opportunity that you will never have again. You will look back on [it] and you'll wish that you had taken greater advantage of it.

By contrast, Prescott mothers were preoccupied with the micro-details of their children's classroom life, including their performance in specific subjects, their friendship networks, and their overall emotional state.

Upper-Middle-Class Fathers and Authority

Upper-middle-class fathers were not uninvolved in their children's schooling however. As studies of power dynamics in marriage would predict, there are indications that Prescott fathers made fewer decisions but these decisions were more important than the typical decisions of mothers (Blood and Wolfe 1960; Safilios-Rothschild 1970; Steil 1984). For example, mothers decided which drawings would be hung up on the refrigerator and which would be thrown away, if children would purchase books with a class mail order, and what objects from home children would bring to school for 'sharing' time. Mothers also interviewed tutors, arranged tutoring schedules, and made transportation arrangement for these lessons. Fathers, however, were involved in decisions to hire a tutor or change children's academic program (i.e., move children from one reading group to another), to retain children for a school year, and to complain formally to school officials.

In addition, when fathers participated in routine school events they appeared to take on a more authoritative role than mothers. Because of mothers' more intimate involvement in schooling, couples reported that mothers did talk more in conferences than did fathers. For example, Mr Harris said:

> . . . I am the one that showed up for moral support. I was not the one who was the least bit bashful about talking but because she was in the classroom she could come out with all kinds of things that I heard second-hand from her. She was the more knowledgeable speaker of the two of us. I would do like you are doing, nod my head [laughter]. I had my two cents' worth but really relied on Joanie to do the talking because she was the more knowledgeable of the two. Something [i.e., talking] I didn't know if she would have done ten years ago herself. But she was very familiar with the situation and she really got herself involved.

Still, his wife felt that he played a critical role in the process. Her husband had a college degree; she did not. She keenly felt her lack of education at certain moments and was very grateful for his attendance at conferences:

> I was nervous because I was not well-educated in the collegiate sense. I felt that I didn't ask the right questions. I was glad when Tim went with me because he always seemed to ask the right questions. He always went with me.

Moreover her husband also admitted that he felt he played a more assertive role in the conference than his wife:

> I thought I asked the more penetrating questions. Such as, 'Look what are these three books down here if that is the third level or the highest level, and how come Allen has already read this book?'

The teachers also commented on the tendency of fathers to be more inquisitive in conferences, particularly regarding school success. Mrs Walters remarked:

> The man would be more interested in [the] detail of the lessons, or what things their child has to know . . . like the blue sheet that tells all the math skills that you want at the end of year, things like that; fathers are very interested in that kind of information. And the moms tended to be more interested in [their children's] other friends, and did they get along, and did people like their child.

A few fathers spoke explicitly about the problems they had deferring to teachers' control of the classroom. Mr Smith had a Ph.D. in physics and taught at a local university. His wife volunteered in the classroom bimonthly, but he had only been in the classroom twice over the previous year. In our interview, he said that he wanted to volunteer more but that his schedule didn't permit it. For example, when asked if he considered going to school more often he said:

> I did and I really intended to. It was the same old thing of being torn in 5000 directions. I don't know. I was doing about 10 things over at the place where I [worked]. The schedule wasn't uniform. It was not 8 to 5 or anything. So I was back and forth so much it was hard to guarantee that next week I could be there Tuesdays at 10. On occasion, in fact the occasions that I went over there, I think they occurred because I was available, and so I said to Claire, 'Why don't I go instead of you?'

At first he attributed his lack of involvement to his own lack of discipline:

> Part of it was probably just not getting up and doing it. I should probably have just pushed myself to do it more. I don't know. It was like any habit if you didn't do it enough. But it was hard for me to set up a schedule in advance because things were always popping and things just didn't jar well.

On further questioning, however, it became clear that he was uncomfortable deferring to the teacher's expertise and his own inability to control the situation. For example, when asked about the disadvantages of volunteering in the classroom he replied:

> Well, if I went regularly . . . I would probably have gotten into it too much. I would probably have begun to have gotten some control feelings about it. I would probably have overdone it.
> I didn't want to rock the boat. Mrs Cates was really great. Mrs Walters was really good. And I had confidence in them and I had confidence in the class. The children seemed to work together well. (pause) It was funny because everything was such a mixed bag. On the one hand, I felt like going once or twice. I got probably all I needed in terms of insight as to what was going on as far as what I felt I needed to get. I think I should have gone more for the girls' sake because they liked me going very much. They enjoyed that. So I should have. But I thought I might have begun to have gotten a little control in there.

In his visits to the classroom Mr Smith observed that the math curriculum was organized around memorization. To a proponent of hands-on learning this was like 'nails scratching down a blackboard'. The role of the parent volunteer, however, was to be the teacher's helper. Since Mr Smith found it difficult to fulfill that role his solution was to stay out of the classroom.

Parents' efforts to control classroom activities and/or be critical of teachers also show some evidence of gender differences. For example, mothers were more likely than fathers to reveal doubts and anxiety about their right to challenge teachers' decisions. As Emily's mother fretted:

It was hard for a mother to judge. You know as I had told David so many times: we were not professionals in teaching. How did I know? I walked into a classroom and I knew the way I would like to see it run. But who was I? I did not know whether that was right. I was just a mother who came and observed. Unless I saw my child's work being affected and then that made a difference.

Similarly Allen's mother was anxious when she confronted teachers:

I had to get up my nerve, like the day I went to ask Mrs Walters for the math packets for Allen. I made up my mind that I was going to be friendly but firm. I got what I wanted. I was friendly and firm again [the next year] and it didn't get me any place [laughs].

She attributed her nervousness in dealing with teachers to a general problem of non-assertiveness:

I was a chicken. I was asking someone to do something for me and for my children. That was never a comfortable position for me in any area. Any area, whether it was the baby-sitter or anything. It was very difficult for me to ask someone to do something for me. Other people it just flows right off. Not me. It was very hard.

Prescott fathers did not express similar feelings of anxiety about their interactions with teachers. Some said plainly that teachers did not intimidate them. Nor did fathers appear anxious or withdrawn in their visits to the school. Some, in fact, felt very free to give teachers ideas and criticism. Mrs Smith was embarrassed by her husband's behavior in the parent–teacher conference:

He came into the parent conference the first time and he spent half the time telling her all these ideas on how to teach math!

She had different expectations for the conference:

I felt that we had a few minutes with the teacher ... I went with the expectation that she would be talking fifty miles an hour for the entire time telling us where Carol was ... I really went with the attitude of listening to her tell us about what Carol had been doing.

Mrs Smith did not try to hush her husband:

I figured it was her show and if she didn't like it, then she had to say, 'Well, could you make an appointment tomorrow after school to talk about this but right now I feel the need to get on with this agenda'. And I thought well, she didn't say that and it wasn't my place to say it. So I just sat back and enjoyed it.

Hence mothers appeared to experience more doubts than fathers about the legitimacy of criticizing teachers. Mothers did in fact criticize and challenge

Prescott teachers, but they did so by overriding their own internal doubts and fears. Prescott fathers did not appear to be plagued by such concerns. As a result fathers were present, and often took a leadership role, when parents confronted school staff about problems in their children's schooling. In keeping with traditional gender role socialization, it appears that fathers brought their training in assertiveness, leadership, and direct confrontation to their interactions with female teachers and administrators.

Teachers too revealed a gender bias in their assessment of parent involvement in schooling. Just as fathers often are given praise for carrying out household chores that mothers carry out routinely, Prescott teachers admired fathers' involvement in schooling — involvement that they expected routinely from mothers. In their conversations at school teachers treated the appearance of a father differently than that of a mother. Prescott teachers talked more about a father volunteering in the classroom than mothers coming to school. Mothers' volunteering was routine; fathers' visits were newsworthy. In interviews, teachers also revealed that they interpreted fathers' involvement differently than mothers'. Mrs Walters, for example, took fathers' attendance as an indication of the interest parents had in education:

> If the father came, you got biased in a particular way that that family really was interested in [education]; and, in fact, nearly all Prescott fathers come still. I think as they go up the grades, sometimes . . . the fathers drop out a bit . . . they felt that things are on the road. But the first grades were real busy.

Implicitly and explicitly, teachers' different reactions to mothers and fathers suggest that teachers see fathers' time as more valuable than mothers' time. It also raises the possibility that teachers' expectations are heightened by fathers' attendance at school events.

Parents at School

Despite dramatic increases in women's labor force participation, traditional gender roles in parenting have undergone only slight modification. Women continue to bear responsibility for housework and child rearing. Men do less than women in the home, do less than they perceive that they should do, and, when they do engage in housework and child rearing activities, do more interesting and varied tasks (Coverman and Sheley 1986; Benin and Agostinelli 1988; Berk 1985). Moreover labor-saving devices have not reduced women's labor as much as predicted. Women perform some household chores more frequently than in earlier eras and, most importantly, invest more time in child rearing activities (Vanek 1983).

This study suggests that women's child rearing activities have expanded further in recent decades, particularly for upper-middle-class women. In the nineteenth century mothers were considered guardians of children's intellectual development (Kuhn 1947). Nevertheless contemporary mothers appear to face a more varied, complex, and labor-intensive set of tasks in promoting their children's academic progress than in previous eras. Upper-middle-class mothers attend school events, work to bring their home activities in alignment with the school activities, and supervise their children's progress at school. Fathers are kept apprised of children's developments and make decisions, and their decisions, while fewer in number, are (on average) more significant in shaping their children's school careers than their wives' decisions.[3] Women's labor force participation does not appreciably shape this division of labor. Thus parent involvement remains primarily mother involvement in education while fathers, particularly in upper-middle-class homes, have an important symbolic role.[4]

Notes

1. Child rearing articles clearly show an increased emphasis on cognitive development since the turn of the century (Wrigley 1989). There has been also a spurt in the number of books on promoting educational development (Berger 1983; Trelease 1982). Most of these books have been published in the last twenty-five years. Pre-school programs also show an increasing emphasis on educational development.
2. In this regard Prescott fathers' role resembled that of Colton parents; it was characterized by separation rather than interconnectedness. However, Prescott fathers were occasionally critical and directive of educators. They did not always defer to the notion of professional expertise.
3. Nevertheless fathers were most likely to become involved in formal, institutional activities, particularly parent–teacher conferences. In some cases, as I have shown, fathers took a leadership role in the activities. Thus in contacts with the school (i.e., inter-institutional relationships) fathers' roles exceeded their home activities. This suggests again the notion of a family–school linkage as a distinct set of activities rather than consisting of educational activities at home or at school.
4. Studies of family life suggest that women's labor force participation (and paid child care) does not usually have a negative impact on children, especially school aged children. [For debates regarding the impact of single parenthood and mothers' employment on children's achievement see Milne *et al.* 1986 and Heyns and Catsambis 1986.] Divorce does, however, place a strain (at least temporarily) on children. Most divorced children also lost contact with their fathers, as mothers retain custody over 90 per cent of the time and fathers' visiting patterns (and economic support) are limited (Glick and Lin 1986; Cherlin 1981; Kelly and Wallerstein 1976; Kurdek *et al.* 1981; Wallerstein and Kelly 1980; Furstenberg *et al.* 1987). Since all evidence suggests that separation and divorce severely disrupts family life, particularly in the first year, I would suspect that mothers' involvement in school activities might also subside during this time (Arandell 1986). Although worthy of further investigation, this suggests that parent involvement will shift through the family life cycle, not only according to the age of the child, but according to the stage of separation, divorce, and (in most cases) remarriage that the family is in.

6   Why Does Social Class Influence Parent Involvement in Schooling

Many of the school-related activities in which mothers and fathers participated owe their existence to recent historical developments. For instance, classroom volunteers were virtually unknown only a few decades ago. The growth of private educational services to supplement schooling (e.g., tutors, learning centers, and private testing) is a new trend. And, as noted in the previous chapter, the emphasis on parents promoting cognitive development through specific child rearing practices is also a post Second World War development. These new trends remind us that many types of family–school relationships are possible.

Educators, however, frequently act as if there is only one 'proper' form of parent involvement in school. Even teachers with radically different teaching styles made similar requests for parent involvement. The educators at both Colton and Prescott schools promoted one, and only one, type of family–school relationship. Despite a standard set of goals, the teachers in the two schools encountered very different responses. Colton parents generally did not comply with teachers' requests. Prescott parents did. Social class was associated with a powerful and positive increase in parent participation in schooling.

Why were there such dramatic differences in parent involvement in the two schools? This chapter considers three possible explanations: 1) that parents differed in how much they valued education; 2) that the schools produced these patterns as a result of substantial differences in the quality and quantity of interactions with parents; and 3) that social class provided parents with different resources and outlooks, which in turn shaped their behavior.

1. Values

Surprisingly, teachers and principals in both schools were in agreement as to why parents did, and did not, work with their children more in school: in their view, parents' actions reflected their values.[1] For example, Colton's principal explained the low levels of parent involvement in this way:

> They don't value education because they don't have much of one
> themselves. [Since] they don't value education as much as they could,
> they don't put those values and expectations on their kids.

He felt this low priority placed on education influenced test scores. In the
principal's mind, the children's inferior educational performance was:

> ... because of the home, of the environment that they come from. A
> superintendent that I worked with once said [that] if he had a choice, he
> would choose kids that are capable, [because] any teacher can make
> them look good.

> So, you know, it is the community you serve. You can't get a silk purse
> out of a sow's ear. Lord knows, your job is to keep trying and providing
> all of the opportunities you can. The test scores at this school are lower,
> not the lowest but very low. They have been that way and I suspect
> they will probably remain that way. They were that way before I came
> and they will be that way after I leave.

Colton teachers too pointed to the issue of values when they discussed parents
who were very active in schooling. Both Mrs Thompson and Mrs Sampson
described active parents as being 'concerned' and 'supportive'. In conversations
with aides during recess and after school, in the teachers' room and in interviews,
the teachers consistently interpreted physical presence on the school site as a
symbol of how much parents 'cared' about their children and about educational
success. As Mrs Thompson noted:

> They come to school to see. They are attentive and care. They come to
> school and ask for work if they are out. It is mainly just an overall
> [feeling] ... that they are at school, busy and active in the whole scene,
> and that they are there. It is obvious that they care.

Conversely, parents who missed conferences were seen as lacking this 'concern'
for education. For example, when asked why she thought that Ann-Marie's
mother had missed a conference Mrs Sampson said:

> She was busy, either working or not concerned. Obviously not
> concerned because my children did well [in school] and still I got myself
> to all of their conferences.

At Prescott educators sang the same tune in a different key. They attributed
the large numbers of parents active in school to the values they presumed these
parents embraced. As the principal said:

> This particular community is one with a very strong interest in its
> schools. It is a wonderful situation in which to work. Education is very
> important to the parents and they back that up with an interest in
> volunteering.

To the Prescott principal and to the teachers volunteering was symbolic of the interest parents took in schooling. Moreover the principal felt that parents' volunteering and active involvement in schooling had additional benefits:

> This view that education is important helps kids as well. If parents value schooling and think it is important, then kids take it seriously.

Although Mrs Walters and Mrs Hoffman had very different styles of interaction with parents, they both interpreted high levels of parent involvement as a sign of support. According to the teachers, parents who were involved wanted educational success for their children more than those who weren't involved. They noted that even mothers who worked full-time could read to their children and play an active role in education, if it mattered enough to them. At the end of the year Mrs Hoffman described one girl's mother in this way:

> Gail's mother is the type of mother who would read to the child. She has a full-time job. She also would help on anything Gail needed help on. She wasn't a pesky parent but a very supportive parent.

Both teachers saw fathers' attendance at school events as a sign that the family was particularly interested in education.[2]

Parents: The Importance of Education

Interviews with parents in their homes, however, did *not* suggest that parent participation in schooling reflected the value they placed on education. Most Colton parents said that education was very important: they were insistent that their children attain a high school diploma. Parents whose children were retained were deeply upset by their children's educational failures. Some parents, particularly those who appeared to be upwardly mobile, were fervent on the topic. A few Colton parents did seem to value schooling less, and their children missed substantial amounts of school. But, some parents who seemed to value education extremely highly were *not* involved in schooling and parents who placed a lower value on schooling *were* involved. Knowing parents' values regarding education did not help clarify their patterns of involvement.

In numerous ways in the interviews Colton parents expressed the belief that education was important. Those who did not comply with teachers' requests appeared to value education quite highly. Laura's mother, for example, did not work with her daughter at home, despite Mrs Thompson's explicit request that she do so, nor did she always attend school events or parent–teacher conferences. But she expressed the belief that education was very important and she bitterly regretted her own failure to graduate from high school. She passionately wanted her daughter to graduate from high school:

> I want, I desperately want her to graduate. I had a business class my senior year and they got me a job at a new shopping mall. And I

figured, 'Why I got a job, I don't need to [voice trails off]'. And so I quit
school two months before graduation. And I regret it to this day. But, I
desperately want her to graduate from high school. If she can do that,
that would satisfy me.

Another Colton mother also did not work with her daughter consistently, even
though the child was in special education and the teachers had suggested that the
mother work with her at home. When asked what she would like Jill to be when
she grew up, she said that she would like her to be independent. Then she added:

I'd like for her to have a good job, get a good education, be smarter
than me. I only went as far as the tenth grade in school. I feel I cheated
myself.

She wanted her daughter to graduate from high school:

I want her to for sure go through high school. I'd like to see her get
some college education, but only if she's willing to.

Overall, Colton parents had strong feelings about the importance of their
children graduating from high school. Johnny's father mirrored the views of
other parents when he described how much education he would like his children
to get:

They are going to finish high school. I don't think I will accept 'No' for
an answer for that. You have to have that. Without that, you are lost.
And then if they want to go to college or trade school or whatever I will
help them as much as I can.

An insistence on high school graduation and a tentative interest in having their
children attend college was typical of Colton mothers' and fathers' educational
aspirations for their children. Nor was Colton parents' interest in education
confined to future aspirations; they were very concerned about their children's
success in first grade as well.

A further sign of this commitment to education was parents' attitude
towards failure in school. If Colton parents did not value educational success
very highly compared to Prescott parents, then they should have been less upset
by educational failure. This was not the case. Parents whose children had
repeated first grade were very distressed. As noted in Chapter Three, Mrs Morris
was upset over her son's retention and her husband and her mother 'took it
hard'. Another Colton mother felt that a kindergarten teacher had 'picked on'
her daughter and that this had negatively influenced her daughter's attitude
towards school. The mother's anger over the treatment her daughter received
endured. Three years later she could not bring herself to speak to the teacher:

You know, I just saw her yesterday at the Book Fair. And she was
saying, 'Hi' to Jill and she turned to me and said, 'Hi'. And God forgive
me but I can't talk to the woman. Every time I see her, I just get so mad.
I can't believe she is still there.

Another mother was disappointed over her daughter's retention; she resigned herself to it because she felt that repeating the grade would be best for her child. These Colton parents' feelings about retentions — their disappointment, tears, anger, and resignation — also characterized the reactions at Prescott school. None of the parents at either school showed indifference to the subject.[3]

There were parents for whom schooling was less important. In particular some Colton parents failed to get their children to school regularly. Mr Wagner, the Colton principal, was surprised to find children who were habitually truant:

> I had a problem with three or four parents this year, that their kids don't attend school. They were missing 30 to 50 per cent — chronic absenteeism. That is different from many other schools. I only had one at the other school I was at [which was three times bigger].

Among the families interviewed only Ann-Marie's mother appeared to value schooling less than other Colton parents did. She did not have strong feelings about whether her daughter did or did not receive a high school diploma; nor did she press her daughter to conform to the teacher's wishes. In addition she allowed her daughter to miss school frequently. The second grade teacher estimated that she missed school as often as once a week and was tardy (sometimes by an hour or two) once a week as well.

Ann-Marie's mother's background, however, was not typical of Colton (or Prescott) parents. As a child, she traveled with her parents, who were musicians. After fifth grade she did not attend school regularly. In her job as a clerk in a twenty-four hour convenience store she worked late at night. Although Ann-Marie was only in second grade her mother reported that Ann-Marie got herself up, got dressed, and then woke her mother up to have her brush her hair. When her mother did not have the use of a car, or 'did not have it together' to get a bus pass, she presumed that Ann-Marie would miss school. Ann-Marie did not like to miss school and she would sometimes badger her mother to call a friend with a car so she could get to school. To her mother's surprise Ann-Marie always wanted to go to school, even when this meant arriving an hour or two late. The teachers felt that Ann-Marie's mother neglected her. As Mrs Sampson said:

> Ann-Marie comes to school looking kind of dirty some days. Not much on, on a cold day. [It] looks like nobody is really taking care of her sometimes. Her hair needs brushing and her socks were kind of falling down her legs and she had on a dress and slip — and it was one of the cool days not long ago — with no sweater.

Compared to other parents in the study Ann-Marie's mother did not appear to value education highly. Yet this apparent lack of commitment to schooling was not a good predictor of her level of involvement at home. In fact she enjoyed reading as a hobby and read two books a week on the average. She also encouraged her daughter to read to herself, and Ann-Marie read almost every afternoon, often for two hours or more. Ann-Marie's mother also made up math problems for her child to do at home. These educational activities were not coordinated with the school curriculum. Ann-Marie's mother did not take the initiative in choosing books for her daughter, nor did she supervise her daughter's reading. (When I visited the home, Ann-Marie's current selection was John Knowles' *A Separate Peace*.) Ann-Marie's mother did not know what her daughter did when she came to a word she didn't know, nor did she use her daughter's reading as a way to boost her school performance. She did, however, buy numerous books at flea markets and second-hand stores and collect books from friends. Ann-Marie was a very good reader; she ranked second highest in the class. She was also at the top of the class in the number of hours in the school's Read-at-Home Program.

From her own perspective, Ann-Marie's mother valued education more than some others in the community. She felt that her former sister-in-law's failure to enroll her six-year-old son in school was a serious mistake:

> He was supposed to go to school and she just didn't feel like enrolling them or sending them. It's kind of shocking to me that she didn't even care whether she did or not. I would say, 'Well, I'll give you a ride to get his physical and his shots and stuff like that'. She [was] just real lethargic. She had no purpose, so 'why bother?' . . . She taught them things at home, you know, but not enough.

Her account of her efforts to persuade her sister-in-law to enroll the boy are revealing:

> I said it's important that he goes, because he's got to learn how to interact with everyone else . . . I know; I did go to elementary school, but not for very many years. And I know how damaging it is not to be able to learn how to get along or whatever. When you get a job, you have to know how to get along with all those people. I think school helps a lot that way, not just learning.

Ann-Marie's mother appeared to value schooling primarily for its social benefits. Nonetheless, in encouraging Ann-Marie to read and helping her with her math she was among the most active parents (in terms of educational activities at home) in the second grade class.

Prescott School

Prescott parents educational aspirations were higher than that of Colton parents. Prescott parents insisted that their children acquire college degrees, and many were tentatively in favor of post-graduate work. As one mother said when asked how much education she would like her children to have:

> No question about it, four years of college. They have a father who went to an Ivy League school and feels very strongly about his school

... There is no doubt in my mind and they know that. They just can't think about anything [else] until four years of college is over.

About post-graduate work one parent remarked:

I would never say, 'I'll pay for two years or three years or four years and then that is it.' As long as anyone will go to school around here I will pay for it, as long as I can afford it ... I would like to see them dabble in a number of different fields ... Then, maybe somewhere along the line they [will] find out what really turns them on and concentrate on that ... certainly by the time they are ready to go to graduate school.

Prescott parents' higher educational aspirations do not, however, provide an explanation for the difference in parent involvement between the two schools. Colton and Prescott parents did not differ enough in their attitudes about the importance of schooling to account for their differences in behavior. Some Colton parents who valued education very highly still did not comply with teachers' requests to work with their children at home, while at least one parent who did not appear to value education did work with her child. In selected cases, parents' values towards education may significantly influence their behavior, increasing or decreasing their involvement in their children's schooling. Overall, however, the value that parents placed on education is an insufficient explanation for why Colton parents adopted a pattern of separation between home and school while their counterparts at Prescott adopted one of interconnectedness.

2. Institutional Discrimination

Some of the most dramatic works in the sociology of education recount tales of teachers, in one case, on the eighth day of kindergarten, sorting children into classroom groups on the basis of social class (Rist 1970). These and other findings have led some social scientists to argue that there are cases of systematic discrimination in how children are treated at school. Studies of high school guidance counseling (Cicourel and Kitsuse 1963) concluded that upper-middle-class children were directed towards college; working-class children were directed away from it. Independent of ability, social class has been found to influence children's day-to-day experiences in school.

These studies provide powerful examples of how social class influences school outcomes. But evidence for this line of argument has not been consistently sustained by other research. Eder (1981), for example, examined the influence of social class on assignment to reading groups. After taking into account children's ability, social class did not appear to play a role in the assignment process. Studies of tracking within high school have found similar patterns: social class is highly correlated with college track placement, but after examining students' performance on ability tests, the impact of class becomes insignificant.[4] We know that high ability children of humble social origins (i.e.,

Table 6 *School Sponsored Activities, by Month of School Year*

	Schools	
Month	Colton	Prescott
September	Back-to-School Night	Back-to-School Night
October		Halloween Parade
November	Fall parent–teacher conference	Fall parent–teacher conference
December	Holiday program	Holiday program
February	Grandparents' Day	Spring parent–teacher conference
March	Spring parent-teacher conference	Open House
April	Open House	Grandparents' Day
	Easter Hat parade	

Note: Includes only the events that all parents are invited to attend.

smart poor children) are less likely to attend college than privileged children of low ability. But with a few dramatic exceptions, research has found little evidence that teachers apply standards unequally.

In my field observations, I searched for a pattern of institutional discrimination. I looked for examples of Colton teachers discouraging parent involvement and Prescott teachers encouraging parent involvement. My classroom observations focused on (among other things) this question: Did Colton and Prescott teachers make different requests of parents or, even in subtle ways, encourage upper-middle-class parents to be involved more than working-class parents?

My research findings suggest that Colton and Prescott school staff were similar, and at times identical, in their requests to parents. As Table 6 indicates, both schools invited parents to attend the same kinds of events, including Back-to-School Night, parent–teacher conferences, Open House night, a holiday program, and a series of other activities. They used similar methods (e.g., colored ditto-fliers) to apprise parents of coming events. At both schools teachers pressed children to persuade their parents to attend these events. On the day of Open House they reminded children of the event and told them to come to school that night with their parents. On conference day teachers sometimes mentioned to a child that they would be meeting with the child's mother that afternoon. In both schools teachers actively sought parents' attendance at school events.

In each school some teachers were warmer, friendlier, and more outgoing than others. At Colton parents said they felt more comfortable with Mrs Thompson in first grade than with Mrs Sampson in second. When parents didn't attend conferences, and Mrs Thompson thought their child needed help at home, she took the step of visiting the mother at home. Similarly at Prescott the kindergarten teacher, Mrs Taylor, was much friendlier and chattier with parents than the more stern Mrs Hoffman. In each school one teacher (not in the study) had a reputation for using parents extensively in the classroom. Thus within each school there was variation; some teachers appeared to be more comfortable and more interested in working with parents than others (Becker and Epstein 1982; Epstein 1987; Epstein and Dauber 1988).

Although teachers covered similar topics with parents, the tone, breadth, and quality of the interaction differed between the two schools. Prescott parent–teacher interactions appeared to be more social and more conversational. As a result the parent–teacher interactions at Prescott were often longer, more casual, and included more purely social exchanges. This was particularly true in conversations between the teachers' aides and parents. At Colton conversations between parents and teachers were shorter, more explicitly focused on school matters and more stilted. Prescott teachers attributed the smooth and generally pleasant flow of conversation to parents' socio-economic position:

> They [parents] will be very friendly because they're people who ...
> because of their status in the world are used to making conversation and
> being polite and being open. All those sorts of things make them
> successful people.

Mrs Walters moved to Prescott from an inner city school. When she first came, she 'misinterpreted' parents' actions as overtures to friendship:

> ... when I first started teaching, I misinterpreted those kinds of
> encounters as being friendships — I don't mean close friendships. And
> then I found out that, depending on whatever, their minds can be
> changed very quickly. You'll be getting (what feels like) a stab in the
> back.

Mrs Walters complained of parents always being 'happy and positive about everything' to her face, but then going to the principal to lodge complaints against her. As a result she had come to view parent interactions as a 'game':

> So I tend just to really play their game. And I think of it as a game
> because I don't feel a closeness to most of the parents. I'll just be very
> friendly and polite and pleasant and cheerful.

In my observations the differences in face-to-face interactions between parents and staff at Colton and Prescott seemed due to the parents more than to the teachers. With a few exceptions teachers at both schools seemed equally awkward in their interactions with parents. Teachers seemed intent on managing the interaction to meet their goals (i.e., imparting information about children's academic performance). The first and second grade teachers often seemed more comfortable and relaxed in their interactions with children than with parents. And, to my knowledge, teachers at Prescott did not work harder than those at Colton to get to know parents, see parents socially, or have warmer relations with parents. In what became a play within a play, my relations with parents differed, particularly in my interactions with them during Open House. Although I tried to maintain a similar manner in my interactions with parents at each school, I found dramatic differences in their responses. Colton parents appeared nervous, answered my questions in short sentences, and did not usually ask me any questions. By contrast Prescott parents appeared relaxed, gave lengthy answers, asked me many questions, and offered their own theories of what results I might find in the study. These observations suggest that although parent-teacher relations were sometimes warmer and more social at Prescott than at Colton, this does not represent a systematic difference in teachers' treatment of parents.

There is some evidence that Colton teachers were more vigorous than Prescott teachers in recruiting parents to work with their children at home. During the first year of the study, Colton school had three formal programs: a Read-at-Home Program, a parent education workshop to help parents work effectively with their children at home, and a class on parenting directed at single parents.[5] The teachers announced these programs in their classes. Each classroom had a chart on the wall showing students' progress in the Read-at-Home Program.

Although Prescott school had a more frequent newsletter (issued weekly) than did Colton (where fliers were sent home sporadically, averaging once a month), it did not have a formal school program aimed at getting parents to work with their children at home. At Back-to-School Night and in conferences, Prescott teachers did talk about the importance of reading to children, but their pitches did not appear — from my observation — to be as aggressive as the program at Colton. At Colton some teachers (especially Mrs Thompson) showed a missionary zeal as they stressed the importance of reading at home to children; efforts at Prescott were less vigorous. On the other hand, because of a very active parents' club, Prescott provided parents with more opportunities — and more explicit invitations — to join in activities at the school. The parents' club sponsored a number of fund-raising activities and, perhaps most import- antly, organized and coordinated the classroom volunteer program. When Prescott parents came to school, they found an active group of parents with whom to join forces. In some cases this may have encouraged parents' involvement. Still, these activities were managed by parents. While appreciated by teachers, the parent volunteer program was not initiated and controlled by teachers.

In summary, the schools were very similar in their relations with parents. No pattern of institutional activity emerged that could account for the differences in parents' family–school interactions. In terms of *teachers'* activities Colton school appeared to have a *more* vigorous outreach program than Prescott school.

3. Class as Providing Cultural Resources

Researchers in education often either assert or assume that social class is important because it influences the quality of schooling children receive. Yet in the schools studied here, there is little evidence that the differences in parent involvement are linked to teachers' actions.[6] Instead the actions of parents seem linked to the resources that their education, occupational status, income, and differences in family life provided. Social class does make a difference, but its effects are less direct and more complex than commonly believed.

Educational and Occupational Status

Objectively Colton parents' educational skills were inferior to those of Prescott parents. Most of the Colton parents were high school graduates or, especially among the fathers, high school drop-outs. Colton parents reported having poor educational skills. For example, Johnny's mother, Mrs Trenton was a high school graduate. She confessed to having a reading problem. She noted that when she started reading pre-school books to her son, her own reading improved:

> I used to have a reading problem. I couldn't read very well. I mean I could read well enough to do applications. But when I was nineteen and married my husband, I had to ask him words. I didn't know how to sound words out. Then when I started reading to Johnny, my reading improved.

Tommy's mother, Mrs Morris, described her husband's educational limitations:

> My husband didn't graduate [from high school]. He went back to school for the carpentry. He failed the [contractors' licensing exam] the first time. He failed part B and he passed part A. Then he passed. It was hard for him. It was hard to read and to concentrate.

Colton parents lacked educational *competence*, and they were aware of their shortcomings.

In some cases, even when parents had difficulty with basic material, they felt more capable and more fortunate than others they knew. Mrs Morris had a high school education. She depended on the school to educate her son, but she was clearly better educated than her aunt, who was about her age:

> My aunt went to eighth grade. She is three years older than I am. She went to eighth grade. She got a job, well she lasted two days. Where I feel — I am confident — she has no confidence in herself whatsoever to go out and fill out an application. Now to work for the school district [in the cafeteria], she didn't want to go because she was ashamed to put on the application that she didn't graduate.

When her aunt took an adult education class, Mrs Morris helped her with the material. In addition she felt her education gave her an edge in the job market:

> At the time [I graduated] I thought it was no big deal. Well, now I think, yeah, it is a big deal. I am sure if we went out to get a job, I think I would get a job easier than she would because I have graduated.

The inferior educational skills of Colton parents were real. In my observations of parents in meetings with teachers and in interviews in their homes, Colton parents frequently broke rules of standard English in their conversations, used words incorrectly (e.g., 'insuperior' instead of 'inferior'), and appeared to have much smaller vocabularies than Prescott parents. In addition, when Colton parents talked about working to improve their own skills so that they could help their children, they were referring to elementary school material. One father, for example, boasted that he had taken a 'refresher course' at work which enabled him to help his daughter in school. The refresher course was on fractions.

Colton parents' lack of educational skills hampered them in their interactions with teachers. Some mothers had trouble understanding what teachers were saying. Laura's mother liked Mrs Thompson and felt comfortable with her; she had trouble understanding other teachers, however, particularly her daughter's kindergarten teacher. She said her difficulty varied with the teacher:

> It all depends on the person and how they treat you. If they start using big words, you think, 'Oh God what does that mean?' You know, it is just like going to the doctor's. And it makes you feel a little insuperior to them. Because I don't have the education they do. You know, I just *don't*.

Laura's mother doubted that she would be able to continue to help her daughter as she advanced in school:

> You know, school has changed so much, and I know that when she gets into the higher grades, I won't be able to help her, math especially, unless I take a refresher course myself. Because it has changed so much, and it is so different.

These changes in schooling, and her own lack of education, led her to rely heavily on the teacher:

> So I feel that it is the teacher's job to help her as much as possible to understand it because I know that I won't be able to. . . . I can sit down and try to help her figure it out, but I don't think that I'll be able to help her like I should be able to.

Jill's mother also complained of having trouble understanding the vocabulary of teachers. She expressed her frustration after an Individual Education Plan conference in which she agreed to place her daughter in special education for the next year.[7] At the end of the conference, Mrs Brown was asked to sign a paper summarizing the results of the conference and the decision to place Jill in special education for most of the school day:

> She put that paper in front of me with all of this stuff, and you know, half of it I didn't understand. But everyone wanted to get up and go. The psychologist couldn't wait to leave, and I thought, 'Why sit here and ask all these questions? I am going to talk to the one next year there when Jill goes to school. I will get all of the information from her that I

need to know. There is no sense in me asking it all now so that I can forget it all or have to repeat the thing next year. Better just to go in there fresh next year with a new teacher.'

Parents' limited educational competence increased their doubts as to whether or not they were helping their children correctly. Although aware that teachers wanted them to work with children at home, these parents resisted the teachers' suggestions. Jill's mother's comments give voice to other parents' doubts as well as her own:

> You know, a lot of things that I might do with her here at home might frustrate her, or, you know, confuse her or something. They have a different arithmetic system now and they are doing all kinds of different stuff with the kids. So, rather than taking two or three hours to sit down and have them explain it to me and make sure I know what I am talking about [laughs nervously], it is better just to leave it at school.

In some cases, Colton parents' self-doubts were further fueled by their children's resistance. Children insisted that the parents were trying to get them to do the school work incorrectly. One mother described a typical encounter with her older son:

> My kid will come home and I will sit down and help him do homework. [And he says], 'My teacher didn't do it that way. You are doing it *wrong*, Mom!' When you get to that point, [you say], 'Forget it! Do it at school!'

Colton teachers confirmed that parents felt that they lacked educational competence. For example, Mrs Thompson recounted how, when she first requested volunteers, some mothers were eager to help. For them it was an opportunity to break the isolation of being at home:

> We wanted mothers to come to school to help. In the past, I have found we can offer even a social advantage. Some of the parents never got out of the house; and I would have mothers come to school dressed up because it was a social event to come to school.

But the volunteer program ran into difficulty, in part because, as Mrs Thompson noted, parents felt they were not competent to help:

> A lot of the mothers [who came to school] felt that they would grade a paper wrong or they didn't have the ability, even in the first grade level, to even spell the words.

Mrs Thompson discounted this and felt that the parents could, and should, have worked more with their children:

> I think that more of them would be competent than they know that they would have been. I think that so many of them hadn't been to high school and so forth. They didn't feel that they had the abilities. I think

they could have done more than they have. But they feel since they didn't complete school that they couldn't help the child.

Educational competence was not an issue among Prescott parents. In contrast to Colton, all of the fathers were college graduates and three had advanced degress (i.e., a JD, an MBA, and a Ph.D); five of the six mothers had attended college. Prescott parents' vocabulary, grammar, and general ability to articulate their thoughts was objectively superior to that of Colton parents. A few of the mothers appeared to be concerned about math and science material at high school level and expected to defer to the fathers at that time. But with first and second grade work, none of the Prescott parents expressed concern about their competence to help.

Occupational Status

Colton and Prescott mothers and fathers approached teachers from different positions in the status hierarchy. Colton parents held jobs with lower occupational status than teachers jobs. The fathers in the sample were employed as an assembly line worker, a cement worker, an unemployed tire retreading worker, a self-employed construction worker, and a police officer. The mothers were employed as an assembly line worker, a salesperson in a convenience store, and bookkeeper for the family business. Colton teachers affirmed that these occupations were typical of parents' work lives, over one half of parents were employed in skilled or semi-skilled occupations. Mrs Thompson often tried to keep track of the parents' jobs so that she could ask a mother or father to come in to talk if the class was studying a related topic. According to her, the most common jobs for fathers were 'construction work, factory labor type of thing, gas stations'. For mothers, the most common job was 'waitressing', with 'cleaning, some office work, store clerk', rounding out the list.

By contrast, Prescott fathers were in jobs of equal or superior occupational prestige to that of elementary school teachers. In addition, as other writers have noted (Lipman-Blumen 1984), the gender status of males is generally accorded higher social ranking than that of females.[8] Hence, in the overwhelming majority of cases, Prescott fathers' status outranked the teachers'. The occupational prestige of Prescott mothers was more mixed; the mothers who were working at the time of the study were employed as an administrator in a bank, a nurse, and a (part-time) bookkeeper for the family business.

These differences in occupational status appeared to influence parent–teacher interactions. Much as Sennett and Cobb (1972) have theorized, these parents seemed to consider their occupational status (and general class position) as a 'badge' representing their ability. Colton mothers and fathers looked up to teachers; they did not see themselves as equals. One mother explained it in this way:

A teacher goes to school for a long time. They know a lot more than a regular person. I don't consider myself stupid, but I'm not extremely smart or intelligent. I could not go into a classroom and teach a class and expect them to come out knowing as much as the teacher teaches them. So I rely on the teacher's opinion a lot more than my own opinion.

Colton mothers and fathers saw teachers as *professionals*, having a specialized body of knowledge that they had acquired through training. Just as they viewed doctors as having a specialized body of knowledge that was beyond their comprehension, the parents felt that they were not capable of understanding the specialized knowledge of teachers. Colton parents granted teachers a 'backstage' — a world from which they, by virtue of their lack of ability and training, were excluded.[9]

Perceiving teachers as professional and themselves as educationally incompetent influences Colton parents' beliefs about their own proper role in their children's schooling. They readily assigned responsibility for their children's education to the teacher. There were variations of course. Some Colton parents were much more active than others in preparing children for school. For example, some parents went over math papers and had children correct their mistakes. Other parents simply looked at the math papers and praised their children.

Colton parents' relatively low occupational and educational status also appeared to shape their evaluation of schooling. For example, Ann-Marie's mother liked her daughter's kindergarten teacher and first grade teacher a great deal. But she was unhappy with her second grade teacher (Mrs Sampson) and felt that the teacher 'yelled' at the children too much. She had not complained, however, nor did she have any plans to do so. She was fearful that if she protested the teacher might retaliate, making the situation worse:

> I am sure if I went up to her and said something to her about her yelling, it would just make her madder and that might put more pressure on Ann-Marie ... I am sure it would be in very subtle ways. Just the resentment she might feel towards her that she caused trouble.

Ann-Marie's mother also did not think that complaining to the teacher would do any good:

> The teacher would probably explain why she does things the way she does. I don't think she would change it or listen — you know — really listen.

Nor did she see consulting with the principal as a viable option. When asked, 'Have you ever thought about complaining to the principal?' she answered:

> No, I don't think I'd want to do that. If it were a big problem, I'd have her transferred to another class and then I would have to [speak to the principal]. I wouldn't go to the teacher first, I definitely would go to the office first, and talk to somebody there if it was a big problem.

To Ann-Marie's mother, a 'big problem' was something very serious: if she thought her daughter was being 'discriminated against', then she 'would have to do something'. She had not experienced that type of problem nor did she expect to in the future. Moreover she thought that very few parents complained to the school. When asked why, she said:

> I don't know. A lot of people around here have lost a lot of confidence . . . People are living here because they can't afford to live other places. So they don't have much self-esteem. It's probably harder for them to speak up about things.

This lack of confidence in their ability to understand, challenge, and face teachers as equals was a key factor in shaping Colton parents' behavior. It influenced their views on their role in education and their demeanor at the school. School was an alien world: Colton parents neither understood the inner workings of the educational system nor had sufficient social status to validate their assessments of teachers' actions. Instead, Colton parents appeared to depend on teachers, as professionals, to be self-regulating. Generally they did not believe that they could or should oversee and try to manage the behavior of teachers. There were a few parents who took a more active role in the school, visiting teachers regularly and expressing their views. Other studies (Clark 1983) have also described mothers who, despite low levels of education and occupational status, take the view that teachers can 'make mistakes' and are assertive in their interactions with teachers. Such an approach was rare at Colton.

At Prescott parents did not exhibit similar feelings of dependence, passivity, and insecurity with teachers. Only one mother — the only Prescott mother in the sample with no more than a high school education — reported a similar feeling of deference to teachers. Feeling her lack of higher education keenly, she said:

> Teachers intimidate me. They have always intimidated me. To me they are right up there [pointing to the sky] next to God and doctors.

The remaining mothers and fathers in Prescott did not express self-doubts. Their college education seemed to grant symbolic access to the world of professionals. These parents tended to view teachers as equals. They did not defer to them as having superior social status, nor as having a 'backstage' of knowledge which the parents were not capable of penetrating. As one father made clear, he saw himself as capable of being a teacher. It was just something he had not chosen to do:

> I don't think of teachers as more educated than me or in a higher position than me. I don't have any sense of hierarchy. I am not higher than them, and they are not higher than me. We are equals. We are reciprocals.

This sense of equality helped him take the initiative with teachers. If he felt there was a problem he talked to them about it:

> So if I have a problem I will talk to them. I have a sense of decorum. I wouldn't go busting into a classroom and say something. Obviously,

for they are professional people. But there aren't any barriers in that sense. They are not working for me, but they also aren't doing something that I couldn't do. It is more a question of division of labor.

Prescott parents were also very comfortable going to the principal to complain about a teacher, and they did not hesitate to make demands of teachers. Their occupational experiences may have contributed to the apparent ease with which Prescott parents pursued their own interests. For example, Mr Harris, Allen's father and a store owner said:

I am . . . accustomed to dealing with authority figures and not being concerned about it. If the mayor of the city walks into my store, I don't get all concerned about it. It is, 'Hi, how are you'. It is not a big deal.

Mr Harris and his wife complained to the principal on several occasions. Reflecting on his behavior and that of other parents in the community, he said:

I suspect that in this community, especially with people who are in positions of authority themselves, they think nothing of going to somebody else who is in a position of authority and talking to them face to face and saying, 'You are wrong.'

Occupational experiences also appeared to play a role in the way Emily's parents, the Svenssons, chose to handle a recommendation from Mrs Walters that their daughter be retained in first grade. Although Mrs Walters knew, and reportedly understood, why the Svenssons had decided not to have Emily repeat first grade, she once again wrote that recommendation on Emily's report card on the last day of school. Emily's father considered asking Mrs Walters to write down that she had misdiagnosed his daughter's reading skills and placed her in an inappropriate reading group (a mistake that Mrs Walters had admitted to the parents in a conference).

I almost asked Mrs Walters to write down the statement that she made to us that she had misevaluated Emily and that Emily had fooled her . . . I could have said, 'Well, Mrs Walters, I would like you to write down the reasons why you feel she should be retained.'

He decided ultimately not to ask her to do this, but not because he was afraid to make such a demand. Mr Svensson's occupation as a lawyer gave him a great deal of experience with conflict but he decided it was not constructive or necessary to insist that Mrs Walters admit her mistake. Instead he 'gave her the benefit of the doubt':

I am a trial lawyer. There is a lot of conflict and controversy . . . Teachers have been [people] I have always enjoyed being around. I have always done well and gotten along well in school. I just gave Mrs Walters the benefit of the doubt . . . And I didn't know what purpose, other than perhaps my personal satisfaction, of having her write down that one of the reasons she was retaining Emily was because Mrs Walters had not made as good a professional evaluation as she might have.

Thus both the relatively high occupational standing and the occupational experiences of Prescott fathers and, to a lesser extent mothers, gave them an advantage in their interactions with teachers. In particular they rejected the idea that they — as lay persons — were not capable of evaluating professionals. Rather than automatically deferring to professionals many of the parents were assertive and controlling with educators. They tried to take a leadership role in their children's schooling. They were not shy about informing teachers about weaknesses in their performance, nor did they hesitate to tell the principal and superintendent that a teacher was not up to par and should be replaced.

Not all Prescott parents approached school staff the same way of course. Some parents felt sorry for teachers because of the demands other parents made of them; these parents were almost uniformly supportive of the school in their formal interactions. If they had complaints, as Mr and Mrs Simpson had, they left them unexpressed. Even in these cases, Prescott parents critically evaluated the teachers' performance rather than presuming that they were incapable of such judgment. Their position of being social equals (or superiors) to teachers appeared to buttress their view that they had the right and responsibility to participate in their children's schooling. It also increased their criticisms of the professional behavior of school staff.

Dimensions of Work

Prescott and Colton parents, especially fathers, worked in occupational settings which had a different labor process and a different criterion for occupational success. Prescott fathers worked longer hours, carried their work over into their homes, traveled away from home as part of their jobs, and socialized with co-workers in the evenings and weekend hours. These encroachments into evening and weekend time were not, as others have found, an optional work experience. Engineers, lawyers, and managers in this study and others (Kanter 1977; Margolis 1979) felt they had to carry out these tasks in order to achieve occupational success. Relocations related to promotions were also part of the demands placed on the family by the father's career (Margolis 1979). As Margolis (1979) demonstrated in her study of managers, mothers and children played a role in supporting the fathers' careers. In a 'two person single career', wives release husbands from home obligations, thus increasing the time they can devote to their careers. Wives also carry out occupationally related duties (e.g., when they entertain their husbands' co-workers at home) and families as a whole make sacrifices for the fathers' careers, through loss of friendships in moves. This pattern of support was evident at Prescott. In these families, there was an interconnectedness between work and home.

At Colton there was a different relationship between work — especially the father's work — and family life. Here, fathers worked set hours at a specific site.

Some of the fathers had shifts that rotated around the clock (i.e., day, swing, and graveyard shift); these were disruptive of family life. Unlike Prescott fathers, however, working-class parents never carried out work tasks in the home. Their children never observed them at home doing labor linked to their occupational success, nor did children have to withdraw or be quiet so that the father could complete work assignments. Similarly, Colton parents were not required to travel away from home during the week for their jobs, nor had any of the families relocated for the sake of the husbands' careers. The criterion for advancement was the husband's performance at work; socializing with co-workers or business associates was not part of job requirements. While the content of the work was much more routine, closely supervised, and far less complex than the labor process in upper-middle-class jobs (Kohn and Schooler 1983), at the end of the shift, Colton parents left the job behind. Thus there was a separation between home and work in these families.

The amount of separation or interconnectedness between work and home appeared to influence family–school relationships. First, it shaped parents' conception of the educational process. All of the Colton fathers and mothers viewed their children's education as a form of work not unlike their own experiences on the job. Colton families saw schooling as something that took place on the school site. They drew a clear line between school and home. By contrast, Prescott parents saw education as a twenty-four hour a day experience which took place both at school *and* at home, just as the fathers labored both at work and at home.

Second, the amount of interconnectedness between work and home also influenced the parents' flexibility and ability to attend school events during the day. Upper-middle-class fathers had jobs with self-direction and autonomy; all of the Prescott fathers could, theoretically, rearrange their schedules to attend parent–teacher conferences in the middle of the afternoon or volunteer in the classroom. Some working-class fathers worked evening or graveyard shifts, so (theoretically) they, too, could attend school events; but overall, working-class jobs offered parents less flexibility and autonomy for making changes in their schedule to accommodate their children's school events.

Third, the amount of interconnectedness between family life and work influenced the social networks of the family. Among the working-class families, social interactions with colleagues did not have a positive influence on occupational advancement. In addition, none of the families moved because of career advancement. Among upper-middle-class families, however, social networks could and did influence occupational advancement. Unlike working-class jobs, where the routine character of work makes it clear when someone is or is not working efficiently, many upper-middle-class jobs lack clearly identifiable criteria for evaluation.[10] Kanter (1977) suggests that this indeterminacy leads supervisors to evaluate the social characteristics of the worker, the degree to which he or she is a 'team player', and the characteristics of the worker's home life. Evidence shows that upper-middle-class families socialize with co-workers in evenings and weekends and that this socializing can influence occupational advancement (Kanter 1977; Margolis 1979; Packard 1964). All of these factors increase the class homogeneity — rather than heterogeneity — of social ties.

Class, Networks, and Information

These differences in networks, linked to the character of work, shaped the amount of information about education available to parents. The lack of geographic mobility associated with working-class jobs meant that Colton parents had many relatives in the area. As other studies have found, kinship ties among working-class families are intense (Fischer 1982a; 1982b; Lee 1979; Litwack 1971; Caplow et al. 1983; Bott 1971). Four of the six Colton mothers spoke with their mothers by telephone several times per week; and parents frequently mentioned their sisters and parents in interviews. Most members of these kin groups were of working-class status, as were neighbors, co-workers, and other parents in the school community. As a result Colton parents did not have social ties with teachers, principals, and school administrators.[11] Nor did the mothers of children in the Colton classes I observed socialize with one another; none were friends with other mothers in their children's class. Colton parents did not enroll their children in formal lessons. After school Colton children rode their bikes, watched television, and played. Their free time was informally, rather than formally, organized. 'Educated people' were not part of the daily lives of people living in Colton. This meant that Colton parents were heavily dependent upon the teachers for the information which they received about school, the nature of their children's learning patterns, and the ways in which parents could be involved in schooling.

By contrast, at Prescott, professional, upper-middle-class parents had informal ties to educators. Sprinkled throughout the car pools, Mothers' Club, and neighborhoods, there were many current or former teachers. Without a survey it is difficult to be precise, but a conservative estimate is that twenty to twenty-five per cent of the children at Prescott had a teacher in their immediate family or in the networks of family and friends with whom they maintained regular contact. For example, in the six families interviewed, three families had a relative or a close family friend who was a teacher.[12] This web of educators was particularly important when Prescott parents were searching for answers to their children's school-related problems. For example, when Emily's parents became concerned about Emily's lack of progress in first grade, they turned to a family member for additional input:

> I talked to my sister-in-law, who was a teacher. We talked at great length about it. She actually worked with Emily a little bit. She had been a first grade teacher and had some reading games.

In other instances teachers and parents lived near one another. For example, Allen's family lived next door to Bernice Cates, a teacher hired to teach first grade at Prescott during the second year of the study. When Allen's younger brother Jacob was in first grade Mrs Cates was his teacher. When Jacob was not doing as well in school as his mother had expected, being neighbors with his teacher helped. Mrs Harris felt more comfortable pressing her neigbor for an explanation for Jacob's disappointing performance:

> He [Jacob] had this innate intelligence. He just had it. And he did have it. That was [what was] so disturbing. It bothered Tim and I that we had to say, 'Now Bernice, what is really wrong with Jacob? Why isn't he producing on at least an average level?' He was just average. And we felt that there probably should have been a little bit more than just that. We had to, not browbeat her, but basically twist her arm and say, what is wrong here? Why isn't this going the way we perceive that it should be going?

This strategy paid off for the Harrises in a parent–teacher conference. Mr Harris gave the following description of the events:

> Bernice did not tell us until the end of the year. . . . The conference had ended; she said to us, 'OK, I am going to tell you something as neighbors. You ought to have Jake tested for OT [Occupational Therapy]. He might need OT'. There was no 'might' about it. Jacob desperately needed OT. And we would have sat here, fat, dumb, and happy today if she had not had the courage to override the school authorities and the school rule and take us aside.

The occupational therapy in which the Harrises immediately enrolled their son worked to improve his muscle control, particularly the way in which he held up his head, used his arms, and sat in a chair. His parents reported a dramatic improvement in his posture, his handwriting, and his motor coordination in soccer.[13]

In addition to knowing educators Prescott mothers also had more intense ties to other parents in the school community. All six Prescott mothers knew other mothers of children in the same classroom; three mothers knew all but two or three of the mothers in the class. In the interviews, mothers noted the 'close friendships' that developed among mothers of children in the same class. Some of these friendships developed because parents lived in the same neighborhood and attended the same extra-curricular events. Upper-middle-class children at Prescott were enrolled in many formal lessons. All of the children had at least one activity per week and several had three (i.e., soccer games, swim lessons, scouting). In some cases, as with Bluebirds, almost all the girls in the two second grade classrooms in the school participated in the activity. Several mothers shared the leadership of the group, thereby increasing contact with other mothers in the school.[14]

School volunteering also strengthened mothers' friendships. According to teachers and mothers, it was common practice that immediately after helping out in the classroom, the mother–volunteer would go home and telephone another mother to discuss her experience. Teachers estimated an average of eight to fifteen telephone calls per week took place discussing the activities in each of the kindergarten, first, second, and third grade classrooms. Mothers confirmed that they had three to five telephone calls per week with other mothers of children in the school. Some Prescott mothers said that their best friends were mothers of their children's classmates.

These networks among the mothers influenced some mothers' behavior. Mrs Roy, Jonathan's mother, for example, was very disappointed in Jonathan's first grade classroom. She was appalled by her conferences with Mrs Walters, in which Mrs Walters (who had a learning-disabled son) raised the possibility that Jonathan might never learn to read:

> At all our conferences, Mrs Walters dealt mainly with her son. She actually said this to me — this is terrible, 'Things are only going to get worse. Kids with problems like these kinds of problems, things will become worse and they won't have friends.' That is devastating for someone to hear.

Mrs Roy ultimately rejected as inaccurate Mrs Walters' academic prognosis for Jonathan. She did so in part because of her social networks. Although Mrs Roy did not consider herself to be a 'typical Prescotter', through soccer games and other community events, she had gotten to know other parents. The opinions of parents, particularly about Mrs Walters, had a powerful influence on her behavior. Mrs Roy rejected Mrs Walters' professional assessment of her child's educational future, noting that 'I just didn't buy it'. She said the judgments of other parents were critical in this process:

> I felt I *should* [respect her judgment] but I didn't. I think I had enough experience at that time to form my own judgment. *And* by talking to other parents, [I found out] what their perspective was with the classroom and how their children had done during the year.

Her information linkages with other parents in the school played a critical role in her assessment of Jonathan's needs and in her behavior. She 'gave up' trying to intervene in her son's classroom by the middle of first grade. Although the rumors that circulated among Prescott parents were not always accurate, having a critical mass of parents active in school did seem to provide Prescott mothers with information that they considered useful and important.

Thus parents' informal networks — with parents of other children in the same classroom and with educators — shaped their children's school experience. These informal ties between teachers and parents were virtually unknown at Colton, in part because teachers rarely, if ever, live next door to and/or socialize with working-class families. Instead most teachers, including those at Prescott and Colton schools, live in upper-middle-class neighborhoods where they socialize with other upper-middle-class families. Consequently their informal hints and off-the-record comments are unevenly distributed through the population. Upper-middle-class parents, including Prescott parents, are potentially able to benefit from these comments; Colton parents are virtually excluded from this possibility.

Class and Access To Scarce Resources

It is received wisdom that people tend to take for granted what they have. For those with a college or a post-graduate education it may be difficult to imagine what life is like for those whose education ended with high school — or before. The experience of Colton parents suggests that the lack of a college education is an exercise in exclusion: exclusion from understanding conversations at school; exclusion from feeling that one belongs at school and is capable of evaluating the performance of better-educated persons; even exclusion from being able to help children with their school work. By virtue of social class differences in networks, working-class parents typically have no access to the sorts of detailed rumors about the talents and failings of local teachers that were so readily available to Prescott parents.

Moreover evidence shows that a college education and a prestigious occupation are highly valued — and relatively scarce — resources in American society. While the number of persons graduating from college has steadily increased, only twenty per cent of the total population are college graduates. Among the population twenty-five to thirty-four years of age the proportion is higher, but three-quarters do not finish college (Grant and Snyder 1985; U.S. Department of Education 1988). Most adults lack a college education and occupational prestige that matches or surpasses that of elementary school teachers.

School children are not drawn equally from the different segments of American society. The birth rate varies by social class: the higher the social class, the lower the birth rate. Compared with the adult population, children of poor families are overrepresented in American schools (*Education Week* 1986). Thus there are relatively few children from upper-middle-class homes in contemporary classrooms. In most urban districts around the country, the trend is towards school-age children from single-parent working-class homes. Many of these children are non-white (*Education Week* 186; U.S. Department of Education 1988). This means that teachers face different types of parents. Teachers in some districts work with parents very much like Prescott parents. Because of residential segregation by race and class many of these parents are concentrated in the relatively homogeneous suburban districts that ring central cities. Most teachers, however, work with parents in much less privileged positions in the social stratification system. These parents have high school educations or are high school drop-outs. They have lower occupational status and suffer from economic instability.

Because of their position in the social stratification system, upper-middle-class parents are better equipped than working-class parents to meet the requests of teachers. Hidden in relatively benign requests — that parents read to their children, attend school events, volunteer in the classroom, help their children in school, and respond to the teachers's requests — are pre-conditions. Although the children were only in first grade, Colton parents did not feel competent — and in some cases did not appear to be competent — to help their children in school. Parents' reading skills were weak, their math skills elementary, and they had difficulty understanding teachers. The teachers' requests presumed educational competence which some of the Colton parents lacked. Upper-middle-class parents rarely have difficulty meeting this pre-condition of literacy and basic educational skills.

The case of a Colton mother, a high school graduate, who found that her reading started to improve as she read pre-school books to her son might seem extreme, but recent surveys suggest that it is not. The skills of high school and college graduates have been declining. For example, studies have found that in a representative sample of young adult college graduates, over one third could not correctly estimate the cost per ounce of a food item when given the weight (i.e., 20 oz) and the total price ($1.99). High school drop-outs 'suffer from serious literacy deficiencies' (Venezky *et al.* 1987, p. 36), and many have difficulties with very basic tasks. Nationally, estimates are that around fifteen per cent of American adults are functionally illiterate (Venezky *et al.* 1987). Educational skills are a pre-condition to helping children in school; today high school drop-outs or high school graduates frequently lack these skills.

Finally, when teachers requested that parents work with their children at home, a pre-condition to meeting that request was that parents understand and share teachers' views concerning the interconnectedness between home and school. Prescott parents, for the most part, did so; Colton parents did not. Ironically then, Colton parents' greater respect for the professional expertise of teachers, combined with their emphasis on a separation between school and home, decreased rather than increased these parents' likelihood of working with their children at home on educational activities. Unlike upper-middle-class parents, the invisible pre-conditions for parents' responding to teachers' requests for help were not present in most working-class homes.

Notes

1. In adopting this view, educators had embraced the dominant model in the social sciences.
2. Parent involvement was not uniform; over one half of mothers did not volunteer in the classroom. Teachers, including Mrs Walters, attributed this to the labor force participation of women: 'So many mothers are working, it is hard to get help.' When a working mother did participate in the classroom, the teachers often commented on how 'concerned' she was and how 'supportive' she was of education. As at Colton, high levels of parent involvement were seen as an expression of values.
3. I interpret parents' disappointment as a sign that they desire — or value — school success. Other interpretations are possible, however, including that parents see children's poor school performance as a reflection on themselves (and their own intelligence or parenting ability). Although not likely, it is also possible that parents do not value education very

highly themselves, but they know that others value it highly so they try to conform with this social standard.

4. Most of the earlier research looked at differences between schools (i.e., Heyns 1974). More recently, however, researchers have suggested that there are important variations across schools in how they track students (Garet and Delaney 1988; Oakes 1985). Once assigned to a track, however, ability grouping appears to have an influence on students' academic performance over time (Lee and Bryk 1988; Gamoran 1987; Kerckhoff 1986).

5. In the second year of the study, the vice-principal was promoted and the reading resource teacher was transferred to another school. These staffing changes meant that the leaders of the single-parent class and the parent education workshop left Colton and the programs did not operate that year. Only the Read-at-Home Program continued intact. It was unclear whether the school staff members would decide to resume the programs the following year.

6. Epstein (1986) shows that parents in classrooms of teachers who take a leadership role in promoting parent involvement are, in fact, more involved in their children's schooling than parents of children in classrooms where teachers were not leaders in this area. In addition, these parents have more positive attitudes about the school. Epstein also finds that teacher leaders are more uniform in their requests for help, while teachers who are not leaders concentrate their requests on parents of children of lower socio-economic status. The results of Epstein's study suggest that teachers can, and at times do, overcome the pattern of class bias in parent involvement in schooling (a pattern of class bias that works in two ways: teachers concentrate their requests on lower socio-economic parents and parents of higher socio-economic levels respond more readily to teachers' requests). This research, however, attempts to understand why this class bias in parent involvement persists in schools, a pattern which some very active teachers appear to be able to reduce, but not eliminate, by their leadership activities.

7. The conference included the special education teacher, the school psychologist, the principal, a district official in special education, Mrs Brown, and myself. The second grade classroom teacher, Mrs Sampson, did not attend.

8. According to Hodge, Treiman, and Rossi, (1966) the public school teacher has a prestige score of 81. The prestige scores of the fathers were as follows: trial lawyer, 89; corporate executive, physicist, 90; owner of a business, 80; and building contractor, 80. This group appeared to be typical of other fathers in the school; teachers reported that most fathers were professionals or semi-professionals.

9. See Friedson (1986), Larson (1979), and Hughes (1963) for a general discussion of the issues of professional status and Lortie (1977) and Goode (1969) for a more specialized discussion of the professional standing of teachers.

10. For example, when a product fails in the market, it is difficult to sort out how much the marketing manager is responsible and how much the product was doomed, regardless of the talent of the marketing manager.

11. Some Colton parents were friendly with persons filling working-class and low-level, white-collar jobs in the school. When asked if she knew anybody from the school (including parents), Tommy's mother replied:

> Friends of ours up the street; she works in the office there on Thursdays and Fridays. I went in a couple of times this year and talked to her . . . And then Bill, the janitor. I think everyone knows Bill. And I know the woman in the cafeteria.

12. Carol's grandmother was a teacher in a nearby suburban district; Emily's aunt was a teacher in an inner-city school; and Allen's parents had a close family friend and a neighbor who were teachers.

13. They also discovered the reason that Mrs Cates had told them her opinion 'off the record': cuts in the school district's funding had changed eligibility requirements for OT. Previously, students whose performance was at grade level were eligible for the service;

the new regulations required that students be two years below grade level in order to qualify for the service. If teachers recommended OT then the district was responsible for paying for it. Mr and Mrs Harris were not opposed to enrolling their son in private lessons and paying for OT themselves. They were happy to do this. But they were angry at Bernice Cates and at the school system for not letting them know earlier about the problem:

> It made us angry. We were angry because we knew her personally. We felt that
> she should have felt more comfortable to say to us, 'This is what Jacob needs.'

14. Although precise figures were not available, it was clear that Prescott had less turnover in the school population than Colton where, in some years, one quarter of the students turned over in one year. This relative stability at Prescott facilitated the formation of social networks among the parents. This stability and instability in school populations did not appear to be unique to the school, but rather related to class position. Colton had an inexpensive housing market which attracted parents to the community, offsetting the undesirable aspects of the community, including the crime rate, drag racing, drug problem, and limited shopping area. Many parents lived in apartments. Those parents that improved their economic position, moved to other — more desirable — communities. Other families also moved away to other communities in their search for steady employment. Prescott, on the other hand, was an expensive housing market. Families typically owned their dwellings, rather than renting, and moved to Prescott with the intention of staying. Some Prescott families were forced to move for the father's occupational career. Nevertheless, by virtue of their longer career ladder, relative invulnerability to unemployment, and high income, most upper-middle-class families had lower mobility rates than families in the working-class community. These class differences in geographical mobility, in turn, shaped social networks among the parents.

7   Educational Profits: The Positive Impact of Parent Involvement on Children's School Careers

Schools do many things. Educators offer programs that teach young children how to brush their teeth, guard against sexual abuse, use crosswalks, be physically fit, develop artistic and musical talents, and use computers. For most people, however, the 'bottom line' of schools' productivity is children's measurable, academic performance in the classroom and on standardized tests. In this chapter I examine whether or not the different types of family-school relationships — interconnectedness in the upper-middle-class families and separation in the working-class families — influence academic performance. The signs here are rough indicators rather than precise equations, and it is difficult to assess the amount of influence parents' actions have on children's total academic performance. Researchers often maintain that parent involvement is associated with high levels of achievement, particularly in reading.[1] In this study, however, it was not high-achievers who had the most intense family–school relationships, nor were the effects of parent involvement felt only in reading. Rather, low-achievers from upper-middle-class families were the object of the strongest interconnections; these relationships had a positive influence on the work the child completed. In addition parents' activities shaped the degree to which children received a 'generic' or a 'customized' educational experience within schools. Individualized school careers appeared beneficial, for the most part. The negative consequences are treated in the next chapter.

Impact on Promotion and Retention

Parents' behavior influenced promotion and retention decisions. The potential impact of parents' actions was highest for children who were of average ability but who had motivational problems (i.e., they were 'lazy'). In some instances Colton teachers felt that parents' actions made critical differences in school careers; including determining whether children were promoted or retained. Children of average ability with motivational problems sometimes repeated a grade at Colton, a pattern teachers felt could have been avoided with more active parent participation.

For example, the Joneses, Laura's parents, felt that they did try to promote school success at home; they had even started a college fund for their children. Mrs Jones's lack of educational skills made her feel dependent on Laura's teacher (Mrs Thompson), but Mr Jones said he helped his step-daughter with school 'all the time'. Her parents bought a set of books from the grocery store for Laura and reported that they gave her a book as a gift on her birthday or at Christmas. Mrs Jones encouraged her daughter to do well in school, to check out classroom books, and to challenge herself:

> I would suggest to her that she bring home a harder book . . . tell her, 'You know you can do that. All you have to do is try.' I would tell her to bring home some books on the weekend.

In interviews, her mother and Mrs Thompson separately discussed the problems they had motivating Laura to work. Mrs Thompson felt that motivation was a serious issue:

> The biggest problem seemed to be motivation. To get her to want to do it. I don't think she had that much help at home . . . We hadn't found a reason to make her want to do it enough.

In her classroom work Laura would rush through tasks making careless errors, as her teacher noted:

> Things weren't well done. The easiest way, she did them. When we wrote stories she would finish before the other children. She took the easy way out.

Mrs Jones's view of Laura's approach to learning is very similar to Mrs Thompson's:

> She is too lazy. She doesn't want to take the time to help count out her change . . . She knows she can. If people sit down with her and try to get her to do things and if she is interested she can do things all by herself. But if you had a handful of change and said count out thirty-five cents, she would say, 'I don't know, you do it for me.' That's her attitude. You do it for me and it will be easier.

Her mother sometimes would become impatient with the slowness with which Laura approached tasks, such as cleaning up her room:

> She can't stop talking to do anything. She just loves to talk. I send her to her room to clean it up and she'll be in there for a half-hour, when all she has to do is pick up a few things and make her bed. You walk in there and everything is not done because she is sitting there singing, reading, or something else. It's enough to drive you nuts.

Although Mrs Jones tried to integrate academic tasks into family life, such as having Laura count out her lunch money, she was frustrated by Laura's slow pace:

> Sometimes I do it for her, which I shouldn't. But because I don't have the patience. I am very bad on patience. I have to admit that ... It would drive me nuts when I give her a bunch of change and it takes her hours and hours. I would just go nuts. I would end up doing it for her.

Her husband, Laura's step-father, criticized his wife for that:

> Roger gets on to me about not letting her complete stuff. He just thinks I should let her finish it. So what if it takes twelve days? That's her problem. She can't go out to play until she gets it done. And I feel bad because she can't go out and play. I am not strict enough I guess. I don't discipline enough. I let her get away with a lot. It upsets me. I shouldn't let her get away with stuff like I do. I'm just soft-hearted, I guess.

In spring of first grade, Laura's mother was pregnant and missed the parent–teacher conference. Mrs Thompson was worried about Laura's lack of progress. Although Laura had the ability to do the school work, failure to apply herself put her at risk of being retained. Mrs Thompson felt that if Mrs Jones worked with Laura at home the retention could be avoided. She visited Mrs Jones at home, brought workbooks, and asked her to work with Laura:

> I did have a special conference with her. That is when I took the extra workbooks and things home saying, 'You can help her, we can get her through this year. But she is going to need extra help.'

Mrs Thompson said that Mrs Jones agreed to help Laura, but she did not see many indications of follow-through, and Mrs Jones did not sign slips for the Read-at-Home Program:

> She said, 'Yes, yes' but I didn't see that much progress ... When I would send books home, her mother didn't sign the slips that much. Most of the reading came from school, that Emily or I would listen to her. So her reading list was compiled by people helping her at school, not at home.

By the end of the year, faced with Laura's lack of progress, Mrs Thompson felt that she had no choice but to recommend retention, given:

> ... the amount of work completed and the quality of her reading at that time. Knowing that she could do so much more. I kept her back for another year hoping that would give her a good basis.

Mrs Thompson's knowledge of Laura as an individual also influenced her decision:

Also, knowing her personality. If she felt that she was at the bottom of the class that would give her all of the more reason to sluff off. Whereas, if she was accomplished and getting a lot of good feedback from the teachers and the children, that perhaps that would give her what she needed to go on.

Mrs Thompson regretted that she and Mrs Jones had not found a way to motivate Laura:

Laura's problem mainly was just practice and doing. She didn't ever really get enough of that. She didn't want to that much either. So I know that the mother would have had to put her foot down and make her do it. I couldn't find a way to make her enjoy it that much.

She was also disappointed that the mother had not taken a more active role in schooling, given Laura's educational needs:

The mother seemed to leave it up to the school. She wanted the best for her child. But she felt more or less that the school knew what was going on and she didn't enter into it that much. She wanted Laura to do well. She cared for her and took good care of her. But she didn't seem to feel that was her role or that she had the capabilities to do that much at home with her.

Indeed, Laura's mother did not seem to have a clear idea why Laura was retained, repeating only that her 'grades weren't up to par'. She was disappointed by the retention, as was her daughter, but felt that she wanted what was best for her:

I don't want her to go ahead and not know what she's doing next year; that is just as bad. So I said, 'Well, sure, if that's what she needs.'

At both Prescott and Colton parents resisted giving, and at times refused to give, their permission for their child to repeat a grade. In fact longitudinal research on the impact of retentions is mixed, and an increasing number of studies are showing that there is little evidence that childrens' academic performance improves (when compared to children in academic difficulty who are promoted) (Shepard 1986; Walsh 1988). Children feel stigmatized — at times accurately — in late years by peers as well as teachers. At both schools teachers strongly believed in retentions and insisted that without a retention children continued to have difficulty in school all the way through the grades.[2] Overall, Colton recommended far more children for retention than Prescott, but the refusal rates appeared to be roughly comparable. At both schools teachers said that each year a few parents refused to allow it.[3]

Parents' responses to teachers' requests differed between the schools; so, too, did parents' perceptions of what constituted 'helping' their children. Laura's parents felt they assisted their daughter with her school work at home. What they meant by 'all the time' and what the teachers meant were two different things, just as Prescott and Colton parents said they wanted to be 'helpful' but had different conceptions of their proper role.

Prescott: Covering the Curriculum at Home

Parent involvement studies emphasize the role of parents as reactive rather than proactive. What was striking at Prescott, however, was that the initiative did not always come from teachers. Instead mothers would sometimes propose, arrange, and carry out these activities. In this way mothers would try to create a customized educational experience for their children. Particularly when children were doing poorly in school, mothers would gain the teacher's permission to instruct children at home, *using classroom materials*. This strategy boosted some children's academic performance.

For example, in Mrs Hoffman's class the spelling program was individualized and self-paced. Each child worked on a spelling packet which contained a list of words and a series of steps for practicing each word. The spelling packets were numerically ordered; all the children began on number one at the beginning of the year and progressed through the packets at their own pace. As part of the volunteer program Mrs Harris worked in the classroom for an hour every other week. While volunteering she noticed that her son, Allen, was on a lower numbered spelling packet than many of his classmates. As she explained:

> Allen was getting behind on his spelling. I went in one day and ... I said, 'I really can see, because I am in the classroom, that Allen is getting behind in the spelling. Do you think that he needs to do some at home?' Sandi handles these things so well. She included Mrs Takahashi [the teacher's aide] in the conversation because this woman is her partner in the classroom. She said, 'What do you think, Yuri? Do you think Allen should take this work home?' The conversation went on and [the decision was] yes.

After Mrs Hoffman agreed, Mrs Harris began working with Allen at home:

> So they gave me the paper and they gave me the spelling list. You get a list of ten words. You have to write ten sentences. Then after you write ten sentences you have to do some sort of word activity using the ten words. You either write them out three times or you draw lines around for the shape. I do not understand the purpose of that at all. Or you circle the vowels or you make crossword puzzles with them. Or you alphabetize them 'a' to 'z' or 'z' to 'a'. You write them down in lengths of words. Just anything to re-use the words to re-impress it in their brains.

Allen did not object to the work:

> He enjoyed doing it at home. He was very happy to do them at home. He had to make up sentences, thoughtful sentences. He did it and just

that little bit of a boost — I guess that took him about two months — kept him up with the mainstream of the class.

Allen's mother said that over that peiod they often worked on the spelling daily:

> He would spend about a half an hour [on his spelling]; it depended. At night, after dinner, or sometimes after school . . . The other children are some place else doing something else. I am downstairs doing my bookkeeping so I am not hanging over him. He doesn't want me to hang over him.

Mrs Hoffman was impressed by the way in which Mrs Harris worked with Allen:

> She really worked with him. He was lazy and it took him a while to think of sentences. He is bright enough. She really followed through. They completed the work every day. He would bring it back and forth every day and I would correct it for about three weeks. Once he had gotten caught up, then he didn't need to do it anymore. It wasn't necessary.[4]

After Allen had caught up to the spelling packet that the rest of the class was working on he stopping taking his spelling home every day. In Mrs Hoffman's opinion Mrs Harris's help had a significant and positive effect on all of her children's performance:

> I think that if she didn't work in the class, her boys wouldn't do too well. They are not brilliant at all. But they are going to do well. She is going to see that they are going to get a good foundation. She isn't going to have to do that forever. A child like that would flounder if they let them. It was important that they worked with him.[5]

Other Prescott parents also requested that the teacher send home classroom material to boost their children's performance. Emily, for example, was in the lowest reading group in first grade at Prescott. Her parents requested that Mrs Walters send home a duplicate set of textbooks for them to practice with at home. In second grade Emily spent an hour a day with the reading resource teacher. During that time she missed spelling period. Early in the year her mother made arrangements for her to do her spelling at home. Her mother supervised this enterprise immediately after school:

> Because she spent all her spelling time in her reading resource class, we did all of the spelling at home. We had a little routine. She would do her spelling, which meant putting the words in alphabetical order and writing sentences. Then I would give her a test. Then she would go back to school and Mrs Hoffman would give her a test.

For most of the school year Emily had her classroom spelling lesson at home. About three-quarters of the way through the school year (right before the birth of a second brother) Emily began resisting this pattern.

All of that was fine. Then, in March, she wanted no part of it. I went to school and said, 'What do I do? You tell me.' I am arguing with my daughter! She doesn't want to do this.

On the advice of Mrs Hoffman the mother stopped the home lessons:

She [Mrs Hoffman] said, 'Just forget it. It is not worth going through. [Work with her] when she wants to do it or maybe you do one word a night.' So we *really* backed off on spelling.

At Colton none of the parents I interviewed (nor, to my knowledge, any of the parents in the class) initiated similar activities. The closest parallel was Johnny's parents, who went over his math papers with him. They had him redo the problems marked wrong at home. His mother said Johnny resisted this slightly (i.e., saying 'oh, crumb') but proceeded to do them under her supervision. Colton parents expected teachers to 'take the lead' in education; they did not try to supervise teachers or alter the character of their children's classroom program.

There is no question that without these interventions by Prescott mothers children would have learned less of the curriculum in second grade than they did. According to teachers, parents' interventions positively affected their children's academic performance. Mrs Harris and other mothers were able to raise their children's performance in part because of their definition of their proper role in the children's schooling, and their own spelling abilities. The organization of the school, however, including the volunteer program, the support which the teacher gave to the enterprise, and the structure of the self-paced curriculum, were pre-conditions to their success.[6] In addition to preparation upper-middle-class mothers intervened at school, bringing home and school into a tight alignment. This provided an educational advantage for some children. This type of parent-initiated intervention needs to be addressed in current models of children's educational performance.

Educational Profits: The Experience of Low Achievers

Although upper-middle-class families had tighter home—school linkages than did their working-class counterparts, within upper-middle-class families, the patterns were not uniform. The most intense family—school relationships were not for the highest achieving students in upper-middle-class families. These occurred in families where children were at the *bottom* of their class. Rather than simply accepting the generic education handed out by the school, the parents sought to alter the school experience, increase the efficiency of home activities, and go beyond the school by hiring professional educators. Mrs Walters, for example, recommended in the spring conference that Emily repeat first grade because of her lack of progress in reading. She confessed to the Svensson's that she had 'failed' their daughter by not recognizing that Emily was having difficulty with the reading material. Mrs Walters also felt that she should have used an 'auditory' approach to teaching Emily how to read rather than a 'visual' approach. Emily was socially mature, eager to please, and very cooperative in the classroom; these factors had led Mrs Walters to feel that Emily had 'fooled her'. Mrs Walters did not discover Emily was having major difficulty with the material until one day in spring when, while trying to read aloud to Mrs Walters, Emily stopped reading, began to cry, and told Mrs Walters: 'I can't do it.' From her observation in the classroom Mrs Svensson had a lurking uneasiness about Emily's first grade work. At points in the year she had felt that 'things weren't clicking'. Her husband, however, encouraged her to trust Mrs Walters' 'professional' judgment. Mrs Svensson did occasionally ask Mrs Walters if there was a problem but Mrs Walters, until late in the year, felt there was nothing unusual. To her parents, therefore the recommendation to retain Emily was 'a bombshell'.

Unlike Colton parents, the Svenssons initially neither accepted nor rejected this recommendation. Instead they sought to take control of her schooling, by seeking additional information from professionals other than Prescott teachers, and supplementing the generic program offered by the school. For example, after this conference Emily's parents had a series of conferences with the teacher, the reading resource teacher, the principal, and numerous other educational consultants. In part because their son was only a year behind Emily (and the children would have been in the same grade), and in part because they did not respect Mrs Walters, the Svenssons refused to allow Emily to be retained. They requested (and were given) Mrs Hoffman as her second grade teacher. Through their investigations they learned about the various approaches to teaching reading and the precise character of their daughter's difficulties (in the language used by teachers). They ensured that she worked with the reading resource teacher for the remaining months of first grade, and they paid to have her tutored during the summer after first grade. Emily's mother took the lead in these activities, especially the discussions with private tutors, teachers at the school, and friends and relatives who are educators (although she kept her husband closely apprised of the developments):

> I have talked to professional tutors and to a lot of people. Because we realized that there is a problem with our daughter. You try to find out as much information as you can. I felt like a real fish out of water.

Mrs Svensson was especially bewildered by all of the new terms:

> Ross learned beautifully from the visual approach as opposed to the phonetic approach. I didn't even know about these two approaches to reading. We all learned phonetically. Who ever heard of a visual approach?

During second grade Mr and Mrs Svensson continued to work with Emily. As noted above, they did her spelling lessons at home and they continued to have a series of special conferences — including several with the principal — over their daughter's academic standing. At the end of second grade Mrs Hoffman also recommended that Emily be retained. (Emily was at the bottom of her class; nationally she was in the thirty-sixth percentile in reading.) The Svenssons agreed to it although they did not inform their daughter about it.

The summer after second grade they enrolled Emily in a summer school reading class every morning from 8.30 to 9.30. They also had her tutored by the reading specialist at Prescott school for three hours per week for a month. And Mrs Svensson hired a high school student to read to Emily and practice flashcards with her twice a week for an hour in the afternoons (in addition to the professional tutoring). Her parents took Emily to the library every week and instituted a reward system (i.e., stickers and ice cream cones) for reading books. They read to her and her brother at night. They had additional private testing (which the school district refused to authorize) and continued to discuss her learning difficulties with many educators.[7] In short, Emily's parents tried to develop a customized educational program (which operated twelve months a year) best suited to Emily's needs.

By the end of the summer the tutor felt that Emily had 'a good summer' and had made progress. In addition Prescott — because of shifts in enrollment — had a change in the classroom organization. They decided to have a combination second and third grade class. Through their networks Emily's parents learned of this change in the classroom structure. Again the parents did not simply let the school take the lead, which would have meant sending Emily to Mrs Hoffman in September (or waiting to see what the teachers said after the school year was underway). Instead the Svenssons took the initiative. In August Mr Svensson wrote a letter to the principal 'sharing his thoughts' about the progress Emily had made during the summer. He explained that he and his wife wanted to discuss having Emily enrolled in the combination class rather than repeat second grade, as the teachers had recommended. As Mr Svensson said:

> I sent a letter saying these were our thoughts. We had great confidence in Mrs Hoffman ... but it appeared that some things may have changed over the summer. This was the additional information we were putting in the formula. Based on that, we wanted to talk again about Emily being retained.

The principal (after conferring with the reading resource teacher and Mrs Hoffman) agreed to this change; Mr Svensson also said the principal thanked him for the 'professional way' in which he and his wife had handled the matter.

In other cases at Prescott when children showed dramatic improvement in their classroom performance teachers sometimes ascribed it to the role their parents played. Jonathan, for example, was the lowest achieving boy in first grade. A child with severe allergies, his language development had been slow. He was retained in kindergarten. Diagnosed as learning-disabled (with auditory reception problems), he worked with the special education teacher part-time.

As with the Svenssons, Jonathan's mother sought to customize his educational experience. Mrs Roy watched her son intently during her periods of volunteering in the classroom. She then coordinated her home activities to reinforce the curriculum she had witnessed at school. She would make up math problems for him to do after school. Along with math she would repeat what she had observed in class:

> We tried to do a lot of other things, too. Explaining things to him . . . time, calendar, that kind of thing. He forgets; that is part of his learning problem. He doesn't remember things well. We have to go over and over and over things.

These activities took place at least four times per week and sometimes every day. Mrs Roy said that she tried to scatter these activities throughout the day and in brief encounters:

> I try to break things up during the day because he gets real tired. A half hour is a *long* time for him. So, you know, fifteen minutes is usually the limit that he would do well at anything.

Most of the time Jonathan's mother had full responsibility for these activities. About one fifth of the time, however, she would be working as a nurse in the Emergency Room. She would then leave instructions for her husband or their eldest son to work with Jonathan. With his parents and the teachers Jonathan would get frustrated with his school work:

> He cries when he thinks he can't [do it] — whether he tries it or not — when he thinks he can't do it, he gets frustrated.

Challenging the view that it is educators who shape parents' actions, Jonathan Roy's mother tried to compensate for weaknesses she perceived in his school program. Jonathan was one of the children in Mrs Walters' class who had difficulty with the self-directed math program. A quiet boy, he did not draw attention to himself, but he also did not work on his math in independent time. When Mrs Roy discovered this she tried to increase his coverage of the classroom curriculum:

> I found out Jonathan had not been doing any math at all in class. I was really concerned about that and wrote notes to both of them [Mrs Walters and the special education teacher]. We had a conference — the three of us. Mrs Walters went through what she teaches the class and the different concepts and on and on and on.

The result of the meeting was that Mrs Walters would send home extra homework to help him catch up. This pattern quickly came to a halt, however:

> The outcome of that was that she was going to send work home with Jonathan, extra homework so he could catch up. And it happened about three times and then it stopped. I questioned her about that and she said it was because he never asked for it and so she never gave it to him.

Mrs Roy was irritated by this:

I felt frustrated. I didn't understand that he had to ask for it. He did sometimes ask for it, and she didn't have time to give it to him.[8]

Ultimately, Mrs Roy said she 'gave up', in part because of what she learned from other parents:

I kind of gave up on her ... I considered [going to talk to the principal], but I didn't do it. She has been a teacher that a lot of parents are dissatisfied with, not just me. A lot of parents feel that it is a wasted year.

She tried to 'compensate' for the weaknesses in Jonathan's classroom program by working with him at home:

I worked with him a lot. So I think that is how I compensated for it ... I felt that I had gone as far as I could. I had talked to her several times ... You can only go so far!

She also hired tutors to work with her son during the summers after first and second grades. Mrs Roy gave the tutors guidelines for what Jonathan needed to work on, and Jonathan met with them about ten times during the summer (at a cost of about $150). It was another effort to supplement the generic program offered by the school, to improve his school performance.

Although she had much more confidence in his second grade teacher than in his first, Mrs Roy's interventions continued in second grade. She wrote a long letter to Mrs Hoffman on the first day of school, an effort she said was aimed at getting the teacher to 'zero in on' on her child's academic problems. She made repeated requests (which were denied until the very end of the year) that he be tested for speech therapy, and she had 'mini-conferences' with Mrs Hoffman every other week (rather than twice a year). Mrs Roy also had numerous consultations with his special education teacher, and she continued to coordinate her home activities with her son's classroom program.

At times during the year, Mrs Hoffman felt that Mrs Roy was a 'pesky parent'. During the course of second grade, however, Jonathan went from being a non-reader to being almost a grade-level reader. Mrs Hoffman attributed part of this spurt to her structured classroom program and the improvement in his behavior. She also believed that his academic performance was linked to the efforts of his mother:

If he was supposed to do something, she was right in there. I think she had a full-time job, but she still managed to come in and work in the classroom. She really wanted to see what was going on. I didn't blame her. He had been retained in kindergarten and wasn't reading. Part of it was behavior. He is a bright little boy.

Mrs Roy's home instruction was 'tightly coupled' with the classroom program. Her close supervision, interventions, and compensations appeared to help her son's performance in school. She helped him stay with his class rather than slipping back and running the risk of being placed in special education classes full-time.

This pattern of leadership, close scrutiny, and intensive supplementation of the generic classroom program was typical among parents of low-achievers; it was not typical among parents of *high-achievers* at Prescott. Parents such as the Simpsons, whose children were doing well in school, were generally content simply to read to their children, attend school events, and respond to Prescott teachers' requests for assistance. They did not undertake this extensive pattern of initiative and supervision.

Colton: Differences in Linkages

In working-class families the most intensive family–school relationships were among high-achievers, not low-achievers. It was parents of high-achievers who were most likely to attend school events, read to their children, send back slips for the Read-at-Home Program, ask the teachers for ideas of educational activities to do at home, and carefully review children's school papers. Johnny's parents and Suzy's parents both were considered by the teachers to be 'very supportive' of schooling because of their faithful attendance at school events: because in these families the fathers came to school as well as the mothers; and because these parents read to their children at home and carefully reviewed their children's school papers. The Colton principal said there were not very many parents who were intensively involved, but:

> They are here. They come to the PTA [Parent–Teachers Association].
> They are more involved in the process of raising and educating kids.

These parents were particularly diligent about complying with the formal requests that teachers made of them. Even the most intensively involved parents at Colton, however, did not engage in the kinds of activities that were typical of Prescott parents. For example, almost all Prescott mothers knew that it was possible to request a specific teacher although the educators discouraged it; most Colton parents had no such knowledge. One mother I interviewed was astonished to hear that parents could request teachers. Because of her overall trust in her daughter's teacher, however, this parent was not concerned that she had not been told about the possibility of requesting a specific teacher:

> Is that allowed? I never thought about that. I think if Mrs Thompson thought one teacher would be better for her than another, she would have mentioned it to me. She's very open about that.

As discussed in Chapter Three, Colton mothers also were unaware of special programs offered by the school, unless the classroom teacher recommended that their child be enrolled in a certain program. Nor were Colton parents informed about the use of tutors, private testing, special conferences, or the availability of the principal's advice regarding their children's academic program. Upper-middle-class parents at Prescott knew about these possibilities but did not always draw on them; Colton parents, including the most intensively involved parents of high achievers, were unaware of these resources for improving their children's school careers.

At Colton parents of low-achievers deferred to teachers and their professional expertise; they did not attempt to customize their children's educational careers. As a result these children received a basic, generic educational experience arranged by teachers. The principal insisted that this experience was a high quality one:

> I think they are being provided a fine opportunity for education at this school. I really do. I am very pleased with the services that are available here for kids and the effort of the staff here to provide those services. And the stability of the staff; people have been here forever.

The quality of the school's program notwithstanding, compared to Prescott low-achievers Colton low-achievers did not receive the same intensive evaluation by numerous professionals, educational experiences in the summer, or supplementation of the school's programs during the year. When Prescott parents initiated activities they often anticipated decisions that teachers would have suggested weeks later. And parents' home activities were more tightly coupled with the classroom curriculum at Prescott than at Colton. Colton mothers who did try to help their children in school often found their efforts hampered by their own lack of educational skills and by a conception of schooling that differed from the teachers'. These mothers also lacked experience in negotiating and had no detailed information about the classroom curriculum.

For example, Mrs Brown's efforts on behalf of her daughter Jill did not produce the desired results. Jill was an overweight child who had been retained in kindergarten. Mrs Brown was a high school drop-out who had married and had a son in her late teens. Mrs Thompson believed that Jill's success in school was extremely important to her mother:

> I think the mother has been right behind her really wanting to carry the load for her, if she could. She wants very, very badly — I saw a strong drive — to see Jill succeed.

The mother volunteered to help with classroom activities. She was the 'room mother' two years in a row and also accompanied the class on field trips:

> The mother always seemed harried — as if she had a hard time of it. She wanted to do things for the [class] party. She wanted to come into the room. She wanted to go on field trips. She wanted to come and pick up work if she could.

The special education teacher also felt that Jill's mother wanted to help but was unsure how to go about it. The mother took a passive rather than an assertive role in her daughter's education:

You know, her mom always said, 'Gee, whatever she can do to help' although she doesn't really know exactly what to do to help. I did ask her, when Jill was absent for about six days, I asked her to come by and to pick up some work for her . . . There was no hesitation once I asked her to come, but she didn't volunteer. She didn't offer to come in.

Although she sent school work home, Mrs Thompson felt that little was actually accomplished there:

Once she would get it home, I think she couldn't make Jill do it that much. She wanted to. I did send home a whole bunch of material over the summer. Jill would cry, and that seemed to be the end of it. She would cry with her mother and say, 'I can't do this'. The mother would be frustrated and they would end up with no production.

Mrs Brown told a similar story. She knew Jill was over a year and one half below grade level. Still, she was dubious about her ability to get her daughter to read during the summer:

I will try it with her, but I don't think it will work. I bought her a cassette and the books, like Sleeping Beauty. She put the book in the drawer and will listen to the record. She wouldn't follow along in the books. She doesn't have an attention span long enough to do anything unless it is playing. I will try it with her and see if she'll do it. But I really doubt that she will.

Both her mother and her teacher felt that Jill lacked self-confidence and that her attention span was very short. As her mother said:

Jill can sit down real enthused about doing a piece of work. She'll get a little way into it and if she comes up to something that she can't comprehend — or she had a problem of some sort — she wants to quit right now. She won't sit there and do it. She'll whine or be antsy. I know; the school tells me she does the same thing there.

She has an attention span of about ten or fifteen minutes. You can't push her past that. If you do, then she really becomes frustrated . . . She starts crying and she gets really upset.

As with Emily's parents, Jill's mother was disappointed in one of her child's teachers:

And you know, Jill did good her first couple of months in kindergarten. And then the teacher, just kind of . . . it was a personality clash I guess, but she destroyed everything . . . you know, every motivation Jill had for even going to school.

She felt this incident had had a lasting influence on her daughter. Mrs Brown was bitter and angry at the teacher:

And ever since then, she has had no confidence. And it really was an uphill struggle trying to get confidence back into her. And I'll sit her down and praise her and praise her and praise her for doing stuff and she just — it doesn't get through to her. So it is very frustrating, not only for her, but for the teachers and me, too.

Mrs Thompson agreed that Jill lacked confidence but she felt that the mother may have contributed to the problem:

We had several occasions where the mother would write a note that something had gone wrong. Jill had complained about something on the playground — things weren't going quite right and someone had picked on her there. So I feel Jill used this quite a bit. She would go running home to mother and telling mother and then mother would back [her] up. There again [the mother] not enforcing Jill's confidence that she could do something about it herself. The mother had to do it for her. So she had no confidence at all.

She felt that Mrs Brown was not giving Jill a chance to learn to take on responsibilities and was giving in too easily to Jill's resistance to learning:

Maybe Jill hadn't been made to face up to her responsibilities, in the anxiety of the mother to do things for her. Maybe if she had clamped down on Jill a little bit and said, 'This is your problem you've got to do this or you've got to do that.' I think the mother — things were so hard for her — that she would sometimes take the easy way out rather than fight with Jill.

Jill's mother, along with Emily's mother, was very anxious about her daughter's lack of progress.[9] Mrs Brown was often confused and bewildered in the discussion of her daughter's learning difficulties. Her tenth grade education was no match for what she called the 'fancy terms' bandied about by professionals in the discussion of her daughter's learning difficulties. She had difficulty understanding discussions at school; for example, of the Individual Educational Program meeting at the end of second grade she said:

They weren't really explanatory. I mean they didn't explain things. I didn't get aything out of it.

Unlike Emily's parents, who had worked in upper-middle-class jobs where formal meetings are routine, Mrs Brown found the structure of the meeting uncomfortable and unfamiliar:

I thought it was a little too formal. When I sit down with people, I like to feel comfortable with them. I did not feel comfortable with them yesterday. I felt like I was more in a business meeting where I had no business being there, other than it was Jill they were talking about. I am not used to formal meetings.

Mrs Brown did not have a clear understanding of the nature of her daughter's problems nor of the steps she could take to improve them. Mrs Thompson was worried when she discovered that, at the Book Fair, Mrs Brown chose books that were far too hard for Jill:

> She brought it to the room and asked if it would be all right for Jill. The book was at the end of second grade level or third; it was above Jill's abilities. So I said, 'Perhaps keep that one, she will grow into it.' Then I gave [her] some that were very simple.

> I didn't want to hurt her feelings, but I remember telling her that Jill would feel more competent if she could start it. She really did not have her pinpointed in terms of her abilities.

Jill entered special education classes part-time in first and second grade. All of her teachers commented on her short attention span and her difficulty working independently. Her special education teacher felt she got 'extremely frustrated' and had problems doing her school work unless an adult was sitting next to her monitoring her performance. As a result she did little work in her regular classroom; she would wander around the room, talk to other children, or draw. Testing showed Jill to be of average intelligence, with normal speech and language development, and weak visual motor skills; psychological testing revealed signs of anxiety and insecurity. Her teachers felt there were tasks that Jill could perform in an individualized setting but 'in a classroom situation, when asked to do it, she can't cope.'

Although her academic performance was weak when she entered first grade, between first and second grade, Jill fell farther and farther behind the regular classroom program. The gap between her performance and that of the other children widened. By the end of second grade she was almost two years below grade level, with the reading skills of a child entering first grade. Given her inability to work independently the teachers were not optimistic about her ability to sustain work in the regular classroom. Consequently, although Jill was of average intelligence, at the end of second grade the special education teacher recommended that she be moved into a special education class. The decision, which Jill's mother approved, was that Jill would spend most of her day in special education with two periods a day in the classroom.[10]

As with other Colton parents, Jill's mother defined education as the responsibility of the teacher. She was interested in helping her daughter; in fact in her role as room mother, her help on field trips, and her attendance at school events, she was among the most active mothers in the classroom. She did not, however, presume to take control of her daughter's academic program. Her efforts to work consistently with her daughter at home failed. Mrs Brown did not supplement Jill's schooling during the summer with tutoring, nor did she request additional conferences during the year with school officials, take a leadership role in Jill's educational program, or work with teachers closely during the year.[11]

Jill received special education from the school; her program was not the same as other children's. Nevertheless the school site instruction — as originally formulated by teachers — constituted Jill's educational experience. Her parents did not customize this program; they did not question, challenge, or propose changes in any aspects of the school's academic strategy for Jill, nor did they supplement that education at home or hire professional educators to tutor her. The generic education offered by the school composed nearly all of Jill's educational experience.

Generic and Customized School Careers

Case studies highlight issues for further conceptual and methodological pursuit. The cases reported here suggest that parents' actions were associated with differences in educational performance, a pattern noted in studies of parents' participation in school. In particular, other work has emphasized the impact of parents reading to their children at home and supervising homework (Henderson 1981; Epstein 1987; Rich 1987a; 1987b). The cases discussed here, however, go beyond current research and show that social class influences the level of alignment and interconnectedness between family life and school life. Emily's parents sought to control, shape, and supplement her school program. Jill's mother left education to the school. As a result Prescott low-achievers often had customized educational experiences which operated twelve months a year and were tailored to their specific needs. Colton parents had difficulty pinpointing the nature of their children's educational problems, understanding the dialogues at school, and making certain that their children completed school work at home.

In all probability all aspects of parents' customizing are not equally powerful, nor would one aspect have the same effect on a variety of children. Parents' preparation at home and working with their children in the summer, as suggested by many other studies, is probably one of the most significant factors in shaping performance. For example, social class influences summer learning, with children from higher social classes learning more (and forgetting less) over the summer than children from lower classes (Heyns 1988). Nevertheless the cases presented here suggest the importance of teacher–student chemistry. Given students' individual learning problems and personalities, some children can work more effectively with some teachers than with others; a conclusion bolstered by studies of educational effectiveness which have failed to demonstrate one uniformly effective method of teaching (see Averch 1972 for a review).

Children who rush through their work are not good candidates for a self-directed program but benefit more from a structured classroom, a point made by Mrs Hoffman about Emily Svensson:

> I have a very structured classroom. She was a child that benefited from that. She tried to get done as fast as possible. She made many errors.

Jill's special education teacher felt that if Jill had been in a classroom which was more tightly run (in terms of children's behavior), Jill would have benefited from that, rather than being allowed to wander around the room.

If parents have an accurate and detailed understanding of their children's learning difficulties and if the school is large enough to offer parents a choice of teachers in each grade, interventions by parents to request specific teachers could have a potentially significant impact on children's performance. Administrators, however, have compelling organizational reasons for discouraging teacher requests, including the need for classes which are balanced along racial, academic, gender, and behavioral lines. Parents' use of tutors and other professional consultants, and their monitoring to make sure their children are placed in specialized programs on the school site also may have a significant impact on performance.

Nevertheless some children will benefit from these parent interventions more than others, just as some children's learning may be more dependent upon teacher–student chemistry than others. In a private assessment of Mrs Walters' classroom, Mrs Hoffman felt that some children's progress had been slowed by the experience (including Emily's and Jonathan's) while other children, including Donald Simpson were unaffected. ('Nothing would affect Donald', Mrs Hoffman said.) Low-achievers may be more dependent upon teacher-student chemistry and upon parent participation in school. Mrs Brown very badly wanted her daughter to succeed in school, but she deferred to the school in the design of her daughter's educational program. In the end this meant that Jill was exposed to less material and appeared to make less progress in school than upper-middle-class children at the bottom of their class whose parents brought very different social resources to the process.

A Customized School Career: The Teachers' Role

In their work teachers strove to give their best to every child and, within the constraints of the program, to design a plan that met each child's need. Teachers tried to place children in a reading group best suited for them, referred children to special school programs, and used teaching styles designed to reach each child. Given that classroom size varied between twenty-eight and thirty-four children, out of necessity teachers had universalistic programs, where all of the children engaged in similar activities. There were serious constraints on the amount of individualizing that teachers could do. Some of the special attention that children received in school resulted from teachers' determination of their students' special needs; but some was due to parents' presence at school. When teachers believed that parents valued education and were heavily involved in children's schooling, they took actions which they did not take for children whose parents were less active in schooling.

This was particularly apparent at Colton school. Parent involvement was significantly less at Colton than at Prescott, but the few Colton parents who were involved appeared to have a more dramatic impact on their children's educational program than parents at Prescott school. In some cases parents' actions influenced what information teachers passed along to parents. Mrs Sampson, for example, had learned from the parents of her Vietnamese students that Vietnamese families in the US value education very highly:

> In the case of the Vietnamese children, they have been taught to respect the teacher. You certainly can tell. When those parents come, they tell you that. Education is very important in their country and they respect the teacher.

Mrs Sampson said that she had a Vietnamese boy who, by the end of the year, was at the top of the class. In the beginning of the year he had been talkative. Mrs Sampson did not find the child's behavior to be particularly disruptive. With most parents she might not have mentioned this aspect of the child's behavior at all, or noted it only briefly at the fall conference. Given her sense of the parents' views on education, however, Mrs Sampson sought out the boy's mother at school in the early part of the year and asked her to speak to her son:

> At the beginning of the year, a beautiful child in my room was a little chatterbox. I mentioned that to the mother [to get her] to talk to him about that. I felt kind of guilty doing it, because he was so good. But I knew they expected those children to really listen in school and not goof off.

Parents' actions also appeared to influence teachers' assessment of children's abilities and their potential for achievement. For example, Mrs Thompson was impressed by Johnny's parents. The father attended conferences and remarked about the importance of his children getting a good education. From the Read at-Home slips, Johnny's reports, and his parents' reports, Mrs Thompson concluded that Johnny's parents had worked with him at home, reading to him, teaching him new words, and giving him educational 'advantages'.[12] Mrs Thompson was surprised to discover that despite these advantages Johnny had difficulty with new material:

> We found out that a lot of his learning was because he had all of these advantages and help from the parents at home. Whenever we would present a new concept, it took a long time to get it over to John. Once he got it, he had it ... He could express himself well. You could tell he had a lot of advantages and background materials and so forth. But the learning process didn't come as quickly.

This astounded Mrs Thompson and violated her expectations:

> That amazed me about him. That he had so much background and had learned so much and yet the learning procedure wasn't easy for him. We would explain it and he wouldn't get it, and then we would explain it [again]. He wanted to learn it. He wanted to get it. He had more

patience with it than I thought he would. But we would just have to go over it and reinforce it and reinforce [it] and then he would get it. But it didn't come the first time.

In fact in numerous ways throughout the year Mrs Thompson expressed surprise at Johnny's average performance, given his family background. On the last day of school for example, we were reviewing the test scores for children. At the end of second grade, Johnny's scores were the grade level equivalent of only 1.9 in reading and 2.2 overall. The highest in the class was 2.9; Johnny's score was only slightly above the class average. Seeing this, Mrs Thompson sighed deeply and said:

> Isn't that terrible? And after all of that help.

Despite her conviction that Johnny was not a gifted student and her knowledge that he was only slightly above the class average, Mrs Thompson recommended that he be selected for the school enrichment program:

> We used to have the children we would send out to MGM [Mentally Gifted Minors]; he wouldn't have qualified for that . . . But they have changed the rules on that. It was for children who needed some enrichment in school. John did need that because he was used to having a lot of things to think about and interests. Sometimes we would go a little too slowly for him in that respect.

Mrs Thompson did not recommend that children with similar, or even slightly superior, academic records be admitted to the program; each class could only refer a few children. This suggests that Johnny's parents may have influenced her decision about his classroom program. In addition her frequent comments of surprise about Johnny's actual performance suggests that his parents' behavior raised her expectations. Knowing that they worked with Johnny at home, she expected high levels of academic performance; she was both surprised and disappointed when that did not occur.

Parents' actions could have a negative influence on teachers' perceptions as well. Mrs Sampson believed strongly that children's home environments influenced their classroom performance. In second grade, Mrs Sampson was disturbed by the behavior of Ann-Marie's mother, particularly her tendency to party, the rumors that there were frequent parties at her house, Ann-Marie's neglected appearance, and her frequent tardiness and absenteeism. She felt that because of her home situation, Ann-Marie did not have as positive an attitude toward school as children whose parents were more conventional. For example, in comparing Ann-Marie with Suzy, a child whose father was a sheriff and whose mother brought her to see the classroom the day before school started, Mrs Sampson said:

> I think that the child [Suzy] has a better attitude about school. They know that their parents know what is going on. It would help her with her learning. Suzy's attitude is better to start with than Ann-Marie's.

Her relations with children were without poking and knocking and kicking and name-callings. So it would seem to me that perhaps the stable home life and what had gone on there have helped her.

Mrs Sampson was annoyed that when she chastized her, Ann-Marie would say that 'her mother was going to call the school board'. Mrs Sampson felt that 'she heard this at home or she wouldn't have said it.' Although Ann-Marie was at the top of the class in her hours for the Read-at-Home Program, was second in the class in the SRA Reading Program, and had greater reading fluency when reading aloud than most of her peers, Mrs Sampson did not focus on her reading skills until the end of the year, when she looked at the standardized test scores:

> I realized that Ann-Marie was sharp near the end of the year. I realized maybe I should have put her name in for testing for the gifted program. I looked at her test scores and her reading score was real high. I realized that in their workbooks on the pages they really had to think about, Ann-Marie did all right. And she was really working away on SRA when it gets up to the third grade level . . . I had forgotten about that; she was really motivated. She was up there with Minh.

By the time Mrs Sampson came to this conclusion it was too late in the year for Ann-Marie to be tested for the gifted program.

It is possible, even likely, that Mrs Sampson's negative assessment of Ann-Marie's home life clouded her view of the child's classroom performance. Mrs Sampson seemed to presume that an unstable home environment would have a negative influence on classroom performance. That view persisted until challenged by test scores. With other children, especially Minh, the Vietnamese boy and Suzy, whose father attended parent-teacher conferences, Mrs Sampson appeared to expect good performance and was on the lookout for evidence of academic promise. This raises questions about how long it may take a teacher to discover that a child with very active parents is slow or that a child with indifferent parents is 'sharper' than expected. In some cases the teacher may discover the discrepancy in the first few days of school; in other cases, as with Ann-Marie, it may be delayed until near the end of the year. In the meantime children's schooling — particularly their access to special programs — could be shaped more by teachers' perceptions of the parents' role in education than by the children's performance in the classroom.[13]

Ironically this was less of an issue at Prescott than at Colton. At Prescott almost all parents were involved and there was greater competition for scarce resources (i.e., access to special programs or special teachers). Teachers responded to parents' direct requests for action; for example, they sent home spelling lessons or math packets. Unlike at Colton, however, there were no signs at Prescott of teachers — on their own initiative — altering a child's school program based on their assessment of the student's parents' values. Hence Colton parents were less likely to be involved in their children's schooling, but the ones that were involved appeared to have a greater impact on their children's school program than at Prescott.

Alignment Between School and Home: Educational Profits

Status attainment research maintains that social class influences children's school performance by shaping the preparation parents give to children at home. This study challenges that picture. It suggests that parents do more than prepare children for school and supervise homework. They intervene and shape children's school programs. It also reveals that teachers may change their behavior based on their perception of family life and their interactions with parents at school. There were many interconnections between home and school for upper-middle-class families.

Many parents did influence their children's schooling. Although school staff discouraged it, parents requested specific teachers. Some parents badgered the school to have their children admitted to special programs, gaining an educational experience for their children that otherwise would not have occurred.[14] Parents supplemented classroom instruction at home, enabling their children to move through more of the curriculum than they otherwise would have done. Parents' and teachers' actions had reciprocal effects. Based on their impression of parents' wishes, teachers sometimes took steps to alter children's school programs. Mrs Thompson recommended Johnny for an enrichment program, and Mrs Sampson took steps to have Minh — who was already at the top of the class — become an even better student. For their part, parents responded to the behavior of the teacher. Doubting the efficiency of Mrs Walter's hands-on approach to math some parents stepped up their instruction at home. Parents' observations when they volunteered in classroom were useful. By coordinating their home activities with the classroom program Prescott mothers more effectively reinforced the curriculum. Colton parents also taught their children new words and math facts. By repeating the material emphasized in class that week, however, Prescott mothers focused their actions more effectively or — put differently — received a bigger return on the time and energy they invested in their children's schooling.

Although it is difficult to quantify the contribution that parents' interventions make to children's performance, for some children the impact is not trivial. Teachers were convinced that parents' interventions in classroom activities gave children a critical boost, keeping children who were 'not brilliant at all' from 'floundering' in the classroom. For low-achievers, parents could, like Jonathan's mother, maintain a 'floor' beneath their children. This could help them — despite their learning difficulties — keep pace with their class. These children appeared to read better, know more spelling and math, and be given access to additional resources more quickly than children at Colton. Parents' actions were important for children with particular problems, especially children of average ability who lacked motivation. This pattern challenges the current view within status attainment research that the superior educational performance of middle-class and upper-middle-class children is related to the activities of the children alone. Parents intervened in their children's schooling in important ways; some children profited from these interventions.

Parent's actions were not tied to how strongly they wanted their children to graduate from high school. Instead parents' performance was linked to their educational competence, their social confidence, the information they had about their children's schooling, their conception of parents' proper role in education, and their children's classroom performance. These social resources forged a closer alignment between family life and school life for upper-middle-class families than for working-class families Some working-class families fully complied with teachers' requests, by reading to their children, attending school events, and reviewing classroom papers and reinforcing the material. Nevertheless the most active working-class families were less involved than the least active upper-middle-class families. Working-class families rarely engaged in any of the unadvertised patterns of family involvement, nor did they seek to customize and control their children's schooling. They expected the teachers to take the lead in the educational process.

Social class did not, however, *determine* parents' actions. In contrast to prevailing models of cultural capital and social profits, the benefits from social class status were not automatic (Bourdieu 1977a; 1977b; 1984; Cookson and Persell 1985; Lamont and Lareau 1988). Social class provided resources; parents had to *activate* these resources. It was through social practices that parents transformed social resources into profits.

Upper-middle-class parents had many latent social resources. Parents of high achievers, for example, were aware that they could request that their children be tested for a learning disability, complain to the principal, and hire tutors. For a variety of reasons, often beginning with their children's level of performance, they did not activate these resources. Possession of a high status resource did not automatically lead to a social profit. Depending on the social context, parents did — or did not — activate their social resources. In addition, among parents who did draw on their resources (mainly those whose children were low-achievers), some used these assets more shrewdly than others. Mothers routinely ran into resistance from their children; some mothers also encountered resistance from teachers in their attempts to intervene in their children's schooling. For some mothers this resistance became a road block, for others it was only a hurdle. After a few attempts Jonathan's mother 'gave up' on Mrs Walters' sending math packets home; that same year, Allen's mother was able to get Mrs Walters to send home math packets weekly. Similarly, hearing that Prescott school discouraged parents' requesting specific teachers some mothers left it at that, others wrote a formal note and managed to secure the teacher of their choice for their children. As in many other situations parents differed in their social interactional skills; these influenced parents' behavior in their children's schooling.

Finally, not all resources associated with upper-middle-class life were salient. Teachers appeared to be relatively indifferent to the size of children's homes, the quality or quantity of house furnishings, the destination of family vacations, parents' taste in music, and the style of clothing worn by children and parents. There was no evidence that these had an impact on family–school relationships or contributed to the educational profits associated with parent involvement in schooling. Rather it was social resources that facilitated parents' compliance with teachers' requests for their participation (i.e., reading to their children) that appeared to be significant.

This suggests that social and cultural resources are not equally valuable (i.e., forms of capital) in all settings, nor is the same resource potentially profitable all the time. The value of these resources depends on the social context. In this setting it was the standards of teachers — their requests that parents read to their children and their modes of evaluation — that made elements of upper-middle-class life potentially more profitable than those of working-class life. It was up to parents to take these resources and transform them into social profits. Working-class families lacked the social resources upper-middle-class families had to facilitate parents' involvement in schooling. For some children this produced a critical difference in the educational profits which parents could provide their children as they made their way through school.

Notes

1. Epstein (in press) shows positive effects on reading achievement scores from parent involvement; Henderson (1981) provides an annotated bibliography of studies on this topic.
2. Prescott had more elaborate pre-kindergarten screening, and when they retained children had a more formal program for parents and children than Colton. Prescott also had fewer children with difficulties related to English as a second language than did Colton.
3. Parents' style of resistance differed substantially between the two schools. At Colton mothers typically simply refused, at times without providing an explanation. Some Colton mothers gave a brief explanation, often that their husbands would not allow it. At Prescott parents' refusal was more indirect and framed in the language of educators, as when parents expressed a desire to pursue other alternatives (i.e., tutoring). As at Colton, however, some mothers indicated that they would approve it but their husbands would not.

   When parents were unhappy with educators' recommendations, they also pursued different pathways. Colton parents rarely lodged formal complaints against the school. Prescott parents, however, did complain to authorities, including the principal and district officials. Within the district, Prescott school retained more children than other elementary schools. This had generated discussion among parents in the community and complaints at the district office. As a result, during the study the superintendent came to a special meeting of the principal and the teachers to discuss (and ultimately reaffirm) the Prescott school's policy of retaining children in kindergarten.
4. Mrs Harris said that this went on for two months. At one point in the interview Mrs. Hoffman also said it went on for 'a couple of months', although here she said that she graded the spelling for 'three weeks'. I was not observing in the classroom, and I cannot confirm the duration. It is clear, however, that it did not go on any longer than two months and possibly less.
5. In first grade, Mrs Walters worried that Allen's parents, particularly his father, put too much pressure on him. She remarked:

   > In fact Allen is somebody whose father seems to put a whole lot of pressure on him from my sense of it. He wants him to do more advanced things.

Mrs Walters reported trying to 'protect' Allen from this pressure. When Allen's mother asked that Mrs Walters send home extra math packets, Mrs Walters resisted the idea at first. In the end, she gave in and sent home math packets on Friday and graded them after Allen completed them.

Mrs Hoffman, however, did not perceive Allen's parents as placing undue pressure on him:

> She didn't insist that he be at the top of the class. But she insisted that he work to his capacity. She established a good work habit . . . They would be putting too much pressure on him if they had continued pushing him in spelling after he caught up. I think they asked him if he wanted to continue [to work at home] and he said no. I think that I said no, I didn't want them to too. You can't put so much in a vessel; at least not without getting leakage.

6. Of course, it was the self-paced character of the curriculum which allowed Allen to get behind on his spelling. Even in a more structured program, however, children usually spend class time writing the words in sentences. Unless Allen was given the sentences to write, he probably would have had the same difficulty of keeping up with the rest of the class since he had trouble thinking up sentences and working steadily on the task.

7. Not all of these actions were encouraged by the school. In particular, Prescott teachers often looked askance at private educational testing.

8. Another effort by Mrs Walters and Mrs Roy to improve Jonathan's concentration in class also fizzled:

> She [Mrs. Walters] felt he was easily distracted. We were going to set up some reward system. Every Wednesday they have a newsletter which comes home. She would put a note on his paper regarding how he was paying attention. She was going to tell him that I was going to get this note. It was going to be something that he would know about and I would know about it. And it only happened once.

> Mrs Roy felt disappointed and felt that her preparations at home were for naught: I had him all prepared to bring [home] his paper with his little note on it. 'Where is your paper? Where is your note?' It wasn't there . . . It was really hard to deal with that. Because nothing was followed through.

9. Jill's father played no obvious role in Jill's schooling. Mrs Brown said that her husband, a carpenter, was very shy. He never came to any school events.

10. As Mehan and colleagues point out, special educational meetings are heavily constrained by legal and administrative factors. Legally parents are given a significant role; parents must annually approve the Individual Educational Plan developed by the school. In reality, however, the educational decision is often made before the meeting or during the session with limited input from parents. Parents merely ratify the decisions made by the professionals (Mehan *et al.* 1986).

11. In an interview Mrs Sampson, Jill's second grade teacher, said that if Jill had been her own daughter she would have looked into having her tutored. To my knowledge Mrs Sampson did not propose this strategy to Jill's mother.

12. At the beginning of the year Mrs Thompson had been apprehensive about Johnny's father. She had worried that he would monitor *too* closely his son's schooling:

> When I first met the father I . . . [pause] got the impression that we not only have to deal with John but we would have to deal with the father. The way he came on at the beginning . . . I thought that he would watch every step of the way because he was *so* enthusiastic about John and so sure John was going to be — just telling us John's achievement. The feeling that John was above the average.

She thought that the father's high opinion of his son might be detrimental to Johnny's relationships:

> I really thought that perhaps the father would interfere by making John feel that he was above average. And often that can be a detriment in relationships with other kids.

Her fears, however, were not realized:

> That didn't turn out to be so much that way. The father didn't interfere that much and was supportive and was appreciative of what we could do.

13. Research on the impact of social class on teachers' expectations is mixed, but researchers have generally defined social class in a very general fashion (i.e., parents' occupation) (Baron *et al.* 1985). Most studies have also looked at the interactions between teachers and students in the formation of teacher expectations rather than teachers, students, and parents in elementary grades. For more detailed discussions of the issue of teacher expectations and labeling, see Cooper and Good (1983); Dusek (1985); Rist (1977); and Mehan *et al.* (1986).

14. Some actions by parents appeared to be largely symbolic. Parents of high-achievers, for example, showed up at school events, listened to the teachers' praise for their children, and were given encouragement to read to their children. The parents' attendance at school events appeared to have largely a symbolic role with the indirect effect of making the teacher believe the parents were concerned about schooling. These actions appeared, as Hoover-Dempsey *et al.* (1987) suggests, to increase teachers' sense of efficacy in the classroom. Teachers did not feel abandoned, as they did when parents failed to show up for the conferences.

8 The Dark Side of Parent Involvement: Costs for Families and Teachers

This study suggests that parents' assertiveness in school-related matters can give their children an educational boost. But along with the advantages the pattern of interdependency between home and school also produced distinct disadvantages for Prescott children, families, and educators. These negative intrusions into family life have been largely ignored by researchers and by proponents of parent involvement; many fail to admit any significant costs (Rich 1987a; Walberg 1987; Seeley 1984; Atkin *et al.* 1988). The negative consequences for teachers of some types of parent involvement have received more attention (Waller 1932; McPherson 1972; Lightfoot 1978; Lortie 1977). Also, high levels of parent involvement can have important adverse consequences for organizational dynamics, particularly the principal's role at the school. These deserve closer attention.[1]

Costs for Children and Families

Some Prescott children whose parents were heavily involved in their schooling showed signs of stress. When I was observing in first grade I noticed, for example, that Emily developed stomach aches — sometimes two or three times per week — during the reading period. Her mother, Mrs Svensson, noticed this as well:

> It got to the point where she started at reading [period]; during reading, she would get sick. [Mother sighs deeply.] Rose [the school secretary] would call me and say, 'Well, Emily is in here again'.

In the spring of first grade Emily also started not to want to go to school, and she would cry when her mother quizzed her on words in the morning, before school:

> In January I put those words up on the refrigerator. She was coming home with words like 'thrill' and 'what' and 'that'. Every morning . . . she would cry because she didn't know these words.

Emily's misery was compounded by the fact that her brother, who was in kindergarten, could read these words. Comparison was as inevitable as it was invidious:

> The thing was that Ross was knowing these words. He could damn well read all the lists of words.

Other low-achieving children at Prescott also showed signs of stress. Allen, for example, would steal small objects from time to time. His mother accepted their pediatrician's explanation that this behavior probably was linked to Allen's 'frustration level' and his problems at school. Jonathan was well-behaved in class but he was afraid to try new things for fear of failure. His mother was concerned about this. His father also complained about Jonathan's passivity and said that when his son reached second grade, he would 'push' him to try new things.

Prescott teachers were convinced that parents' actions could harm as well as help their children in school. For example, although Emily was tested extensively and her case was reviewed by the first grade teacher, second grade teacher, principal, reading resource teacher, and a private educational consultant, the factors impeding her educational progress were never diagnosed precisely. Emily's lack of progress was said to be 'developmental'. The teachers believed that her reading would improve with further growth.

Reflecting on Emily's year, Mrs Hoffman concluded that some of the child's academic difficulties were linked to the excessive pressure which she experienced at home:

> They [Emily's parents] put quite a bit of pressure on her, quite a bit of pressure. In terms of education and in terms of athletics. She swims every day and that puts education in second place. You only have so much energy; I don't care how old you are. Swimming for an hour a day, five or six days a week, it makes you tired.

Mrs Hoffman also felt that Emily's parents continually compared her to her younger brother (a pattern I also noticed in my interviews) and that this was detrimental:

> You know, I had her brother this year. I almost had the impression from his parents that he was gifted. He was not. He is at grade level and his work habits need attention. I think the two had been compared. It really slowed her up. It really discouraged her. I had many conferences with them and the mother volunteered in the classroom. She would say, 'Ross is doing so well'.

In fact Mrs Hoffman believed Emily reached a plateau in the spring and did not make any more progress in school because of her anxiety about the birth of a new baby:

> There was a lot of difficulty in the spring before the baby came. She had a miserable time with Emily. She didn't know what to do . . . The child

had one sibling already and didn't want another. I didn't tell her that . . . they were always saying how wonderful Ross was. I am not a psychologist. Many of the other teachers do bring these things up. It is not my place. I didn't feel as if I had a right to judge them.

Although both Mrs Hoffman and Mrs Walters had recommended that Emily be retained, in each case the parents decided not to do so largely because of their concern about Emily and Ross being in the same grade. In Mrs Hoffman's opinion the parents' concern that Ross would outflank Emily academically was unrealistic:

That wouldn't have been the case at all with her skills and behavior. They didn't have a realistic view. They hoped it — that he would pass her up. Maybe because he is a boy; [they think] of course he will pass her up. You would be surprised how many parents are very retarded in terms of their thinking of girls and boys. Thinking boys are surpassing girls in intelligence and of the girls wanting to be airline stewardesses and teachers.

Although the family rejected the retention Mrs Hoffman was not upset by this:

Some of the problems are just natural and iron themselves out. Emily had a good summer . . . I wasn't wholeheartedly in favor of retention unless they were in different schools. The family was not in favor of that. The boy would have been pretty nasty . . . If she didn't have a brother I would have felt strongly that retention would have been good for her.

Emily's parents were clearly involved in her schooling; they 'educationalized' the home environment (Epstein 1987). These educational activities included having Emily work with tutors in the summers and in third grade; hiring a teenager to read to Emily and Ross during the summer; the mother helping Emily with missed spelling words; and emphasizing reading at home.

Emily's failure to keep up with her class and the parents' involvement in her schooling took a toll on family life. There were signs that Emily's failure to learn to read had triggered a crisis within the family. Emily's mother was angry at Mrs Walters for not diagnosing Emily's reading problem earlier:

She totally misplaced her in her reading group. Which really put Emily behind, terribly. I really resent that . . . I just get so mad when I even think about it. It really bothers me. She [Emily] went through such frustration and I don't think a child should have to go through that.

The mother said that for the last five months she and her husband had talked daily about Emily's difficulty with reading. The mother was 'consumed' by her daughter's problem. She interviewed tutors, spent time learning the appropriate educational terms for Emily's difficulties, and had special conferences with the first grade teacher, second grade teacher, reading resource teacher, and principal.

Not only time but money was involved; the father estimated that the costs of tutoring and testing totaled around $500. The mother, and reportedly the father, were emotionally distraught about their daughter's academic failure:

> There isn't a day that goes by that in the moring, David will say, 'Gosh, I woke up last night. I just had knots in my stomach about this whole thing'.

Other families, including Mrs Morris in Colton, also were seriously disappointed by their children's problems in school. But with intense levels of parent involvement in schooling educational failure took on a new twist. Emily's mother seemed to feel that *she* had failed as a mother in her role in supervising, intervening, and compensating for the weaknesses in her daughter's schooling. She was angry with herself for 'not keeping on top' of Emily's education:

> I should have gone in and said 'What is going on?' I should have just been much more demanding.

Mrs Svensson also felt humiliated by the whole experience:

> It is a really hard thing. It is really hard. You struggle with this. It hurts your feelings.

She had not acquired the same emotional distance that her husband claimed to have achieved:

> David was commenting the other night, 'You take these things personally'. David was saying that he was really surprised that he wasn't taking this personally. He was very sad for Emily, and that he really wanted to help her, but he wasn't feeling that way [hurt]. And I thought, 'That's great. I'm glad you aren't feeling that way. Because I'm taking it all. One of us has to be on track of the whole thing.'

There were also signs that Emily's school problems affected her relationship with her parents. Noting that their daughter was always eager for their approval, the Svenssons worried about the potentially destructive consequences of their educational involvement. Despite their intense efforts Emily did not learn the materials as quickly or as well as they wanted her to. Thus, try as she might, Emily was unable to please them. When she began to rebel — refusing to clean her room, 'mouthing' off to her mother — the parents 'backed off' the educational instruction:

> I was not real sure how we could work at home without being destructive. Without having it be a frustrating situation. What can we do? Finally, I decided that the best thing we can do is read to her . . . That is a non-threatening situation between parent and child.

While differing in the intensity of their emotional reactions, Mr and Mrs Svensson seemed to share similar views about how to approach Emily's problems. Only occasionally did they disagree over strategy. For example, Mrs Svensson wanted to have her daughter tested for learning disabilities; Mr Svensson, because of his concerns about the effects of labeling, was 'very opposed to it'. There were no signs, however, that this disagreement was creating significant tensions in their marriage. They both agonized over Emily's problems:

> You go over this in your head so many times: 'Where did we go wrong?' David keeps saying, 'Well, obviously we didn't read enough to them'. But yet that's not true because Ross has had the same thing. Well, Ross is developing just fine. There is nothing wrong with him.

The decision about whether to retain Emily drew comments, some critical, from their relatives:

> David's mother thought we should put her in a private school. That it would be awful ... Mother thinks that this is going to ruin Emily. I don't look it at it that way at all. We are not doing this to ruin her. Heavens! So we have to contend with that.

Overall Emily's problems in school created many problems outside the classroom. As in Colton the parents and relatives were disappointed by the child's low achievement. But the negative consequences at Prescott went beyond this. Because family life and school life were viewed as interdependent in that community, the child's academic problems had reciprocal — and more serious — effects on family life. Emily's academic failure created worries, strains, and tensions in family interactions that had no parallel in Colton families with low-achieving children.

Conversations with teachers, observations on the school site, and interviews with other parents made it clear that the negative influence of children's school problems on family life was not unique to the Svensson family. Some parents reported having regular and serious conflicts with their children over homework. Mr Simpson, Donald's father had a weekly battle with his junior-high-school-age daughter over the amount of television she watched and the thoroughness with which she did her math homework. Although he was eager to help her to do well in school he resisted what he perceived as her attempts to manipulate him:

> I don't think that she is coming to me to really understand it; I think that she is coming to me to get an answer. If she could look in the back of the book and get the answer she would do that. I don't give her the answer. I just tell her where she is wrong. And then she will go back and do it — usually right. And I will say, 'Why didn't you do it that way before?'

His daughter's tendency to guess, and her apparent lack of desire to 'understand how she arrived at that answer' irritated Mr Simpson. Complaining that 'she just wants to get the answer,' he confessed:

I get terribly frustrated. And I lose my temper . . . and then I give her a long lecture about you are not taking advantage of this, you are not applying yourself, you are not working at it, you are not spending time on it.

Knowing his tendency to lose control, he had to 'watch himself'. Still, he estimated that two to three times per week he and his daughter had a conflict over her watching television, listening to rock music, and generally doing anything but her homework.

Although the children in first and second grade did not have homework, Prescott and Colton parents reported similar, although milder, conflicts between themselves and their children. Children resisted having parents read to them, work with them, and go over papers. Some mothers felt that they had to 'corner' their children. Mrs Harris described a typical scenario:

He is not an easy child to sit down with. [I say,] 'I think we should go over what you brought home.' [He says,] 'Nope.' [I say,] 'I see. Well I want to do it.' [He says,] 'Nope. I don't want to.' So I usually have to corner him.

Prescott parents, including Mrs Harris, worked out elaborate strategies to get their children to work on school materials at home:

He is a reasonable child. I will say, 'Okay. I understand that you are tired from coming home from school and I am tired from just coming home from work. So how about if you play and I'll do my bookkeeping and then at 4.30 we will work on it but for a short period'. And then he is willing to say, 'Okay'. He gets to play and have his snack. I get to do my bookkeeping. I am not tense because I am thinking I have all of these things I should be doing. He is not angry because I am taking him away from his play because he knows it is going to happen. So that seems to be an amiable resolution to the problem.

At times, however, parents' strategies created new family conflicts. One common problem appeared to be sibling rivalry about educational performance. For example, Allen was sensitive to the fact that his brother — who was a year younger — was an accomplished reader:

He reads to us at night after his two brothers go to bed. For some reason, he doesn't want them around. One reason he probably doesn't want Jacob around is because Jacob is an excellent reader.

The unequal levels of children's performance were painfully clear in other families as well. Carol, for example, was doing very well in school. Her sister Anna, who was a year younger, was having more difficulty. Carol pointed this difference out to Anna to their mother's chagrin:

Carol at first was very critical of Anna. She said, 'Well, at this time last year I could read much better than you read'. So I took Carol over to the side. I explained to her that it would take the fun away if she made Anna feel as if she couldn't do anything well. So now she turns it around and gets very excited when Anna can read a new word or read a book and she reads to Anna and lets her read to her. So now she has become very supportive.

Carol complained, however, that her mother worked with Anna on reading more than her mother worked with her. Mrs Smith felt placed in a dilemma. On the one hand she wanted to help Anna in school, on the other hand she did want not to call attention to Anna as being slow. In addition, because of concerns with equity, if she helped Anna with her reading then she felt she should also help Carol with her numbers. This increased the magnitude of the task.

As the Smith family's situation illustrates, parent involvement in schooling can become intertwined with enduring family tensions over sibling rivalry and competition for parental attention. This is less likely to occur where there is less emphasis on family–school interdependency. At Colton parents spent less time working with their children on academic work, and as a result they did not create new conflicts. The exacerbation of sibling rivalry by parent involvement in schooling was compounded in some Prescott families by marital conflict. For example, Mr and Mrs Smith disagreed vigorously over how to deal with Anna's lapses of memory and general problems in school. Mrs Smith explained:

> When she worked on these flashcards, he would put her down. He would say, 'Oh come on, Anna you know these. You have seen these words before'. In the past, when she was real small, he would pressure her to come up with answers. Simple things that she could have handled.

Mr Smith was irritated by his daughter's memory lapses when she was in kindergarten and took steps to deal with them, as his wife recalled:

> She was in kindergarten. She was real young and he would say, 'What is your teacher's name?' and she couldn't remember. Something real obvious like, 'What is your friend's name?' and she couldn't remember. He decided that in this family there is no such thing as, 'I can't remember.'

In general Mrs Smith vigorously disagreed with her husband's approach to Anna's learning problems:

> Anna has a mechanism that when she feels pressure she freezes. When she freezes, Tom tries to force the answer out by pressure. And I know her, because she has my personality style. And that is the exactly *opposite* way to get the answer.

Mrs Smith preferred her own, more understanding and indirect, pattern of interaction with Anna:

The problem is that her mind just blanked — actually went blank. My solution is to get around it: to talk about it indirectly and try to make it more casual. 'Oh, who was that girl you were playing with?' Then it comes out on the spot. Instead of saying, 'Okay Anna, what did you do today?' Then the atmosphere is squelched.

Their disagreements over child rearing often centered on the handling of educational matters. As Mrs Smith explained, she and her husband went through many stages of interaction:

We do have tensions over the children and we do know that. One stage we went through is that I would scowl at him and the child saw me. I realized that wasn't good. So then I would talk to him afterwards and normally we would get into a giant argument. So that wasn't very productive.

Mrs Smith was particularly annoyed by her husband's tendency to make pronouncements about Anna's relative lack of intelligence. Mr Smith contended that:

Anna wasn't as bright as Carol. That she has to work harder. That she was slow. And all these terms *pigeonhole* a child and lock them into being exactly that — even before there is any evidence that they are like that and need help.

Mrs Smith eventually turned to Anna's teachers as a source of professional expertise to use in her arguments with her husband:

Anna learns very differently than with Carol. Tom used to draw conclusions about that. I got uppity every time he tried to draw conclusions... So I would ask the teacher at conference time, 'What are the normal expectations at this grade level?' It was real comforting to have some authority to quote: 'You can't measure these things until after the third grade.'

She believes her husband benefited from this information:

He didn't understand that children could be in 25 different places at the same age level and still be perfectly fine ... So he accepted that Anna's symptoms weren't indicative of something negative. He decided not to pressure her anymore.

Nevertheless Mrs Smith feels that her husband's behavior has had a negative effect on Anna, and that his behavior still is a problem. Anna continues to seem afraid of her father at times:

This had gone on for about a year and I could see that tension in her. He thinks that she is sometimes afraid of him. He can't understand why she would feel that way. And then he gets angry with her. It's almost humorous.

Mr and Mrs Smith's marital conflicts also spilled over and influenced Mrs Smith's relationship with Anna. Mrs Smith tried to 'relieve the pressure' on her daughter by deflecting challenges from Anna. She admitted that she tried to 'protect' Anna in this way because she felt she and her daughter were very much alike:

> I would much rather be left alone than be pressured, so naturally I suggest that for Anna. So I come in and try to get the pressure [taken off]. But that is probably what she needs. Some expectations but in a proper way. So I have to watch out.

Mrs Smith said that, in the light of Carol's outstanding academic performance and Anna's difficulty, she tended to be 'protective' of her youngest. Her reservations about this approach centered primarily on Anna's school performance:

> I've been very protective of Anna. I think that is typical in a second child in the shadow of the strong first child. I don't want to overprotect . . . turning her into a passive role — not demanding enough of her. I have been thinking about that a lot because she is not reading up to grade level.

Mrs Smith feared that working with Anna at home would call too much attention to the fact that Anna needed help, thus underlining Anna's sister's and her father's already low estimation of her abilities. Although Mrs Smith dismissed this fear as 'silly' she found her fear and her desire to protect Anna difficult to overcome. Even as she spoke she tried to convince herself to change her behavior:

> It's a silly fear — my overprotectiveness. That isn't going to work. I do find myself deflecting challenges away from Anna and that is bad. That could be very difficult for her as she gets a little older. Now is the time to stop. I need to work on that.

Although she was not employed outside the home at the time of the study, Mrs Smith had difficultly finding time to work with her daughter. The teacher had asked Mrs Smith and her husband to go over a word list with Anna. Citing her own lack of discipline, Mrs Smith noted that she had not worked with Anna on her words:

> I only have one month to go and it's my new resolution, so I have got to do it. It's kind of shocking to me because I am a highly motivated mother. I am educated. I take it seriously. And I am aware of the consequences of her not picking up at this level: 'You can't go back and do it over. You are always struggling to keep up.' All these things I know. It's a lack of will. It doesn't come down to a matter of intelligence. It is dedication.

It seems unlikely that Anna's mother lacked the requisite 'dedication.' Instead, tensions within the family probably made Mrs Smith 'protect' Anna from working on her words every day. Mrs Smith was amazed at how much work Anna got done when she went to visit her paternal grandmother:

> She is a neat person. She is aggressive and she really works with the children. The children will go stay with her for a week. She had Anna working on her words every day. She'd say: 'Now here are five words. Now just write them over three times and you're finished.' With words she was having difficulty with — where, when, went, want — to recognize the differences. On vacation, here she is down here working on her words every day. She was so proud.

Overall then, in some Prescott families parent involvement in schooling had negative consequences both for individual children and for family dynamics. Tensions were most apparent in families where children were below grade level. All of the Prescott children who showed signs of stress and almost all of the Prescott families with a low-achieving child (often a sibling of a child in the study) also describe routine negative family interactions triggered by the educational problems. These negative encounters occurred at all levels of family dynamics: between parents and children, brothers and sisters, husbands and wives, and families and extended kin.

Some of these tensions, particularly those involving discipline problems also occurred among Colton families. But the problems at Colton were not so intense and they did not penetrate into family life as they did at Prescott. Colton children who 'acted out' over educational problems did so at school, or in the morning when they resisted going to school. Colton mothers did not have persistent conflicts over academic issues with their children. This is because most Colton parents did not believe it to be part of their duty and obligation as parents and when they tried and their children protested, most Colton parents seemed to give up. By not working with their children at home very much Colton parents were spared potentially difficult and divisive conflicts. Also gender roles were more segregated in Colton homes than in Prescott homes. When Colton families did become involved in education, progress fell almost exclusively to mothers (who typically had more formal education than the fathers). Thus family tensions at Colton, including parent–child conflicts and marital conflicts, were reduced by the less intensive involvement of parents in schooling. This was an advantage for children and for parents.

Teachers' Views

Prescott parents' actions, particularly placing pressure on children to do well in school, not only influenced family dynamics but had a reciprocal influence on the school site. Mrs Walters was alarmed by the excessive pressure which parents placed on children. A desire to protect children structured many of her classroom activities, including her view that homework was not good for first grade children and her resolve not to exhibit work on Open House night because 'the parents compare.' Prescott's principal, Mrs Harpst, also complained that parents placed too much pressure on children:

> We are noticing more and more children with real nervous problems. Children who are acting up or acting in ways that would indicate unhappiness or pressure or tension at very early ages.

Mrs Harpst said that she and the teachers had discussed this at length. While acknowledging that these problems could be linked to the changing social milieu, the educators were very concerned about excessive parent involvement and pressure, as Mrs Harpst's comments indicate:

> Children can be very troubled by parental pressure and it comes out in strange ways . . . If parents could just step back and just relax a little bit. Enjoy, hold high standards, expect good things of their child, and at the same time remember that their child is a child. It might be to that child's advantage.

Teachers felt that parents' actions backfired in some instances, giving children new anxieties and leading to new discipline problems in the classroom. Parents could thus discourage as well as encourage success in school.

Parents and Teachers: Natural Enemies

Over fifty years ago, Willard Waller, author of the *Sociology of Teaching*, called parents and teachers 'natural enemies.' He was right. Parents and teachers have a different relationship *vis-à-vis* children. Parents are concerned with a single child in a class; teachers need to be concerned with all of the children. These particularistic concerns of parents and universalistic concerns of teachers can, and do, create conflicts (Lightfoot 1978; McPherson 1972; Parsons 1961; Waller 1932). These enduring tensions between parents and teachers are widely recognized and acknowledged. What academics and other commentators have failed to realize is that parents' social class position influences the resources which they bring to these 'battles' with their natural enemy. The higher parents' social class, the more social resources they can draw on in making their claims. Lower-class and working-class parents also have particularistic concerns for their children, but they do not bring as many resources to their interactions with teachers.

Social class influences the content of the conflicts between parents and teachers. Working-class parents complained to the school rarely; their complaints were primarily over non-academic matters — particularly discipline. Upper-middle-class parents' complaints centered on core qualities of the teachers' professional expertise — especially their ability to teach the curriculum.

Prescott parents directly and indirectly criticized teachers' professional competence, judgment, and decisions. Parents' complaints about Mrs Walters centered on the noise level in the class and the lack of organization. Allen's mother called the classroom 'chaotic'; other mothers said that the boys were 'running wild' in the class. As noted earlier, many Prescott parents also felt that academics were not emphasized enough in Mrs Walters' classroom; that their children were not challenged sufficiently; that she did not cover enough material during the year; and that too much time was spent on art rather than academic subjects. Although these complaints often lacked supporting evidence, the mothers felt their children were not adequately challenged:

> Allen . . . did as good as could have been expected from that teacher. If he had had a teacher who had challenged him more, I think he would have done better. I cannot criticize his reading because he is reading just beautifully. I cannot criticize his math because he seems to have a handle on the math. I cannot say anything especially negative other than that I don't think that she challenged him enough.

Other teachers in the school, as well as the principal, were aware of Anne Walters' reputation among parents. Mrs Hoffman spoke plainly about this:

> The parents come and gossip. [They say] their child didn't learn anything last year with so and so. There is some nasty gossip about Anne.

At times parents were successful in changing a teacher's behavior, including areas that were clearly within the teacher's professional judgment. Mrs Walters did hand out math packets to some parents although she had grave reservations about first graders doing homework on weekends. Other times parents were less successful. The principal conceded that some parents wanted Mrs Walters fired:

> I think there was an attempt this year to [try to fire her] . . . [but] they would not have the grounds to do so. My evaluations have not indicated that. There are very severe, very stringent rules in the contract that set out how the process is used for dismissal of a teacher . . . Knowing the courts and the process I don't see that they [parents] would have a case.

Teachers and administrators sometimes privately ridiculed the unrealistic and ill-informed expectations that many of the parents placed on them and on the children. For example, Prescott teachers laughed at the way parents of first graders were so pleased when a sixth grade teacher was assigned to teach first grade: 'She is going to teach them sixth grade material, of course'. Teachers were also unimpressed when parents tried to force their children to read at home or wanted their children to be working on multiplication in first grade.

Not all of teachers' management of parents, however, was negative. The volunteer program took a great deal of time (teachers had to find activities for parents to do), but the staff was very appreciative of mothers' classroom volunteering. In addition, when a mother was intrusive but the teacher defined the behavior as in the child's best educational interests, the staff was very supportive of parent involvement. Mrs Harris was intruding into her son's spelling curriculum when she asked if he could work on his spelling packets at home, but his teacher felt that Allen was lazy and was not working as hard as he could on spelling. His mother's actions were thus deemed supportive, rather than being viewed as a criticism of the teacher's classroom work.

Despite the uneven quality of parents' suggestions the principal and teachers at Prescott spent a great deal of time and energy trying to respond to, manage, and contain parental complaints. To allay parents' concerns over Mrs Walters, the principal moved her to kindergarten, where parents' expectations were lower. She decided, also, to establish a program to educate parents about the goals of a first grade:

> Next year we have plans to do a better job of educating parents on the diversity of styles of children's learning. We're going to set up some forums and I'm going to spend some time at the beginning of the year [educating] parents on what happens in the first grade . . . in a proactive as opposed to a reactive manner.

In addition to preventive work, however, teachers in upper-middle-class schools tried to rebuff what they perceived as challenges to their autonomy. In the second year of the study Mrs Walters politely but firmly told parents she did not send home math packets on the weekend. In a meeting with parents, which unexpectedly turned into an attack on Mrs Walters' teaching capabilities, Mrs Harpst vigorously defended the quality of her teachers in front of parents. The principal and teachers worked to educate parents about decisions that were within the realm of their professional responsibility as educators. When faced with parents from out-of-state who were eager to have their child placed in first grade, the principal told them that 'we will make that decision' after a careful evaluation of the child's needs and standing. These exchanges were generally framed in a polite but firm manner. Teachers and administrators were trying to retain control over the educational process.

This effort — sometimes a struggle — by teachers and principals to maintain the upper hand in school matters did not publicly dominate the interactions between Prescott parents and teachers. The principal worked very hard to maintain good relationships between parents and the school. She spent a substantial part of her time simply talking to parents. She met privately with many parents, occasionally called special parents' meetings to address a specific concern, and worked closely with the parents' clubs. She tried to improve her staff's communication skills in their interactions with parents. In some instances, she and the teachers circumvented school rules in order to accommodate parents' requests.

Mrs Harpst appeared to 'cool-out' angry parents by a dual strategy of working to lower their expectations and making them feel that everything possible was being done for their child. For example, faced with Emily's parents' anger over their daughter's failure to learn to read in Mrs Walters' first grade classroom, the principal explained that not all children learn to read in first grade; children learn to read between the ages of five and eight. She worked with the Svenssons to arrange placement for Emily in Mrs Hoffman's second grade, encouraged them to have Emily tutored in the summer, repeatedly emphasized to the parents that they were doing everything they possibly could for their child, and stressed that much of learning was 'developmental.'

Sometimes, however, educators' efforts to work with parents were less successful. Mrs Walters had mothers who, four years later, remained so angry at her they would neither look her in the eye nor greet her when they passed. There were rumors among parents that there were two 'terrible' teachers at Prescott who should be fired. Parents also said that the principal was unresponsive, steadfastly backed up her teachers, and failed to listen to the concerns of parents. Prescott educators complained about the 'vicious rumor mill' and the constant stream of parents' criticisms and complaints. As Mrs Harpst said:

> This community has a rumor mill. There is a rumor mill in this community that is really unbelievable. The community rumor mill has it that Anne [Walters] is not a good teacher and that another teacher, Nancy Watson, is not. Both are *fine* teachers. They both have different styles from the general method of teaching kids in this community. The . . . reputation [of a good teacher] is someone who can do a rather traditional job of excellence in education and communicate it to the parents and to the kids.

Mrs Harpst noted that the sharing of information among parents was not only constant but often inaccurate. Teachers complained that parents drew a dramatic line between kindergarten and first grade. Teachers themselves did not take such a view, as the principal explained:

> Parents have adopted a view that this transition between kindergarten and first grade is a big one. I have the view that a good first grade, a really strong and intense first grade program, has many similarities to a good kindergarten program.

Teachers carrying out an innovative curriculum at Prescott were particularly vulnerable to parents' complaints, a pattern noted by others (McPherson 1972).

Teachers such as Mrs Walters, who lacked good communication skills with adults, were more likely to suffer at the hands of parents. For example, Prescott's kindergarten teacher, Samantha Taylor, was widely respected among parents. Mrs Harpst felt that Mrs Walters and Mrs Taylor were very similar teachers, but they had uneven communication skills with parents. Moreover, parents, unlike the teachers, believed that a kindergarten and first grade program should be drastically different:

> Anne and Samantha are in many ways similar. Samantha has the advantage of being an outstanding communicator [and] the expectations of parents in kindergarten are vastly different than the expectations in first grade . . .

The principal observed that parents' criticisms sometimes had a serious and negative influence on staff morale. All of the teachers were discouraged after the meeting where Anne Walters was attacked by parents as incompetent:

> Teachers work *really* hard to have their job well done. Then to have parents come in and, in a sense, knife one of their peers in the back, by vicious verbal abuse ... that really depressed them [the teachers] a whole lot. I think it was depressing because they felt that if there are to be changes, they aren't going to be done that way. It makes people all the more defensive.

Teachers and administrators in Colton school were spared this criticism of their work. For the most part parents sent their children to school and left the responsibility for education with the teachers. Teachers interpreted this separation as indicating that parents were not 'supportive' of education and/or of the teachers' efforts in the classroom. Colton teachers routinely overlooked the advantages which this lack of parent involvement brought them, particularly the increased professional autonomy and status in their relations with parents. When I pressed this point in interviews with Colton staff, however, some teachers conceded the advantages. Although Mrs Sampson felt that discipline would be much easier in an upper-middle-class community, she was not interested in moving to such a school:

> Parents are very demanding ... critical when there is something to be concerned about. I am afraid you would have to be very tactful. You would have to be right on your toes. Those children need a lot more creative experiences in addition to the regular reading and math program.

Ironically, then, Colton's teachers' morale, too, was negatively influenced by parent involvement, but here it was the lack of involvement in schooling that troubled them.

Teachers in communities with high levels of parent involvement devote a substantial amount of organizational resources to managing home–school relations. They must take time away from teaching to coordinate, train, and make effective use of parents in their classroom. They need to develop good communication skills with parents, since those who cannot effectively explain their academic program are more likely to become the target of parents' criticism.

For principals, the picture is even more dramatic. Principals in schools with a very high level of parent involvement in schooling are frequently placed in difficult positions. They must be responsive to parents, or risk anger in the community and complaints to their superiors, yet they also must try to maintain good relations with their staff. Mr Wagner, the principal at Colton, said that he had 'a lot less pressure' on him at Colton than at his previous school in a more affluent community. As I have shown, parent involvement also increases parents' criticisms of some teachers. Parents' demands (having the teacher fired, preventing their child from being enrolled in that class) may directly conflict with organizational demands. In virtually all school districts, principals lack the prerogative to fire teachers easily and must create classes balanced in size, academic performance, race, gender, and certain behavior problems. These organizational needs preclude principals from meeting parents' requests in several areas.

The different role parents take in supervising their children's school site activities changes the character of the principal's job. Principals in upper-middle-class communities confront more complicated relations with their staff than in working-class schools. They are forced to mediate parents' complaints about teachers, without violating powerful professional and organizational norms of teacher autonomy in the classroom. They must also develop skills for negotiating with upper-middle-class parents who believe they have a right to criticize the school and teachers' performance. Previous studies have described principals' roles in working with parents in school site activities, parents' clubs, concerns about busing, and other school site issues. The point here, however, is that high levels of parent involvement may increase teachers' sense of efficacy, school resources available to teachers, and children's classroom performance, but it also produces organizational conflicts.

In schools with high levels of parent involvement, therefore, principals routinely confront parental demands for teachers' performance that are difficult, if not impossible, to resolve to the satisfaction of all parties. Teachers in these upper-middle-class schools face scrutiny and challenges from parents over their professional competence. Some amount of conflict between parents and teachers is routine, but social class appears to influence the content of the 'battles' and, at least in upper-middle-class schools, the intensity and frequency with which parents take the offensive in trying to control the teacher and their children's education. Parents are less willing to grant teachers a 'backstage' and automatically defer to professional expertise.

Changes in Childhood

In *The Hurried Child*, David Elkind asserts that

> the concept of childhood . . . is threatened with extinction . . . Today's pressures on upper-middle-class children to grow up fast begin in early childhood. Chief among them is the pressure for early educational attainment (Elkind 1981, p. 3, 4).

Elkind chastises parents and teachers for placing too much pressure on children to read in early years; he longs for the revival of the reading 'readiness' concept. Other authors have also criticized the 'erosion of childhood' through the steady stream of educational activities for young children (Suransky 1982).

This study suggests that the 'hurried child' critique — at least in the area of educational attainment — may be much more suitable for upper-middle-class families than working-class ones. In adopting a pattern of separation between home and school, working-class parents placed less academic pressure on their children, as well as on themselves. Working-class children were generally spared the repeated efforts by parents to have their children concentrate, think logically, and perform educationally — in short, to 'work' rather than play. Lacking formal lessons and tutoring, Colton children had more time to experience the joy and tedium of childhood. While illustrating class differences, the research also provides preliminary support for one of the key concepts of the 'hurried child' thesis: well-intended pressure to improve educational performance can have negative consequences for children. This dark side of parent involvement is largely unexplored by proponents of parent involvement: it warrants further exploration. Moreover, social critics' list of negative consequences may be too short. Elkind and Suransky have focused primarily on the negative consequences for children when parents and teachers vigorously promote educational attainment. I suggest that the negative consequences of intense parent involvement in schooling include conflicts in educational organizations and families. For educators, family involvement can be bittersweet; while appreciative of parent support, there are costs for them in reduced professional autonomy. Family conflicts can also be exacerbated in upper-middle-class families, particularly when children are having academic problems. Indeed, the ideology regarding children's valuable contribution to families notwithstanding, there is considerable evidence to suggest that children strain marriages. Marital satisfaction decreases with the birth of the first child. It does not dramatically increase again until children leave the home (Spanier *et al.* 1975; Nock 1979; Campbell *et al.* 1976).

Colton and Prescott mothers and fathers worried when teachers recommended that their children repeat first grade; the character of their worries differed by social class. At Colton mothers were less invoved in their children's schooling and their lives were less disrupted by their children's school failure than at Prescott. While the interconnections between upper-middle-class parents and schools had benefits, they also drew husbands and wives, siblings, and extended family into new — and sometimes bitter — conflicts related to children's school lives. In handing over responsibility for education to the school, working-class parents inadvertently protected their family life from the trauma which Prescott families sometimes experienced when the children were floundering in school.

Notes

1. At Colton, parents were less involved in schooling. This had costs as well as benefits. The costs, at least according to the teachers, were that children's academic performance was weaker than it might have been (with, some teachers felt, negative consequences for some children's self-esteem).

   In addition, Colton parents reported that their children were disturbed by their parents' failure to attend evening activities at school. Laura's mother said her daughter was 'real disappointed' that she could not go to Open House Night; Tommy's mother reported that 'it was a big deal' to her son that she and his father did not go in for Back-to-School

Night. Children's pleasure, and disappointment, regarding their parents' attendance at school events was also apparent at school in the comments children made during recess, 'Sharing' time, and class lessons.

The benefits of this separation between home and school were that children had more autonomy from their parents at home, more leisure time after school, and fewer conflicts with their parents over their education. Overall, Colton family–school relationships were less intense than at Prescott and thus produced fewer tensions among parents, children, and teachers. As a result, the discussion of negative consequences of family–school relationships in this chapter centers primarily around Prescott families.

9 Social Class Differences in Inter-institutional Linkages

In introductory classes across America, sociologists teach students a fundamental principal of the discipline: the behavior of individual people is influenced by the social context. In a society dominated by the ideology of individualism, sociologists nevertheless offer undergraduates the proposition that social institutions — family, work, political and economic structures and religion — shape the contours of individual biographies. Moreover, these social institutions are riddled with inequalities: social class, as well as race and gender, influence life experiences in many spheres, from the work place to family life. As part of these introductory lectures, sociologists typically assert that there are inter-relationships among social institutions, which further shape individual experience. No social institution exists in a vacuum: rather, the social spheres are woven together, a social 'fabric', as some would have it.

Yet, both in their empirical and conceptual work, sociologists have been much more effective in demonstrating dynamics *within* rather than *between* social institutions. This almost exclusive preoccupation with intra-institutional mechanisms is, as I have indicated throughout this book, a mistake. In this concluding chapter, I summarize the evidence that social class has a decisive influence on the connections between families and other social institutions. I further suggest that these class-linked patterns grow out of the defining characteristics of social class, rather than being a manifestation of individuals' aspirations. The metaphor of cultural capital fruitfully expands our understanding of this pattern, although aspects of the concept warrant modification. I close by offering policy recommendations and theoretical implications of what I am characterizing as 'inter-institutional linkages' among social class, family life, and schooling.

Missing the Connections

Structural-functionalism offers a coherent theoretical framework for assessing inter-institutional linkages. The structural-functionalist model suggests that social institutions — kinship, the economy, the political structure, and religion —

carry out specialized functions to meet the needs of society. There is an interdependency between each of these specialized parts. The normal status of the social organism is equilibrium, as the parts function to meet the needs of the social whole (Parsons 1961; 1964; Davis and Moore 1966). Behaviors within institutions, including, for example, women's expressive roles in the home, are said to be linked to the functioning of the entire social system (Parsons and Bales 1955). The list of weaknesses in functionalist theory is long and well known, including the circular character of the theory, failure to incorporate notions of conflict, reification of the *status quo*, and of social needs (Collins 1971; 1975). Unfortunately, few theories since functionalism have offered models of the linkages between social institutions. Researchers' preoccupation with intra-institutional dynamics has eclipsed the inter-institutional connections.

When researchers have addressed these linkages, the results have often been disappointing. Some go astray by failing to take into account the pattern of social stratification. For example, Miller (1988) calls for studies of social functions without a concept of social class differences in social functioning. Similarly, researchers have discussed the 'buffering' and 'bridging' between organizations, but they have done so without locating the organizations within the social stratification system (Pfeffer and Salancik 1978). Nor have they studied the relationships between family life — a social institution — and formal, hierarchical, organizations.[1]

Others have the opposite problem: organizations are set within a system of social stratification, but researchers overstate the linkages between organizations and the dominant class. Bowles and Gintis (1976) argue that the interests of the capitalist class have molded the character of schools, so that authority relations at school 'correspond' to the authority relations in the work place. Correspondence theory, however, fails to offer a persuasive portrait of why teachers would act in the interests of the dominant class (Collins 1981a). It also neglects variations in educational organizations.

Some models focus almost exclusively on individuals, particularly individuals' values and aspirations, as they trace connections between social spheres. This ignores the possibility that individuals are not acting alone but as members of social groups, which have different relationships from gatekeeping institutions. This is a decided weakness, as is the tendency to embrace the standards of organizations as legitimate and to encourage individuals to comply with these standards (Coleman 1985; 1987; 1988) or, worse, to judge those who do not comply as deficient (Deutsch 1967a).

Other researchers simply assume that institutions are 'middle-class' and charge that institutions are thus biased and discriminatory in their treatment of certain social groups. Here, researchers suggest — but generally fail to develop — an analysis of the social connections that lead to this outcome. Some social critics, for example, imply that professionals treat children in a discriminatory fashion or allow parents to circumvent the standards routinely. There is little evidence to support the contention that institutions, particularly schools, operate in a capricious and discriminatory fashion (Amato 1980). To be sure, some dramatic examples of social class bias exist, but much of the evidence suggests that most organizations, in fact, plod along rather than function in an arbitrary manner. Still, if institutions behave in a relatively uniform and neutral fashion, why do we find dramatic differences in school outcomes based on social class? The usual answers are unsatisfactory.

Class Connections

Rather than focusing on dynamics within institutions and assuming *inter*-institutional linkages to be uniform, I have proposed distinct and analytically significant variations by social class. As I have shown, the density of connections between parents and schools differs by social class. This variation has been glossed over by social scientists.[2]

In the working-class community of Colton, there was a separation between family life and educational institutions. All of the parents helped to prepare children for school by teaching them manners and rudimentary educational skills. Parents also felt that they were being supportive and helpful in their children's schooling. Some parents were more energetic than others in reading to their children and attending school events. Even the most active working-class parents, however, did not supervise, compensate for, or attempt to intervene in their children's program. Instead, parents 'trusted' the school to educate their children. Parents and children viewed education as something which took place at school, under the supervision of the teacher. Teachers' efforts to have parents take a leadership role in education in the home often were resisted by parents — and children — and frequently met with failure.

In the upper-middle-class community of Prescott, there was an inter-connectedness between family life and educational institutions. As others have shown, upper-middle-class parents devoted more time and energy to preparing their children academically for school than did working-class parents, particularly in their style of verbal development (Heath 1982a; 1982b). Nevertheless, the actions of Prescott parents went beyond what has been documented in existing studies. Rather than preparing children for schooling and helping to support the teacher, parents actively supervised, supplemented, and intervened in their children's schooling. When faced with a weak teacher, some parents compensated with additional tutoring. Parents also hired other educational consultants, particularly during the summer. While not always successful, upper-middle-class parents sought a more individualized education for their children. Although gratified by parents' high levels of involvement, teachers complained about parents challenging and attempting to circumvent school rules. They felt parents' actions were unhelpful at times and placed additional stress on children and on themselves.

Parents in these two schools, therefore, hoped that their children would achieve educational success in first grade, but they took different steps to try to ensure that success. Notably, social class influenced parents' efforts to individualize their children's experience within bureaucratic institutions. By turning over responsibility for education to the school, working-class parents depended on teachers to provide an equitable and suitable education for their children. Their children received a generic education. Upper-middle-class parents, particularly when their children were floundering academically, worked to customize their children's school experience. They tried to tailor programs and activities to meet their children's needs. There were signs that parents' interventions (or lack of interventions) influenced children's classroom perform-ance, and that the mothers' experiences at school (as well as their friendships with other parents in the community) shaped parents' actions at home.

The current research tradition, then, makes the mistake of lumping together various educational activities that parents undertake with their children without investigating the purpose of these events. Mothers in both schools reported engaging in the same activities (i.e., teaching their children new words), but social class had a significant influence on the meaning and purpose of these activities. Thus, this study points to an important gap in our thinking. Families may be very similar in how much they stress the importance of education or how frequently and diligently they attempt to teach their children new words, but they may differ in how closely these activities are tied to the school's curriculum, how much they monitor their children's school per-formance, and how much they complain to educators.

Our understanding of individuals' careers within gatekeeping institutions must, therefore, move well beyond knowing personal values and aspirations. Upper-middle-class parents had more detailed information about what schools wanted of them, complied more fully with teachers' requests, criticized and challenged teachers more frequently, and adopted a view of their proper role in their children's schooling which more closely matched teachers' wishes than did working-class parents. In short, social class shapes the alignment of social groups with the standards of institutions.

More than Values

Both practitioners and social scientists generally have portrayed class differences in the educational activities of families as a matter of *values* and *concern*. I would contend that, teachers' explanations notwithstanding, parents' values on the importance of an education cannot adequately explain the notable differences revealed in this study between Colton and Prescott schools. Parents did have different levels of educational aspirations, and a few, whose children chronically missed school, did not make education the same priority as did others. Values alone cannot account for all the variation observed between the upper-middle-class and working-class, nor can the differences in family–school relationships be attributed to the educational institutions alone.

The pattern of parent involvement (or lack thereof) provides testimony, I would argue, to the enduring power of social class in American society.

Researchers presume (incorrectly) that once parents are taught the importance of being involved in their children's education, all parents would have an equal chance to participate in ways teachers would approve. But, as I have indicated throughout, social class — specifically, education, occupational status, income, and the characteristics of work — provides parents with unequal *resources* and dispositions, differences that critically affect parental involvement in the educational experience of their children.

First, as discussed in Chapter Six, upper-middle-class parents have the capacity to understand the diagnostic and instructional language used by teachers, or, more generally, the *competence* to help their children in school. Most of the time, these parents could easily handle the material their children were learning in school. When Prescott parents were not familiar with a particular task (for example, Carol's mother did not know that what she called 'borrowing' in subtraction was now called 'regrouping'), they had the requisite skills to learn it. With low achievers, parents sometimes had to learn a good deal. One upper-middle-class mother complained that she felt like a 'fish out of water' as she began talking to tutors about an auditory reading approach (in contrast to a visual reading approach) and the various types of learning disabilities affecting her child. Yet, even when they did not immediately recognize and understand specific terms, upper-middle-class parents were still bolstered by their schooling. A college education provided them with the confidence that they were capable of understanding teachers. As college graduates, they gained symbolic access to the world of educated people and thereby to the world of education itself. Parents with only a high school education had neither these educational resources nor the expectation that they could be acquired. Colton parents complained about the 'big words' teachers used. Some left parent–teacher conferences confused. They could not understand what the teacher was saying, or felt they could not, which in turn influenced their willingness to engage teachers in routine interaction.

Second, social status itself also provided a resource. Upper-middle-class parents approached teachers as social equals, and in some cases parents were actually from higher status positions. Their occupational success led most Prescott parents to believe that they were capable of being school teachers themselves but simply had not chosen to. Few Prescott fathers and mothers were, therefore, intimidated by teachers and social status provided them with *confidence*, as well as competence, in the educational setting. By contrast, working-class parents looked up to teachers. They saw, quite correctly, a social gulf between themselves and 'educated people'. Working-class parents talked, sometimes with awe in their voices, of people they had known who were 'brains' or 'walking encyclopedias'. As high school graduates (or drop-outs) who had never been to a college, the working-class parents felt keenly their lack of social standing and educational training in their visits with teachers (Sennett and Cobb 1972).

Parents' education and social status in turn influenced their belief in their proper role in schooling, especially their right and responsibility to take a leadership role in education. Working-class parents found it a struggle to deal with fractions and pre-school readers — how could they take a leadership role in schooling? They felt they had no choice but to depend on the school and defer to the professional expertise of teachers. In fact, working-class parents expressed a belief in the classic notion that a professional (Hughes 1963) possesses a 'backstage' of professional expertise and belongs to a professional association responsible for self-regulation. They had neither the confidence nor the competence to criticize the actions of teachers (or other professionals).

Third, *income and material resources* also played a role in facilitating family–school relationships. Mothers with other young children at home needed child care and transportation to attend school events. For upper-middle-class parents, of course, this was seldom a problem. Almost all Prescott families had paid house cleaners and two cars. Transportation problems and money problems were a constant strain at Colton. Prescott parents frequently bought casual gifts for their children, sometimes simply because they were out shopping. Many of the parents at Colton did their shopping at the flea market, and new books and coloring materials for their children were special events.

Fourth, there were indications that the style, routine, and purpose of parents' *work* affected family–school relationships in important ways. As discussed in Chapter Six, occupations place different demands on workers regarding the amount of connectedness required between work and family life. Upper-middle-class workers appear to have a pattern of interconnectedness between work and home, while working-class workers have a pattern of separation between the two spheres.[3]

These differences in work-home connections shaped family–school relationships. Work–family connections of many upper-middle-class jobs mirror teachers' preferred school–family relationship much more closely than the work–family connections in the working class. For example, upper-middle-class jobs give employees a vision of work — as a diffuse, round-the-clock experience taking place at home *and* at the work place — which is similar to the vision held by teachers. Parents, particularly fathers, provide role models for children, as they labor at home in the evening and on weekends. Parents also embrace a notion of children's school work as legitimately taking place in the home on a regular basis. Working-class jobs provide a different vision of work—as discrete, time-limited, and taking place only at the work site. Workers holding these positions have less experience and less enthusiasm for work taking place at home on a sustained and regular basis. This conflicts with the teachers' vision of children's school work as well as teachers' own diffuse work experience. Corporations' expectations that upper-middle-class wives will be involved in their husbands' careers also are similar to teachers' expectations for parents' involvement in school. There is not a similar quasi-occupational role for working-class wives in their husbands' careers, nor do they embrace such a role in their children's school careers.

Finally, *networks*, themselves linked to social class position, provide parents with different amounts of general information about schooling. Upper-middle-class parents had teachers, resource specialists, principals, counselors, and special education teachers among their aunts, uncles, sisters-in-law, grandparents, friends, and neighbors. By contrast, working-class parents had gas station attendants, carpenters, convenience store salespersons, janitors, factory workers, and policemen among their relatives and neighbors. A few working-class parents did have relatives who were upwardly mobile and attended college, but often these relatives were geographically removed as well as socially distant and were not a frequent or reliable source of insight and information. Moreover, upper-middle-class jobs often carry informal demands for socializing with co-workers and business associates; through these relationships upper-middle-class parents are drawn into tighter connections with other parents and educators than are working-class parents, and they are more closely aware of the ever-changing standards of institutions.

Without any occupational pressure to socialize with colleagues, working-class people build their social lives around their kinship groups. Colton parents had frequent — weekly and often daily — contact with their parents, siblings, and cousins. These relatives provided other forms of support but they could not share details about teachers or practices in the school community. By contrast, upper-middle-class parents were more likely to have relocated for their careers and were further away from kinship groups. Even when living in the same area, Prescott mothers spent less time with their relatives than did Colton mothers. Instead of spending time with their relatives, Prescott families spent social time with neighbors, other parents from Prescott school, and co-workers. Many Prescott mothers counted other Prescott mothers among their best friends and they also met one another when they enrolled their children in lessons and formal activities outside of school. As other researchers have shown, these organized lessons are rare in working-class communities (Medrich et al. 1982).[4]

These social networks mediated parents' connections to the school. It was through their connections with other Prescott parents that they learned, for example, of Mrs Hoffman's reputation as a 'Hitler,' Mrs Walters' reputation as a terrible teacher, the criteria for getting children into the gifted program, and the problems parents had in pressing their case with the principal, Mrs Harpst. Prescott parents had, then, sources of information and advice not available to even the most active of Colton parents. These resources were particularly valuable when children were in academic trouble.

I would maintain that higher social class provides parents with more resources to intervene in schooling and to bind families into tighter connections with social institutions than are available to working-class families. Of course, parents sometimes had resources that they did not use. There is, also, evidence in the literature of working-class parents overcoming their lack of resources and building interconnections with schools despite their relatively lower education, social standing, and informational resources (Clark 1983). Even then, the relations do not appear to be as intensive as in upper-middle-class families. Parents do not begin their family–school relationships from the same or equal starting points. The standard belief in the desirability of parent involvement rests on certain hidden pre-conditions. It was easier for upper-middle-class parents to comply with teachers' requests than for parents at a lower position in the social stratification system. Moreover, while virtually uniform across the two schools, teachers' requests have varied across historical periods. Educators have always wanted parents to be supportive of schooling and to promote the best interests of children. What educators mean by this, however, has varied through time.

Institutional Standards

In 1948, a distinguished sociologist said that low academic performance of working-class children was linked to the 'permissive' child rearing practices of their parents. He and his colleagues found middle-class children had more 'restrictive' child rearing environments which, they asserted, improved their academic performance (Davis 1948). Two decades later, parents' child rearing practices apparently have changed considerably (Bronfenbrenner 1966). It is now middle-class and upper-middle-class parents who are offering a more 'permissive' environment while working-class children have the relatively 'restrictive' one. Nevertheless, upper-middle-class children continue to perform better in school than working-class children.

This change in child rearing practices demonstrates that standards for socialization in families and schools are historically specific (Aries 1962). In seventeenth century France, it was common for mothers, particularly working-class mothers, to swaddle their infants in cloth and hang them on the wall for long periods of time (Shorter 1977). Researchers have argued that in the eighteenth and early nineteenth centuries, American mothers had a much less intense emotional bond with their children, took less responsiblity for their physical and emotional protection, and had less affectionate or playful interactions than mothers in later years (Dye and Smith 1986).

Schools, too, have changed considerably and across time. For example, in the period of immigration and Taylorism, schools were organized along a factory model: long rows of desks, rigid time clocks, and 'productivity' were emphasized in schools (Cohen and Lazerson 1977); Tyack 1974). Forty years later, open classrooms, relevant curricula, and reduced lines of authority became popular in many districts (Swidler 1979). This was followed by a 'back-to-basics' curriculum that emphasizes basic educational skills. Goals for school administration have shifted routinely, including the recent emphasis on school effectiveness, with visible principal leadership and well-defined curriculum goals (National Commission on Excellence in Education 1983).

These interdependent and dynamic changes in family life and school life shape family–school relationships, including the demands teachers make of parents, and vice versa. A complete history of family–school relationships remains to be written (but see Kaestle 1978a; 1978b). All indications suggest that the current emphasis on developing cognitive skills in the home environment and parents working intensively with their children in school settings is a distinct and new development. Until two decades ago, there were few indications that teachers expected or asked parents to take on an aggressive educational role at home or that parents acted in this fashion.

Today, however, teachers across the nation want parents to provide an advantageous educational environment for children at home, to participate in school events, and generally to support teachers' efforts (Gallup 1985). As I have indicated in Chapter Two, at both Colton and Prescott schools, teachers want parents to carry out the 'four Rs': to read to their young children, to reinforce the curriculum, and to respond explicitly to teachers' requests. They also want parents to respect their professional expertise. This emphasis on parents promoting cognitive development at home has attained the position of a kind of credo in education. It is supported by virtually all professional educational organizations as well as by state and local school systems.[5] There is almost no organized opposition.

Nevertheless, information about the way in which parents can be supportive cannot be fully communicated in the current structure of interactions between parents and teachers. In most schools, parents and teachers of young children meet twice a year for twenty minutes in individual conferences. Parents also hear teachers speak at a few other formal events per year. In these brief meetings, teachers cannot, and do not, provide parents with all the relevant information for involvement; although they may feel they have done so. For example, teachers do not give parents the titles of the fifty to one hundred books they would like parents to read with their children during the school year, nor do they tell parents how to handle difficulties that frequently emerge when parents attempt to work with their children at home (e.g., what to do when children stumble over words, anounce that they do not know a word, or read haltingly or too fast). Furthermore, teachers rarely initiate discussions on how parents should handle the way children squirm, whine, plead to stop, or tell the parent that they are 'doing it wrong' in order to resist the extra work the parents want them to do.

Teachers often do not volunteer that schools allow parents to engage in actions that are not officially sanctioned. Although not told formally they could do so by teachers, Prescott parents requested — sometimes successfully — that their children be placed in the gifted program, be tested for a learning disability, be assigned to a teacher with a good reputation, or be given individualized homework packets on the weekends.

In sum, schools have historically specific standards for parent involvement which are only partially explained by educators (although Colton and Prescott were almost identical in the amount of information teachers shared with parents). Because of this, the informal networks in families' lives — friends, relatives, co-workers — play a critical role as supplemental sources of information. As shown above, these networks are relatively homogenous by social class. The well-meaning advice parents receive differs in how closely it is aligned with the standards of professionals.

A Home Advantage

In an article on mate selection in a French village, Bourdieu (1976) suggests that social stratification is like a card game. Social outcomes are the combined result of the quality of the cards one is dealt and the skill with which they are played. In the contest of advancing their children's education, Colton parents were dealt inferior cards compared to Prescott parents. Some of the Colton parents were skillful players but, given their hand, their outcome was poor. Conversely, some Prescott parents had good cards but, for a variety of reasons, did not play them as shrewdly as other parents.

Social stratification systems (and card games) operate under rules. Gatekeeping institutions — notably schools — have admission standards and performance criteria which individuals must meet to get ahead. The failure to meet these educational standards prevents individuals from attaining elite positions. Educational performance remains strongly linked to occupational success (Hout 1988). One can quarrel with the degree to which admission and performance standards reflect the interests of the dominant class, but it is difficult to argue that the standards are neutral. Institutions' standards are selected from among many possibilities. These standards have pre-conditions for compliance — pre-conditions which are often invisible until subjected to close scrutiny.

As I have shown, social class offered parents, and ultimately children, an advantage in discovering and complying with these standards. It facilitated — or impeded — parents' educational involvement in terms of the amount of work they did with children at home, the kind of work they did at home, and the interpretation they made of why they attended school events. Most importantly, social class position largely excluded working-class parents from taking a leadership role in education and gave upper-middle-class parents the opportunity to take such a role (if they wanted to). Class position particularly affected the likelihood that parents would supervise and/or try to control educators. When parents complied with teachers' wishes, and took an active role in their children's education, positive results often emerged. Conversely, teachers felt that parents' failure to read regularly to children at home could lead children to repeat a grade unnecessarily. Parent involvement could, and sometimes did, become destructive and increase the stress placed on children. Overall, however, there are signs that higher social class provides resources which parents can draw on to help their children excel in school. Social class gave children a home advantage.

Class Cultures and Cultural Capital

In the last decade, the concept of 'cultural capital' has emerged to help explain the relationship between social position and educational success. Developed by Bourdieu, the concept usually is defined as high status cultural resources which influence social selection (Bourdieu 1977a; 1977b; Bourdieu and Passeron 1977). According to this view, possessing key cultural resources provides social advantages, facilitating the inclusion in (and exclusion from) high status positions. Bourdieu has built his case primarily on French society, showing how participation in high status cultural events is powerfully influenced by class (Bourdieu 1977a; 1984), and the ways in which culture penetrates the details of everyday life, providing tastes in furniture, glassware, and home decorations, as well as the capacity to understand and appreciate certain central cultural experiences (for a discussion see Lamont and Lareau 1988). Empirical investigations of the role of cultural capital in the U.S. have increased in recent years. Not all studies have shown a significant effect (Robinson and Garnier 1985), but most studies, particularly by DiMaggio and colleagues (DiMaggio 1982; DiMaggio and Mohr 1985), have generally shown the concept of cultural capital to be helpful in improving explanations of school grades and marital choice. In these areas, gender does appear to mediate the influence of cultural capital on outcomes (DiMaggio and Mohr 1985).

The concept of cultural capital has the potential to produce significant improvements in conceptual models of the linkages between social structure and individual biography (Lamont and Lareau 1988). It retains a notion of individual variability: while individuals possess capital, they must 'invest' these class resources to yield social profits. Privilege associated with class does not automatically yield benefits, for individuals must 'activate' those resources. This approach is an improvement over existing models, which often posit an association between class position and behavior without addressing the notion of human agency or the pattern of internal variation within social classes. The concept also holds the ideas of social structure, classes, and structured inequality which are frequently missing from micro-level studies of social interaction by sociologists and anthropologists (Heath 1983; Erickson and Mohatt 1982; Cook-Gumperez 1986). By highlighting the intersection between social structure and biography, cultural capital has the potential to provide a conceptual bridge (Duster 1981) as sociologists move between 'macro' and 'micro' levels of analysis (Collins 1981b; 1987; 1988).

In this study, the concept of cultural capital illuminates why social class has such an important influence on family–school linkages. In these two schools, parents were not drawing on high status cultural resources — such as taste in classical music or impressionist art — but they were drawing on cultural resources linked to social class. The study suggests that key elements of class cultures become forms of cultural capital because they give parents a pool of resources which they can activate. Through this activation, parents try to bring their children into compliance with the performance standards of educational institutions. The concept of cultural capital significantly expands the current explanations of class differences in parent involvement, notably the emphasis on individual aspirations and institutional discrimination.

The study also highlights dimensions of cultural capital worthy of modification. As I have suggested, the potential of the concept has remained unfulfilled. At the theoretical level, Bourdiew conceives of cultural capital as referring to the process through which individuals realize advantages from their habitus—the dispositions acquired in their socialization process. In his empirical work, however, Bourdieu has not clearly demonstrated the micro-level social interactional process through which dispositions·become activated into capital and function to realize a social profit. Instead, he has either drawn on the socio-linguistic works of Basil Bernstein that show differences in language use in the classroom (Bernstein 1972; 1975; 1982), or, as in his works with Passeron, he has described patterns of cultural consumption or social class differences in educational performance in France. The empirical process through which initial dispositions translate into educational profits has been left unclear.[6]

This problem has also surfaced as others have incorporated the concept of cultural capital into different theoretical systems, particularly models of status attainment (DiMaggio and Mohr 1985; Teachman 1987). These studies have suggested that one can measure how much cultural capital a person has by assessing his or her high status cultural resources. Hence, persons who attend boarding schools where they are exposed to classical music, fine arts, and other elements of an elite education are referred to as having a large amount of cultural capital (Cookson and Persell 1985). Similarly, DiMaggio (1982) creates a scale measuring individuals' exposure to certain types of art and other elements of high culture. He then systematically evaluates how much cultural capital individuals hold and the association between cultural capital and social success. Such work on cultural capital, however, confuses *possession* of cultural resources with *actually realizing a social advantage* from these cultural resources. Members of the same social class may possess similar cultural resources but may not use them (or need to use them) to gain educational and occupational advantages. The transformation of cultural resources into activated cultural capital has frequently been glossed over in the literature.

This particular study of family—school relationships is a preliminary step towards unraveling the process whereby individuals transform cultural capital into social profit. In Prescott and Colton schools parents did not invest their cultural resources at every moment or in every circumstance to gain advantages for their children. For example, in the upper-middle-class community of Prescott, the Svenssons were satisfied with their son Ross's progress in school. They read to him at night and attended school events, but they did not activate many of the other resources at their disposal. Given their education, income, and social networks, they were aware of other actions they might have taken, but they did not feel such intervention was necessary in view of his level of school performance. With their daughter Emily, however, they felt differently. They requested special teachers, hired tutors, had professionals evaluate her, wrote letters to the principal, and discussed her learning problems with a sister-in-law (who was a teacher) and with other relatives and friends. Possession of high status cultural resources does not therefore *automatically* lead to a social investment. Rather these cultural resources must be effectively activated by individuals, in and through their own actions and decisions.

Not everyone activates resources in the same way, and the variations are not only class-determined. Within social classes, parents play out their resources with different degrees of shrewdness. Parents with roughly similar social class resources (or in Bourdieu's terms, 'habitus') used their resources differently. For example, while many Prescott mothers volunteered in the classroom and all attended parent–teacher conferences, parents differed considerably in how much they actually gained from these interactions. Some, for instance, used their classroom observations as a way to gain additional information about their children's performance, but others did not. Similarly, some Prescott parents were better than others at intervening in schooling and getting teachers to do things that they did not want to do. Allen's mother, for example, used her volunteer time in the classroom to look at math packets, comparing her son's work with that of his classmates. She also managed, at least the first year, to convince Mrs Walters to send home additional math packets, despite Mrs Walters' explicit policy against homework in first grade. Another upper-middle-class mother, Mrs Roy, reported 'giving up' when Mrs Walters didn't send home extra math packets as they had discussed. As a result, Allen did extra classroom math assignments while Jonathan, a poorer student, did not.

Even when Prescott parents invested social resources in similar ways, they realized different profits, depending on the context. Mrs Roy read to Jonathan diligently, helped him with his math, visited the school, and worked with the teacher. During second grade, he went from a non-reader to a grade level reader. Mrs Svensson did all of this and more, yet her daughter Emily was still not reading at the end of second grade. Just as in the economic world, where investments that look certain sometimes fail to yield expected returns, families' activation of cultural resources did not guarantee educational success.

These findings support the importance of rethinking the concept of cultural capital and, in particular, of clarifying the stages by and through which resources are activated. Demonstrating that people possess highly valued cultural resources is only part of the story. It fails to reveal which cultural resources individuals use when and with what effect or, put differently, how cultural resources are transformed into cultural capital. What is needed is a more contextually based analysis of the stages of cultural transformation in the educational process. There are cultural resources which are difficult for individuals to control — an accent, for example, unwittingly reveals social class position in many societies. In general, family cultural resources are concretely and contingently activated into cultural capital within and across institutional settings. Indeed, this analysis suggests strongly the importance of moving beyond the current efforts at showing the association between dispositions and profits. A better approach is to posit a three-part process: a) the possession of cultural resources (or dispositions or habitus), b) the activation and investment of these cultural resources, and c) the attainment of social profits from these investments. In their discussion of cultural capital, researchers need to distinguish between 'activated' and 'unactivated' cultural capital.

The concept of cultural capital has the potential to show how individual biography intersects with social structure, a potential that theoretical and empirical work must take advantage of. Researchers need to be able to explain why art consumption arranged by the family should lead to higher grades in school or why the presence of an encyclopedia in the home should shift college aspirations. Without a focus on the activation of cultural resources, much of the analytic power of the concept is missed. To exploit the concept, a key priority will be to expand the focus to include the standards for advancement in an institution and the way in which individuals activate cultural capital to gain social profits. The restriction of these cultural resources to certain groups in the society should also receive more study. Without knowledge of the specific social context, it does not make sense to say that a person is rich (or poor) in cultural capital. In seeking intense family–school relationships, Prescott and Colton educators built heavily on some cultural experiences (e.g., parents reading to children at home) and were relatively indifferent to others (e.g., the furnishings at home, parents' taste in music). The advantages provided by the cultural resources depended in part, therefore, on institutional definitions of what was important.

Moreover, the value of activating cultural resources varies with time. Cultural resources are not equally valuable at every moment throughout a year. For example, parents' steps to ensure that their children complete college applications on time would be valuable before the specific deadlines; after the deadlines the potential profit of parents' action drops. The research on cultural capital has yet to come to grips with social change. Standards within institutions change, and the potential profit from employing a social resource also shifts.

Educational Policy Implications

While social scientists pursue theoretical issues, educators are primarily interested in improving performance. As they struggle to raise test scores of their students, the goal of understanding how social structural patterns shape behavior has a lower priority. This study does have policy implications for schools' efforts to increase parent involvement, but educators might also rethink the goals of parent programs. Parents' attendance at school appears to have a strong symbolic component, particularly when children are performing at average or above average levels. At Open Houses and other ritualized events, some information is exchanged, but often the events are not individualized and they are relatively content-free. Teachers interpret parents' attendance at these school events as evidence that parents value educational success, appreciate the actions of teachers, and respect teachers as professionals (Lortie 1977; Lareau forthcoming). Educators might do better to seek recognition and respect from avenues other than parents' nights, including, of course, making changes in the organization of their profession and demanding better compensation.

Teachers who are determined to try to raise parent involvement in schooling find the lower participation rates of working-class and lower-class families disturbing, as we have seen. This study's findings suggest that these teachers should, first, recognize that there are real obstacles to some parents' participation in school, and, second, seek to diversify their strategies for educational support. At Colton, for example, Mr and Mrs Morris almost never read to Tommy, but his fourth grade sister read to him almost every night. Parents often lack sufficient skills and it is foolhardy for teachers either to ignore this lack of competence or to insist that parents upgrade their skills. A better approach is to suggest that parents arrange for others, particularly older siblings, cousins, or neighborhood children to provide help. They might encourage parents to ritualize these experiences, as when cousins read together every Sunday after church, siblings read before bed on Wednesday nights, or children read every afternoon for twenty minutes with the baby-sitter.

In addition, there is persuasive evidence that working-class parents take grades seriously, placing more emphasis on good grades than on having their children 'understand how and why things happen' (often a priority in upper-middle-class homes) (Kohn 1977). Some Colton parents, for instance, who saw only colored stickers and praise on their children's papers, did not realize that their children were not keeping up with their peers in first grade. Colton parents saw grades on papers and on report cards as one of the most important sources of information. They did not understand that these grades did not show children's ranking within the class, nor did they understand the broader curricular goals behind assignments.

Therefore teachers in working-class schools should make children's grades the cornerstone of their program to involve parents in schooling. They might give out report cards only in parent–teacher conferences, give children a separate grade for how much work they do at home, or provide grades on classroom papers which reflect children's place in the class or age group. More importantly, teachers should always connect their comments to parents directly to the goal of improving children's grades, rather than, for example, to the broader curricular goal of improving reading comprehension. Teachers interested in giving children primarily positive feedback or fostering a cooperative rather than a competitive spirit in their classrooms might find this emphasis on grades distasteful, but research shows that rather than focusing on the intrinsic merit of the educational experience, working-class parents stress the importance of children complying with the standards of external authority (Kohn 1977; Kohn and Schooler 1983).

Social class also influences social networks, something that teachers might take heed of as they try to build parent involvement programs. There is ample evidence of strong ties within kinship groups in working-class and lower-class families, particularly black families. Upper-middle-class parents are more likely to have strong connections with other parents, particularly the parents they encounter as they enroll their children in a wide array of formal lessons. Currently, many teachers make their appeals for parent volunteers in newsletters or at school events, but the response rate is often disappointing. They might try a snowball approach to recruiting classroom volunteers by asking mothers to bring in another relative. Recruiting parent involvement in schooling through existing social networks, including kinship ties, church, soccer teams, or a

Tupperware party may increase educational participation. Given the existing burdens on teachers, it would be important for districts to provide funds to hire a community–school liaison to carry out this outreach. The organizational constraint here, however, is that kinship groups are unlikely to share the same classroom teacher. Since they may share the same district, however, parent involvement programs would need to be coordinated and promoted at the district as well as the classroom level.

The study also highlights the unequal access of parents to supplemental and informal information about education. Working-class people have fewer contacts with educated people who can provide them with helpful hints, suggestions, or information about how schools work.[7] The usual semi-annual conferences are inadequate for giving parents this information without the use of other avenues. Providing parent 'mentors', asking parents to share information with other parents, running newspaper, radio, and television advertisements, and distributing leaflets are possibilities that should be explored.

Finally, Epstein (1987) has shown that some teachers are 'leaders' and appear to be more interested in (and more talented at) recruiting parent involvement in schooling that others. These teacher–leaders could, as Epstein suggests, play a leadership role in training their colleagues. Administrators might also, however, place teacher–leaders in grades where parent involvement is felt to be particularly important (i.e., first grade) and provide additional compensation to these leaders (either in money or release time) for their work.

Social Structure, History, and Biography

In *The Sociological Imagination*, C. Wright Mills asserts that:

> Social science deals with problems of biography, of history, and of their intersection within social structure ... These three — biography, history, society — are the co-ordinate points of the proper study of [humans] (Mills, 1959, p. 143).

The study of social class differences in the connections among social institutions is, as I have maintained, one such juncture of biography, history, and social structure worthy of our attention. Although this analysis has focused on family–school linkages, there are signs that the study of these linkages between families and other social institutions (i.e., economic, legal, and health care) also holds promise. For example, we know that the social networks available to individuals vary by social class. These networks probably provide different levels of informal information which, in turn, supplements the knowledge acquired in formal interactions with professionals. Upper-middle-class persons can turn to friends and relatives who work as doctors, lawyers, and social workers for 'inside information' about the inner workings of bureaucracies. These informational resources are important because organizations inevitably give clients incomplete information. By contrast, working-class persons rarely have access to this kind of information from persons in powerful positions.

Second, the standards of institutions are always changing. Bronfenbrenner (1966), among others, noted that 'segments of society' had differential access to the 'agents of change':

> Child rearing practices are likely to change most quickly in those segments of society which have closest access and are most receptive to the agencies or agents of change (e.g., public media, clinics, physicians, and counselors) (Bronfenbrenner 1966, p. 376).

When schools change their ways of teaching math or grammar, working-class parents are likely to find out later than those whose relatives and friends work in the school system. Upper-middle-class families also have a better chance of learning the latest standards of admission to medical school, computer science departments, and management trainee programs than their working-class counterparts. Upper-middle-class parents can effectively use this information to help their children in their school and work careers.

Third, even if parents are well-informed about the latest standards, social class provides parents with different resources to comply with these standards. Parents may know that the way to get an arrest charge dropped is to hire a good lawyer, or that if college students aren't employed they may do better in school, but — despite this information — parents may be unable to provide these opportunities for their children.

Fourth, and perhaps most subtle, class influences the resources parents have available to circumvent and challenge social institutions. For example, most upper-middle-class children are accepted by colleges because they comply with the standards of application; they apply on time, they submit relatively well-written essays, and they apply to colleges that are likely to accept them. Occasionally, however, upper-middle-class parents will appeal decisions by admission boards or (through informal networks) circumvent standard organizational procedures. It is difficult to know how often families break the rules or pull strings for their children. Flagrant violations of organizational standards (as when parents buy their children's admission to college) do not appear to be routine. However, more modest challenges, as when parents request a particular teacher (despite school rules discouraging teacher requests), ask that their children be assigned to a particular probation officer, or threaten to hire lawyers to press their complaints, probably are. Once again, social class influences this process, in part because of the different levels of information and economic resources at the family's disposal.[8]

Guided by an individualistic analysis, sociologists have found social class differences in organizational outcomes — in the health care system, the legal system, the work place, and the higher education system — but have often failed to provide convincing documentation of social class differences in social processes. There are, however, folk terms for the advantages of class here: people

183

'know how to work the system', 'have connections', or know people who can 'cut red tape'.

Some of these folk explanations, particularly among working-class families, appear to exaggerate the importance of social networks on organizational outcomes. Some working-class and lower-class individuals believe, for example, that simply having a social relationship with a judge, lawyer, or college professor means that a person 'has it made' and the friend will exert influence on the other's behalf and 'fix' the outcome. Upper-middle-class individuals may be tempted to dismiss these conspiracy theories as paranoid delusions or as an insult to moral and professional obligations. In fact, outright violations of organizational rules appear to be rare, but professionals can and do provide their friends with inside information about the best way to frame a complaint, as well as the best person to apply to. Informal information about the proper timing of a protest, the proper office, and the proper questions to ask can make a difference to the outcome. It is these kinds of informal information and linkages between families and social institutions that need to be studied. Working-class families are probably correct in their estimation that they are excluded from many social institutions, but they may be wrong about the exact ways in which they are penalized. Consequently, documenting the separation or interconnections between families and other institutions may provide a new vantage point for old questions in sociology.

This analysis of connections among families and other social institutions can also improve our conceptual models. Sociologists have been haunted by the determinacy (and indeterminacy) of ascribed status in shaping social outcomes. It is this mixture of certainty and uncertainty which has proven so difficult to address. We know that, overall, ascribed status influences the probability of individuals' achievement, but it is hard to show how and why some people don't follow the class-biased pattern.

In earlier historical periods most adults were farmers, and parents were able to pass on physical capital to at least some of their children. The number of farmers is now a very small proportion of the population, and educational credentials have taken on a critical role in ultimate occupational attainment. In American society, occupational status shapes key parameters of life, including access to health insurance and, by virtue of the type of neighborhood one can afford to live in, vulnerability to crime.

Parents are aware of the stakes — that education shapes their children's work careers and, ultimately, their lives — and the uncertainty in the system. Upper-middle-class parents, including Prescott parents, do not rest on the certainty that they will be able to pass on their class position to their children, nor do working-class parents, such as those at Colton, feel that their fate is sealed. Rather they see the schools as gatekeeping institutions where children's access to social goods will be heavily determined. Parents in both schools worked to support their children's educational success. As I have shown, however, parents had very different ideas about what it meant to be supportive and developed different levels of connections with schools. Even as early as second grade, the children's positions in the educational system seemed destined to re-create — rather than challenge — the social position of their own parents. Focusing on social class differences in family–school linkages thus provides a unique vantage point for viewing the unfolding of the stratification system.

Notes

1. In addition, researchers have usually studied these linkages by measuring the frequency of contacts. This fails to capture the existing, but inactivated, connections between individuals and gatekeeping institutions.
2. Many researchers pay lip service to the idea of family–school linkages and assert that they are, in fact, studying these home–school connections. These protests notwithstanding, few studies actually conceptualize or study inter-institutional connections. As noted earlier, researchers tend to study an incomplete list of connections — focusing on parents' compliance with teachers' requests and ignoring parents' actions which challenge and circumvent school norms. Other researchers focus heavily on the alleged benefits of parents' actions; adopting the perspective of the organization, they seek to document the benefits of compliance. This, of course, misses the possible negative consequences of compliance. Few studies examine variations in the linkages between parents and institutions; most, as noted above, focus on the dynamics within the institution. The concept of linkage — as in a well-traveled road or a small path — is not developed in the literature.
3. Ironically, although working-class jobs offer little independence for workers at the site, they provide more freedom for workers in their time at home, for formation of social networks, and gender roles. Work continues to have a central impact on the quality of family life for both working-class and upper-middle-class families, especially as protection against the disruptive effects of unemployment. In addition, some working-class men attempt to compensate for their relative lack of autonomy at work with positional authority demands at home (Rubin 1976).

    On the other hand, among upper-middle-class men in corporations who move from community to community for promotions, occupations place severe constraints on family life and bind family members and corporate demands into a tighter and tighter circle of interaction (Margolis 1979). Work is a central feature in the lives of all families, but upper-middle-class and working-class jobs appear to offer different levels of inter-institutional linkages.
4. Social class differences in family life also shaped family–school relations. Upper-middle-class couples adopted less rigid gender roles than working-class couples. Because of this Prescott fathers were more likely to attend parent–teacher conferences. Working-class parents saw that as the mother's role. Teachers in both schools were very impressed by the presence of a father in the school grounds; in some cases it appeared to raise teachers' expectations for academic performance.
5. Educational systems, while formally local, are increasingly shaped by national forces, including social science research, national professional organizations, textbook companies, and an increasing federal role in the definition of educational issues (Cohen 1978).
6. Conceptualizations of cultural capital also usually embody a rather vague image of the class structure of society, frequently leaving the origins and contours of the class structure ambiguous. For example, Bourdieu is preoccupied with the distribution of 'high culture' within elites and the conflicts within these groups. He also suggests that some members of the society are dominant and others are dominated by 'symbolic violence.' But it is clear that he does not primarily define classes in relationship to the means of production. In his empirical work, the professional middle-class is the dominant group (i.e., wealthy in

cultural capital) and the French working-class is the dominated group (i.e., deficient in cultural capital). As DiMaggio notes (1979), Bourdieu offers a materialist, albeit non-Marxist, analysis of social relations.

7. For example, working-class parents need detailed information about strategies for handling their children's resistance to doing school work at home, as well as other routine problems that emerge when parents try to convert home life into schooling.

8. As researchers take up ways of specifying the processes which produce cultural capital, a key task will be to illuminate the way in which organizations and professions produce standards. Studies of organizations, professions, and social cultures will be helpful in tracing the historical processes through which professionals embrace, enact and then discard various standards of operation.

Appendix
Common Problems in Field Work:
A Personal Essay

In his appendix to *Streetcorner Society*, William Foote Whyte describes why twelve years after his book was originally published he decided to write a detailed portrait of how he did his famous study. He reports that he was teaching a methods course and had trouble finding 'realistic descriptions' of the fieldwork process:

> It seemed as if the academic world had imposed a conspiracy of silence regarding the personal experiences of field workers. In most cases, the authors who had given any attention to their research methods had provided fragmentary information or had written what appeared to be a statement of the methods the field worker would have used if he had known what he was going to come out with when he entered the field. It was impossible to find realistic accounts that revealed the errors and confusions and the personal involvement that a field worker must experience (Whyte 1981, p. 359).

Three decades later the problem remains: realistic descriptions of how research data are collected are unusual. Most studies by sociologists who use qualitative methods devote a short section to the research methodology: they describe the number of respondents, the selection of the sample, and general procedures for data collection. But, as Whyte complained, these studies — some of which are exemplary works — rarely portray the process by which the research was actually done, nor do they give insight into the traps, delays, and frustrations which inevitably accompany field work (but see Walford 1987).

This lack of realistic portraits is a problem, for they are not simply to assuage readers' desires for more personal information about the author, or to get — for those of us with more malicious inclinations — 'the dirt' on a project. Rather, they give qualitative researchers a formal avenue for reporting how they proceeded with data collection and analysis. Without these details, it is hard to tell when researchers did an exemplary job in the data collection and analysis and when they did a 'quick and dirty' job. It is agreed, of course, that one should establish a rapport with one's respondents, be sensitive to the field setting, take comprehensive field notes, analyze your data carefully, and write it up in a lively and accurate fashion. What that actually means, and what researchers actually do, is often anybody's guess. Most studies do not reveal their inner-workings, and good writing can cover up awkwardly collected and poorly documented field work.

In his appendix Whyte chose to do his 'bit to fill this gap' (1981, p. 359), and in this appendix I have decided to do my bit as well. One of the biggest problems is that this entails writing up my mistakes as well as my successes. In most lines of work, including teaching, almost everyone is forced to admit to having made mistakes from time to time. But admitting mistakes in field work seems more difficult. Partly, this is because we often have an overly romantic notion of field work, which emphasizes the glory of 'going native' and glosses over the difficulties and problems of the endeavor. The implicit message is that mistakes are rare. Partly, this reluctance is an artifact of a scholarly tradition in which a public discussion of 'inner-workings' is considered unseemly and unnecessary. Finally, admitting to mistakes in fieldwork raises questions about the quality of the body of the research and the conclusions drawn from it. Given these considerations, it is hardly surprising that so little has been written about actual experiences in the field. Likewise, it is clear that all of us who are engaged in qualitative research could greatly benefit from a more frank sharing of our experiences.

My project has strengths as well as weaknesses. There are parts of the data set in which I am fully confident and parts which I think are considerably weaker. This assessment is implied in the way in which the work is written up, but in my view it is worth making this more explicit. So, in a fit of immodesty as well as honesty, I provide my own assessment of the strengths of the project, and I identify my successes as well as failings as a researcher.

This appendix consists of two parts. In Part I, I review the background for the study, access and entrance to Colton and Prescott, my role in the classroom, the selection of families, the interviews, and my assessment of the major mistakes I made in the research. I also briefly summarize the logistics of data analysis. In Part II, I turn to the development of the conceptual model and my struggle to formulate the research question.

It is my hope that readers will find this 'exposé' of a research project useful, not only for gaining insight into this particular study but for detailed examples of how to cope with common problems in field research. As I bumped about in the field not knowing what I was doing I often felt — incorrectly, as it turned out — that I was making a terrible mess of things, that my project was doomed, and that I should give up the entire enterprise immediately. This negativism came from my persistent feeling that, despite my having had a research question when I started, I didn't truly know what I was doing there. In part, my gloom signaled the continuing struggle to clarify the intellectual goals of the project.

As I have discovered, using qualitative methods means learning to live with uncertainty, ambiguity, and confusion, sometimes for weeks at a time. It also means carving a path by making many decisions, with only the vaguest guide-posts and no one to give you gold stars and good grades along the way. It has its rewards. Yet, there were times in the field that I would have killed for an inviolable rule to follow — an SPSSX command to punch into the computer and let the results spill out. I found it exhausting, as well as exhilarating, to be constantly trying to figure out what to do next. It is unlikely that qualitative work will ever have specific research rules to punch into a computer, but it can — and in my opinion should — offer novice researchers more concrete guidance on matters of data collection, data analysis, and the writing up of qualitative work. This appendix is one, small contribution toward that process.

Part I: The Method of Home Advantage

Personal Background

I grew up in a white, upper-middle-class family; my father and mother worked as school teachers.[1] When I was in college, I spent three months in a small, predominantly black community in rural California, working in the schools as a teacher's aide and helping children with their homework in the evenings in their homes. After I graduated from college I thought about becoming a school teacher, and had there been jobs available I might have done so.

Instead, I got a job interviewing prisoners in City Prison for the San Francisco Pre-Trial Release Program. The program was commonly called the OR Project because it released defendants without bail on their own recognizance (OR).[2] Every day at 6.30 a.m. or at 5.00 p.m. I went inside City Prison. There, with one or two other co-workers, I made a record of who had been arrested, called them out to be interviewed, and spoke with them in the waiting room, through double-paned plastic windows and over telephones. Typically, I interviewed three to eight persons per day in the prison itself, then, in the office, I usually interviewed (by telephone) another ten or fifteen persons throughout the day. Each case needed three references — people who knew the defendant well and could verify the information collected, particularly the defendant's address, contact with relatives, and employment history. Over the course of two years, I did a lot of interviews.

The conditions for interviewing in this job were not exactly ideal. The telephones in City Prison did not work well; one or two were regularly out of order, and the ones that did work sometimes had static, so conversations were often conducted in a shout. Another OR worker was often sitting right next to me (about one foot away) also shouting interview questions. For each interview I would talk over the telephone (through the window) to a defendant, using my right hand to plug my ear so that I could hear her/his response. Once I heard the answer, I would balance the telephone on my left shoulder, use my left hand to secure the paper, and write down the answer. Throughout the interview other defendants stared down at the scene, and bailsmen, lawyers, families, and the guard with the door keys were all within ear shot. The defendants were often in crisis: many were dazed, angry, and adjusting to City Prison.

When I finished that job, I thought (modesty aside) that I had become an outstanding interviewer. I knew, particularly in telephone interviews with the families of respondents, that I often could get people to cooperate when other interviewers failed. I also knew that my interviews were very detailed, accurate, and, despite my truly terrible handwriting (a tremendous liability in field work), were considered to be among the best in the office. From that job I developed a love of interviewing as well as a firm desire to avoid ever being arrested and put in prison.

After I quit this job, I entered graduate school at the University of California, Berkeley, where I also worked intermittently as an interviewer. The twin experiences of working for two years as a full-time interviewer and working part-time on several research projects meant that I approached the field work for this study with uneven skills. In retrospect, I believe that this background had an important influence on the quality of the data I collected. I discovered I was more comfortable as an interviewer than as a participant–observer. While the months in the classrooms provided crucial information for this study, my field notes, for a complicated set of reasons which I explain below, were not as comprehensive, focused, or useful as they should have been. The interviews were much better. I felt I had a good rapport with the mothers and fathers I interviewed and I have confidence in the validity of the results.

The fact that the interviews were tape-recorded was also a major advantage. As my research lurched from studying everything in front of me in the field setting to a specific topic, my interests in a particular interview also shifted. Had I taken notes instead of tape-recording, I am certain that the comprehensiveness of my interview notes would have varied according to which question in the field setting seized my interest at that moment.[3] Although tape recorders do introduce an effect, particularly during the initial stages of an interview, I would not plan a new research project without them. In my opinion, they provide a form of insurance on the accuracy and comprehensiveness of data collected in the face of shifting intellectual concerns.

The Beginning of the Project

The research proposal, in its original formulation, was to study social class differences in family life and the influence of these family patterns on the process of schooling and on educational performance. I had grand plans. I was going to link class differences in family–school relationships to achievement patterns. I had hoped to study three rather than two schools; interview six families in each school; and I wanted to supplement the qualitative study with a quantitative analysis of a national data set of family–school relations. Almost immediately reality began to set in. Although I still think it would have been a good idea to have had a third school that was heterogenous in students' social class, I also still think it would have been too much work. Without any real idea of where to begin, even comparing two schools seemed like two schools too many.

I did have a rough idea of what types of schools I wanted. I decided to study two specific social classes — white working-class and upper-middle-class parents. In this regard, as I note in the text, I followed in the footsteps of others in defining social class, notably Rubin (1976) and Kohn and Schooler (1983). I also wanted schools with a large number of white children to prevent the confounding influence of race. I ultimately sought two homogenous schools with a concentration of children in each of the two social classes. Since most schools in the greater Bay Area are, in fact, segregated by social class, and to a lesser extent by race, this initial focus provided hundreds of schools as possible sites. I was timid about approaching schools. I worried about why a school would ever admit me. At times simply getting in seemed insurmountable, a problem discussed extensively in the literature.[4] In the end I used a different strategy for each school.

Access and Entrance at Colton

About two years before I began, I visited Colton school (and four other schools in the district) and interviewed the principal and vice-principal as a graduate research assistant on another project. The principal investigator of that project had asked for schools with a range of students by social class and Colton was the low socio-economic school. It was considered to be one of the best run schools in the district and I liked the principal and the vice-principal. In addition the school had a large number of white working-class students, a relatively unusual pattern. After a lot of stalling, I wrote the principal a letter (which unfortunately I have lost) asking for permission to visit one first grade classroom to learn about family–school relationships. I then called him and set up a time to talk about the project with him and the vice-principal.

To my astonishment, both of these administrators were very positive. We met for about fifteen minutes in the teachers' room (they had my letter in front of them) and most of the discussion centered on choosing a teacher. They had five teachers to choose from; I left the choice to them. They recommended one of their best first grade teachers, Mrs Thompson, and I accepted their choice. I knew it would be difficult to get one of their worst teachers and there were not, at least in my mind, any compelling analytic reasons for asking for one. (In fact, I preferred to have two good teachers in schools with good leadership. If I did, indeed, find class differences in family–school relationships, I didn't want those findings commingled with and confounded by questions about the quality of the teachers or administrators.) After our brief chat, the principal and the vice-principal said they would talk to the teacher for me and suggested that I return the following week. I left the school completely elated. I felt as if I might, after all, get this project off the ground.

The next week I returned, fifteen minutes late (I forgot my map and got lost), and the vice-principal took me to the classroom, where class was in progress. After the children went out to lunch, Mrs Thompson joined me at the table in the back of the classroom where I had been sitting. My notes from this encounter are sketchy at best:

> I summarize [the] project as an effort to learn about non-school factors [influence on achievement]. She says what do you want to do next; I say just observe, and then select five children and start to interview the parents. In the meantime, though, just observe and if I can help out in any way in the classroom then I am happy to do so. I also say that I realize that it is a busy time of year (tell her my mother was a teacher for 18 years) and that if I become a burden she should feel free to tell me. We then talk about when I will come next; she doesn't know exactly when class starts (she says, 'I just listen to the bells') and so checks chart on the wall ... We determine I will come Monday at 9.04.

From our first encounter on, Mrs Thompson was extremely nice, very friendly, and always tried to be helpful. Although I would like to think it is something I did to put her at ease, I think that basically she is a very nice person who goes through life being considerate and helpful.

In what became a play within a play, Mrs Thompson and other Colton staff were very helpful with the project and, without consulting parents, provided extraordinary materials. The teachers and staff simply gave me the test scores for all of the children in the class without any concern about consent forms or parents' permission. The principal, in considering the project, did not express any concern about the burden on parents and never suggested that I clear the project with the district office. And I never asked him if this was necessary. This was a mistake because for the rest of the project I was unnecessarily worried about what would happen if the district research officer found out about it. I also needed some district statistics and finally had to call the office and ask for them, without mentioning why I needed them. In addition, the principalship changed between the first and the second year of the study; both the principal and vice-principal left. I wrote a letter to the new principal and he agreed to cooperate and to be interviewed, but he might not have. This would have been extremely costly since I was almost one-half of the way through the study. As a result, I now believe in getting the highest official's formal approval for a project early on. I think it is very wise to contact respondents through informal channels but, once having secured access, it is important to gain official approval as well. This is usually not very hard to do (after you are already in the door).

Sometimes I puzzled about why Colton teachers and administrators co-operated so easily. The principal and vice-principal were interested in the research question; all of them thought family involvement in education was important but, although it was never articulated, they mainly seemed to think that being studied was part of their job. They had other researchers before me and expected others after me so they did not seem to treat it as a 'big deal' and were unruffled, helpful, and a bit *blasé* about the entire matter.

Access and Entrance at Prescott

At Prescott it was another story. There I was not given any real difficulty but the goals of the project were closely scrutinized. The district and school administrators expressed concern about the perspective of parents and the burden on parents, but the fact that both a district official and the principal were also graduate students appeared to be helpful in ultimately securing permission. Whereas I was never even asked about consent forms at Colton, the principal at Prescott asked that I get a separate slip from the six parents giving her their permission to release test scores to me. She felt that the human subjects permission form, although important, was not specific enough to cover the release of those materials. Knowing I had consent forms for only six families, the principal would never have released the test scores for the rest of the class to me.[5]

Part of this greater formality and rigidity at Prescott may have been related to my point of contact with the school. At Prescott I went through the district office which increased the emphasis on the procedures for approval of research projects (such as consent forms). I ended up at Prescott, rather than another school, through informal networks or the 'strength of weak ties' (Granovetter 1973). When I was looking for an upper-middle-class community Charles Benson, a very helpful member of my dissertation committee, suggested I think of Prescott. One of his graduate students (whom I knew slightly) worked as a district official, and at his suggestion I called her and then wrote her a letter.

That letter is reprinted in an end note.[6] It has many problems and it is much too long. Access letters should state the problem very briefly and then summarize accurately what the officials are being asked to do. In my letter the most important part (what I was asking them to do) is buried. The content of the letter I wrote to the district official was different than what I planned to tell the teacher and principal. Given that the district official was another graduate student I felt that I somehow owed her a longer, more academic explanation, but I had planned to adopt a much more vague approach with the teacher and parents. This strategy backfired because the district official forwarded the letter I wrote to her to the principal, who in turn gave it to the classroom teacher. I was quite upset at myself for this at the time as I should have known that might be a routine procedure. The lesson from this for me is that it is foolish to think, even if you are fellow graduate students, that one person should get one version of your project (when you are requesting access) and another person should get another. It is better to draft one version suitable for everyone.

Moreover in this age of bureaucracy, unless you are lucky, you will have to write a letter formally requesting access to a site. Another end note presents an introductory letter which, given what I know today, I wish I had written.[7] It is much shorter, more direct, and it focuses primarily on what I need from the site. Respondents do not need to be told, nor are they generally interested in, the details of the intellectual goals of the project (but see Walford 1987a). They seem mainly interested in knowing how much work you are asking them to do.

I now think that before I go into the field, I need a very short and very simple explanation for what I am doing there. When I began I had a one sentence description I was comfortable with: 'I want to learn more about how families help children in school'. If the listener wanted more information, however, I floundered. My answer, inevitably long and rambling, made both the person who asked the question and me squirm. Since that time I have been bored and perplexed when a simple question to a graduate student ('What are you studying?') produced a long, ambiguous, and defensive treatise.

As a matter of politeness, many people ask researchers what they are planning to do while in the field. It is essential to have a fleshed-out response prepared well in advance. In fact, in my bossy moments, I think that no researcher should begin a field study without memorizing a jargon-free summary of her/his intentions. This will save many awkward moments, increase rapport with people in the field, and help prevent the problem of respondents feeling particularly 'on stage' when they begin to engage in the activities in which they know that you are interested. A brief, accurate, and general statement will not of itself produce good rapport, but it is a better beginning point than a long and confused one.[8]

After receiving a copy of my letter (which was a mini-paper) the principal called me. She explained that the school was concerned about overburdening parents but that she was a graduate student as well and was sensitive to problems of research. Her biggest concern seemed to be the choice of the teacher. I wanted a self-contained first grade classroom; that year Prescott had only one first grade and one split classroom. There was only one choice and that was Mrs Walters.

I don't know what the principal, Mrs Harpst, told Mrs Walters. I do know that Mrs Walters was originally reluctant to have me in her classroom. As she told me later, she was afraid I would be a 'critical presence.' She agreed to participate, however, and the principal, in another telephone exchange, told me what day to begin the field work. Consequently I entered the school without ever meeting the principal face-to-face, and although I was at school regularly I did not meet her for several weeks. The first day I appeared at school, Mrs Walters' welcome was cool. She showed me where to hang up my coat and put my purse but said very little in answer to my questions. Her aide, Mrs O'Donnell, was much warmer and bubbly. Mrs Walters told the children who I was while they were waiting in line outside the classroom. Her comments were:

> Today we have a visitor named Miss Lareau. She hasn't been in a classroom for a long time and so she wanted to visit our class and see how you work and talk and play.[9]

Mrs Walters' classroom was much smaller than Mrs Thompson's, and there was no free table at the back of the room. I felt painfully and obviously out of place that first day, as I listened to Mrs Walters talking to the children outside the classroom and watched Mrs O'Donnell work in the corner on some papers. They had not suggested where to sit or stand and I felt continually in the way. Finally, I found a chair in an empty space at the back of the classroom. When the children walked in they all stared at me intently and then walked to their seats, still staring. I was uncomfortable, Mrs Walters seemed uncomfortable, and the children seemed uncomfortable as well, although, as I explain below, they quickly adjusted to my presence.

My entrance to Prescott therefore was less smooth than at Colton for many reasons, including Mrs Walters' general discomfort at having me in the classroom, her lack of control over being selected as a research subject and, on top of that, her having been shown my overly complicated letter. I was worried that the focus on social class described in the letter might have had an important influence on Mrs Walters' behavior. She never seemed to remember what I was studying; she consistently treated me as if I were an educator studying the curriculum (which I was not) rather than someone interested in family involvement in schooling. As I noted in my field notes:

> Mrs Walters seems very interested in explaining the logic of learning activities to me. She carefully explains the bucket program and the 'hands on training' they are receiving ... This pattern, of Mrs Walters repeatedly telling me about the curriculum, makes me think that she sees me as an educator with the tools to evaluate a good or bad learning program. And/or, [it makes me think] she is worried about being evaluated.

Over time my relationship with Mrs Walters gradually warmed up. I considered the day she told me that she originally hadn't wanted me in the classroom to be a watershed. I felt that I had reached some level of acceptance but it took more time and more work than my relationship with Mrs Thompson. As I complained in my field notes, 'I often feel at a loss for words [with her].' Being somewhat shy myself, I felt ill at ease with her when we were alone together and I often seemed to fumble in my efforts to chat with her. But the aide was so friendly and got along so well with both Mrs Walters and me that, when she was there, the social interaction was quite comfortable and pleasant. During recess the three of us would go get a cup of coffee and visit together. When the aide was not there (in the afternoon or when she was sick) relations between Mrs Walters and me were much more formal. Like some older married couples, Mrs Walters and I both seemed to be more comfortable in the classroom with the children between us than trying to negotiate socializing together in a quiet classroom. At first I almost dreaded recess and lunch time with Mrs Walters, and I felt that I truly did not know what to do with myself. If Mrs Walters was doing an errand my choices were to sit in the classroom (which I felt self-conscious about since I never saw any aides or teachers do this), sit in the teachers' room (where I didn't know any of the teachers and conversation seemed to grind to a halt with my presence), or go to the bathroom and then return to the classroom looking busy (I did that a lot).

From this I learned that I had difficulty 'hanging out' and that I was happier in more structured situations, such as when class was in session or when I was interviewing someone. I also concluded that life would have been easier if, during the very first days in the field, I had come to school more frequently than twice a week for a few hours. If I had stayed all day and come three or four days in a row during the first week I would have been introduced to all of the staff and become more integrated. As it was I was introduced to a few staff members, but after that I saw a lot of familiar faces but was never introduced to them. Today I am much better at being able to say, 'I don't think we have met, although I have seen you around. My name is . . .'. But at that time I felt tongue-tied and often moved in and out of the teachers' lounges in both schools without talking or getting to know the other teachers.

Although I came to feel accepted in the classroom in both Prescott and Colton I never felt very comfortable outside of the classroom. This meant that my study was essentially restricted to single classrooms, and I lost the possiblility of learning about the organizational dynamics at each school. Even today I feel that if I had been a more skilled field worker, had become more comfortable on the site, had been better at easing my way into informal settings and simply 'hanging out', that I would have learned more than I did. In particular I might have learned more about routine conflicts between parents and teachers in other classrooms, disagreements among teachers about how to manage parents, and principal–teacher relationships. I also might have gotten onto a more human footing with Mrs Walters and, for example, learned more about sensitive issues, including how she felt about parents breathing down her neck and who she really was. As it stands the manuscript treats these issues only superficially.

My Role in the Classroom

Someone told me once that in field work: *You need to know who you are and what you are doing there.* This is good advice, but such certainty is often hard to come by at the beginning since, even if you have one idea, the context may lead you to different ones. My role in the classroom differed between the two schools and this turned out to be another source of information about family–school relationships.

At Colton it was rare for adults to be in the classroom unless they were teachers or teachers' aides. In addition, children were almost always sitting at desks doing their work; they were not working on projects that needed individual supervision. As a result there was not much that Mrs Thompson needed me to do. Sometimes I would help out with art projects; for example, helping children open glue bottles and wiping up spilled glue. Mostly, however, I watched the lessons from the back of the classroom. This was facilitated by the fact that the classroom was quite large, there was a table in the back of the room at which I could comfortably sit, and the table was five or six feet from the nearest desk, giving me a little distance. I was not grossly disrupting the class by sitting there. I was not completely passive: I helped children line up, I went with them out to recess, I mediated disputes on the playground at children's requests, I went with them to the library, and frequently chatted with children in the class about things that were important to them (e.g., their toys, the pictures they drew). I knew the names of the children in the class and many of the children would wave and say hello to me when I walked across the playground as I came and went at school.

At Prescott, however, the classroom organization, spatial arrangements, and increased presence of parents on the school site led me to interact with children more and in different ways than at Colton. Mrs Walters wanted me to come to school to volunteer during 'independent time.' In these one hour periods three times per week, the class was divided into four 'stations' and different projects were available in each station. Mrs Walters scheduled a parent volunteer to be in the classroom during these times. This left four adults (including myself) to supervise the children as they worked independently. Children frequently had questions and particularly in the beginning of an hour in which the children were working on a new project all the adults were busy answering questions. Once the project got underway there was less to do as children went to work at their own pace.[10]

The problem was, as many parents so bitterly complained, that not all the children worked. Most did work consistently, but many would — for brief periods of time — break classroom rules by poking, hitting, or fussing at each other. Some children, including four or five boys, hardly did any work at all. The children seemed to operate under an implicit classroom rule that if an adult was watching you then you behaved and worked. I was ambivalent about what my role was to be; I didn't want to be a teacher or a disciplinarian. Like a favorite aunt or family friend, I was hoping to avoid discipline issues altogether. I wrote about this ambivalence in my notes:

> I am unsure as to what my role should be when children are not working productively or are 'acting out' with squabbles and minor fights. It is noteworthy that most of the children ignore me and continue their disputes in my presence (while with Mrs Walters and usually with Mrs O'Donnell the dispute is changed or is dropped).

The children quickly realized that I would not scold them and force them to work, as a result they would continue to misbehave in front of me. This made me uncomfortable. On the one hand I didn't want to be scolding children on the other hand I didn't want Mrs Walters to feel that I was not helping out and doing what adults normally did in the classroom. Consequently I sometimes looked foolish and ineffective in the classsroom, as this example makes clear:

> [Today] two boys were pushing each other in their chairs while they were supposed to be playing the numbers game. I came up behind them

and said something weak/mild such as, 'Are you boys playing the numbers game?' They obviously were not as they continued to shove and push each other. Mrs Harris then saw them and came over and said harshly, 'Jonathan, Roger. Stop that this instant! Now sit up and sit in your chairs and behave!' (She physically pushed them apart and pushed their chairs closer to their desks).

Clearly, Mrs Harris was not ambivalent about controlling children. As my notes reflect, I began to think that I might have to get off the fence and take a more assertive role:

> When I started volunteering I wanted to disrupt the [classroom] activities as little as possible and so I made a concerted effort to stay away from the teacher/disciplinarian role. I am discovering, however, that in the world of children the adult/child split means I am often forced into the teacher/disciplinarian role. Otherwise I am seen as powerless, not threatening, and the object of a great deal of acting out behavior when the children are not under the teacher's rule.

I didn't write down the actual date that I finally decided to abandon my passive role, but by about one third of the way through the field work I was controlling the children more and following the roles of the parents and teachers. This seemed to help; I felt more comfortable in the classroom and the children, Mrs Walters, and Mrs O'Donnell began to treat me like another parent or teacher's aide. I helped children with their stories, their art work, and various projects. I gave tests, I dictated problems which they wrote on the board, and supervised children, enforcing classroom rules when we went to the auditorium for a special event. When Mrs Walters left school to have an operation six weeks before the end of the semester, I continued to visit the classroom. By then I was integrated into the classroom, and Miss Chaplan, Mrs Walters' replacement, seemed to accept my presence. I helped organize the report cards and the games on the last day of school.

As I discuss in the text, my relationship to parents mirrored the pattern of family–school relationships in the two schools: I had much more contact with parents at Prescott than at Colton and the parents at Prescott scrutinized my activities much more closely than they did at Colton. There were advantages and disadvantages to this. The advantage of my more active role in the classroom at Prescott was that I worked with some of the parents and was, in many ways, a valuable assistant to Mrs Walters, which she appreciated. The drawback was that I couldn't take notes in the classroom. I only tried that once in Mrs Walters' class. The room was too small to accommodate a desk for me so I had to write on my lap; and I was only two or three feet away from the children's desks so my note-taking distracted them. Also, I was often there for independent time and Mrs Walters needed adults to walk around and help children as they all worked independently. As a result I had to try to recreate notes after I left the site. This increased the amount of time that field work demanded and produced notes with fewer quotes than at Colton.[11]

Access and Entrance to the Families

When I entered the field I had planned to select the parents of children at the end of the school year, after I had observed in the classroom. Seeking a balance by gender and achievement levels, I decided to select a boy and a girl from the high, medium, and low reading groups for interviews. In each school, I wanted five children from intact families (although their parents could be remarried) and one child from a single-parent family. At Colton, since almost one half of the class was non–white, and around a quarter were from single-parent homes, only about one third of the children were potential candidates. One day after school, Mrs Thompson and I sat down with the reading groups. We chose a boy and a girl from each reading group. Whenever possible Mrs Thompson recommended children whose parents she knew from having interacted with them at the school. As a result, the Colton families I interviewed were somewhat more active in their children's schooling than the average parent. After we had made the choices, she gave me a booklet with the names, addresses, and telephone numbers of the families and I copied them out. She also gave me test scores for the entire class.

Mrs Walters was gone from Prescott by the end of the year. One afternoon after school, as we were cleaning up the classroom, the teacher's aide, the replacement teacher (Miss Chaplan), and I talked about whom to select for the study. The decisions were as follows, I selected Donald since he was clearly the highest achiever in the class and I had met his parents at Open House. Mrs O'Donnell also told me that Donald's parents were enthusiastic about the study and were hoping to be selected. Such flattery is hard to resist. I selected Carol and Emily because I had met their mothers and observed them in the classroom. I selected Jonathan, although I had not met his mother, because he was the lowest achieving boy. I added Allen in part because both Jonathan and Donald were well behaved and I wanted someone who was more of a troublemaker. Allen fitted that bill. The children represented almost one quarter of the class but, since five of the six mothers volunteered in the classroom, a slightly higher percentage of mothers active in school. After we selected the children I copied down the names and addresses of the families.

With these two sessions the sample was set. At Colton, however, two of the families moved during the summer after first grade before I had interviewed them. In the second year of the study I needed to add two more families, a boy and a girl, one of whom was from a single-parent family. Because I had not anticipated this, I did not have other names and addresses from which to choose. During the next year I visited Colton occasionally, and I discovered that Mrs Sampson's second grade class had a white girl, Suzy, who was a high achiever and whose parents visited the school frequently. Her father was a sheriff and her mother was a student. The teacher gave me their telephone number and I contacted them. Because of scheduling difficulties I had only one interview with them, but it was a long one and both the mother and father participated in it (with their eight-month-old girl sitting on my lap for much of the time).

The other child I added to the study, Ann-Marie, was in Mrs Sampson's class, and Mrs Sampson frequently mentioned her in informal conversations. I checked my field notes and I had a lot of notes about her from first grade. I decided to add her in the second year because I had been following her; she was from a single-parent family, and she seemed to exemplify important tensions that can occur between parents and schools. This choice was costly, however, as it upset the gender balance and left me with four girls and two boys in the Colton sample. Ann Marie's mother did not have a telephone but Mrs Sampson told me when their parent–teacher conference would be held. So, with a show of confidence I didn't actually feel, I simply went to the conference and spoke to Ann-Marie's mother there. She agreed, with no resistance, to be in the study. This scrambling around to add respondents to the study could have been avoided if I had started the year by following a pool of ten or fifteen families, expecting that some would have moved (or dropped out for other reasons) by the second year.

In reflecting on the choice of families, I continue to feel that the children at both Colton and Prescott schools were a reasonably good sample of the classroom. There were no glaring omissions in terms of discipline problems, achievement levels, temperament, popularity, and parent involvement in schooling. At both schools I had a range of parents, from the most heavily involved to the least involved in school site activities and, according to teachers, in educational activities at home. Still, the sample was small and non-random so I cannot confirm this impression.

In addition to the twelve families in my sample I interviewed both principals, the first and second grade teachers at both schools, and the special education teacher at Colton. I interviewed the first grade teachers in the summer after first grade; the interviews with the second grade teachers and the principals were about a year later. The interviews ranged over a number of issues, including teachers' ideas of the proper role of parents in schooling, and their assessment of the level of educational support which the families were providing for their children. These discussions of the individual children were very helpful; they provided a useful contrast to parents' assessment of their behavior. At times teachers provided me with information which I would have liked to have asked parents about, as when Mrs Thompson told me she sent Jill to the nurse because of body odor. Unfortunately the demands of confidentiality precluded me from probing these issues as much as I would have liked. I did ask parents general questions; if they did not discuss the issue I was looking for, then I simply dropped it. To have done otherwise would have violated the teachers' confidentiality.

Requesting Interviews

In requesting interviews with parents I followed a different strategy for each school. In a qualitative methods class I took, Lillian Rubin cautioned against writing letters to working-class families asking them to participate in a study. She said that it was usually better to telephone, since working-class families did not read as much nor did they routinely receive letters on university stationary. This advice made sense to me and I followed it. I telephoned the Colton mothers, verbally explained the study and asked permission to visit them in their homes. At Prescott, I sent parents a letter describing the study and requesting their participation. I then telephoned a few days later and set up a time for the interview. These written requests for participation did not go out at the same time. They were sent out about a week before I was able to schedule the interview. At both schools the requests and the interviews were staggered over a period of several months.

All of the mothers at Colton and Prescott agreed to participate with little hesitation. The fact that I had been in Mrs Walers' and Mrs Thompson's classes seemed to help in gaining access to the children's homes. After I interviewed the mothers at the end of first grade, I told them I would like to return a year later. All of the mothers were agreeable to this. At the end of the second interview with each mother, I asked if I could interview the father as well. I interviewed all five Prescott fathers (Gail lived in a single-parent family). At Colton, I succeeded in interviewing only three of the five fathers. Mrs Morris and Mrs Brown were doubtful and reluctant to arrange for me to interview their husbands, and I did not press my request. I regret that now — I think with a bit of pressure I could have interviewed Mr Morris, since I met him at school once and at home once. I never even saw Mr Brown. He never went to school and his wife said that he was very shy. I doubt that, even if I had pursued it, I would have gained his cooperation. In addition, because of scheduling difficulties, I only interviewed Jonathan's mother (Prescott) once rather than twice.

In my telephone conversations and my letters to mothers asking for permission to interview them, I said the interviews would last about an hour and fifteen minutes ('depending on how much you have to tell me'). It turned out that the interviews took much longer; they always took at least ninety minutes and in most cases two hours. I discovered this very quickly and should have changed what I told parents but, again fearing rejection, I didn't. Now I would. It is a risk but, if it were happening to me, I would be irritated if I had set aside an hour and the interview took two. Furthermore, for reasons I don't completely understand, when I was in their offices or homes respondents rarely told me that it was time to go. Instead, adopting etiquette norms regarding guests, they seemed to wait me out. It was easy to delude myself and think that the respondents were enjoying the conversation so much that they didn't mind it going overtime, and in some cases that was true. But it was rude of me knowingly to conceal the true length of the interview (even by fifteen minutes to a half-hour) when I made my initial requests. It violated both the spirit and the letter of the notion that a researcher must respect her/his subjects.

My Perceived Role with Parents

The Prescott parents did not have any trouble figuring out who I was and what I was doing. They knew what graduate school was, they knew what a dissertation was, and they understood the concept of someone doing research on education without being an educator. Many had friends and relatives in doctoral programs. My general introduction was followed by questions from Prescott parents about my specific academic and career goals (e.g., 'Is this for your dissertation?').

The Colton parents did have difficulty figuring out who I was and what I was doing there. All of the mothers asked me if I was planning to become a teacher. When I said no, that I was working on a research project for the university, I generally drew nods accompanied by looks of confusion. In the beginning I often said I was a 'graduate student'. I dropped that description after a mother asked me if that meant I was going to graduate soon. From then on, I said that the university did a lot of studies and I was working on a research project to find out how families helped children in school. If mothers continued to ask questions about my plans I often took them through a brief explanation of the higher education system: 'After graduating from high school some people go to college. After four years of college people graduate and get a Bachelor's degree. After that, some people go on to more school, do research and get another degree. That is what I am trying to do now.' Overall, I would say that the Colton parents seemed to think that I was friendly, but that I was from a foreign land 'over there', a world they had little contact with and did not understand. Even without that understanding, however, they were willing to participate in the project.

One consequence of this confusion was that Colton mothers mistakenly thought I worked at the school. My efforts to establish myself as being independent of the school took on new vigor after my first visit to Jill's home, which was early in the interviews. I had finished the interview, had packed everything up, and was standing in the kitchen, chatting. Suddenly I saw that on the wall of the kitchen was a calendar, and on that day's date was written 'visit from school', with the time of our interview. I considered that to be very bad news; it could, and probably did, shape what the mother was willing to tell me. But the interview was over; it was too late to do anything more.

Thereafter, with parents, especially Colton parents, I stepped up my efforts to convince them that I was not from the school by stressing at the beginning of the interview, and repeating it in different ways at different times during the interview, that I did not work there ('Now, I am not from the school and there is something I don't understand very well . . .'). Although I can't be certain, I think these strategies worked; with some probing, all of the Colton parents did express criticisms of the school, although, as I show in the text, they were of a different character than at Prescott.

The Interviews

The interviews took place in the homes, in the living room or dining room. The interviews with mothers who worked in the home were often in the middle of the day, the ones with the fathers and the mothers who worked outside the home took place in the evening or at the weekend. In some cases the houses were quiet; in others children, dogs, house-cleaners, and the telephone frequently intervened. The interviews were open-ended and were set up to be more like a conversation than an interview. I had an interview guide but I sometimes varied the order of the questions, depending on how the interview was evolving. I had a tape recorder and I did not take notes during the interview. Instead, I tried to maintain eye contact, nod frequently, and make people feel comfortable. In the course of these and other interviews, I have discovered that each interview guide has its own rhythm. I have found that there is a particular time (often one eighth of the way through the interview) when the respondent should be 'with you.' If the respondent is not 'with you', it usually means that the interview is in trouble.[12]

In my interviews in people's homes, I found that within fifteen minutes of my arrival we should be set up and ready to begin the interview. Fifteen minutes into the interview things should be more relaxed; the respondent should look less tense and be sitting more comfortably in the chair; the original tension in the room and interpersonal awkwardness should be easing up; and there should be a sense of movement and revelation. Usually that happened, occasionally it did not. Some respondents (like some students in an examination) never seemed to settle into the rhythm. The situation remained awkward all the way through. In those instances I often discontinued the interview and started chatting. I asked the respondents questions about their house, their dog, their clothes, their pictures, their car. (Or I talked about myself, my clothes, local shopping malls I have been in, my family, my childhood fights with my brothers and sisters). My goal was to try to put these people at ease, make myself seem less intimidating, find something that we had in common, and — I suppose — to portray myself as a 'regular person', one that they could talk to easily. In addition, I was interested in hearing them talk about something they cared about and could discuss with ease. That was helpful, for it gave me a sense of the tone and demeanor which I was striving for when I went back to the interview questions.[13]

Sometimes these conversational diversions, while hardly subtle, did seem to help. Respondents seemed to relax and began to forget the tape recorder. (Noticing that I didn't turn off the tape recorder or apparently mind wasting tape on a discussion of the family dog seemed to help some respondents to relax.) A few interviews — my first interview with Laura's mother at Colton and my interviews with Gail's mother at Prescott — never seemed to 'click' fully. There were good moments followed by awkward ones. For example, when I arrived at Laura's house the television was on and the mother didn't turn it off; in fact, she continued to stare at it from time to time, and comment about it during the interview. It was one of my first interviews in a home and I didn't have the nerve to ask her to turn it off. Now I always make sure that the television is off or, if others are watching it, I move the interview to another room. One of the first things I say after I get set up with the tape recorder is, 'Do you mind if we turn off the television for a while? I'm afraid this tape recorder is quirky and the television really causes problems. It shouldn't be too long'. I also thank them when they do turn off the television and again, when I am leaving, apologize if they missed any of their favorite programs because of the interview.

Considering the number of interviews, having two or three awkward ones was not very many, but I found such occasions to be extremely depressing. I tried to take comfort in Lillian Rubin's comment that it 'happens to everyone'. She confided that, after trying everything she could think of to enliven a failing interview with no success, she would simply finish the interview as quickly as possible and 'get out of there'. I still consider that to be good advice.

Data Analysis

I did two data analyses on this project. The first was half-hearted; the second time I was more systematic as I followed many of the ideas in Matthew Miles and A. Michael Huberman's (1984) very good book on data analysis, *Qualitative Data Analysis: A Sourcebook of New Methods*. Fortunately, the results did not change when I analyzed the data more carefully, although the second attempt did highlight themes I had not seen before. Readers interested in data analysis generally are referred to Miles and Huberman. In this section, I simply summarize the steps I took in the two analyses.

In my first effort, I finished collecting the data and then, based on what I had learned, I wrote it up. I felt that I had to portray the data accurately and I carefully reviewed my interviews and field notes. I also drew heavily on the notes I wrote after each interview: a short statement (usually three pages, single-spaced) which summarized the key issues in the interview.[14] During this period I transcribed sections of tapes where I felt there were important quotes, making carbon copies of these transcriptions. One copy of these quotes was put into a file, with the folders organized by child; the carbon copy was cut up and glued onto index cards. I also made numerous charts, sketching out the responses of parents to different issues, a precursor to 'data displays'. But the entire process was informal.

The second time I analyzed the data, the analysis was much more comprehensive and systematic. First, I spent hours listening to tapes: I purchased a portable tape recorder (a 'Walkman') and listened to tapes in the house, as I rode my bike, made dinner, and went about my life. In addition, all of the interviews were transcribed verbatim. It took an average of the to fifteen hours for me or the secretaries in my department to transcribe a two hour interview, depending on sound quality. The shortest interview was ten pages, single-spaced: the longest was twenty-five pages, single-spaced. For a few interviews, only critical sections (anywhere from seven to fifteen pages of single-spaced quotes per interview) were transcribed. In all, had thirty-seven interviews with typed quotes, each interview quite lengthy.

I cut these single-spaced transcriptions up into individual quotes (with a code name on each quote) and glued them on five by eight inch index cards. Colton was yellow, Prescott was white, and the teachers in both schools were blue. I ended up with over one thousand index cards. At first the cards were simply in groups by school and by child. Then they were sorted by basic categories: parents' view of their proper role, their educational activities in the home, and their complaints about Mrs Walters. I also had categories for family life, including children's lessons outside of school and the social networks among parents in the community. Teachers' cards were grouped according to what educational activities they sought from parents.[15]

As the analysis continued, I tried to clarify my research question in the light of the literature. In particular I tried to see how my data could modify, challenge, or elaborate known findings. The cards continued to be in piles by major analytic categories (all over the living room floor), but the composition of these groups shifted as I reviewed the quotes, thought about the research question, looked for negative examples, and tried to clarify the differences within the schools as well as between them. For example, during the first analysis I focused on parents' educational activities at home and their attendance at school events. Gradually I realized that Colton and Prescott parents' actions went beyond helping at home. Parents in the two schools differed in how much they criticized the school and supplemented the school program. I also found omissions in the literature on this issue. This shifted the focus from looking at social class differences in parents' support (i.e., how much parents complied with teachers' requests) to the more inclusive notion of linkages.

As I pursued this idea the analytic categories became more numerous: teachers' wishes for parent involvement; parents' beliefs regarding their proper role, information about schooling, scrutiny of teachers, interventions in school site events, criticisms of teachers, educational aspirations for their children; and possible explanations of why parents were — or were not — involved in schooling. Differences between mothers and fathers and the disadvantages of parents' involvement were two other categories.

During this time I maintained index cards about each child in the study. These quickly became inefficient and cumbersome because the case studies of children were incomplete and I was 'borrowing' cards from the analytic piles to supplement information on each child. Finally I developed a dual system. For each child I had a collection of transcribed interviews on paper for the mother (both interviews) and the father. I also had the comments that the teacher had made about the child. These typed interviews were all paper-clipped together and put in three piles (Colton, Prescott, and educators). In addition, copies of all of the interviews were cut and pasted onto hundreds of index cards which were kept in analytic categories within open cardboard boxes (with rubber bands grouping cards in subcategories), and rearranged slightly as the analysis developed. Ultimately the chapters of this book mirrored the boxes of cards.

Following Miles and Huberman, I also made numerous 'data displays'. For example, I created matrices with the children listed in rows and various types of parent involvement in columns (i.e., reviewing papers after school, reading, attending Open House, attending conferences). I also produced matrices on select issues: in one chart I compared the criticisms Colton and Prescott parents had of school, in another I displayed what parents said was their proper role in schooling. The information on the cards duplicated the data displays (on large pieces of poster board) which provided a quick, visual overview of the evidence. Put differently, the cards showed me what I had, as the groups of cards provided stacks of evidence in support of ideas; the data displays showed me what I didn't have — as the cells revealed missing cases or showed exceptions to the pattern. Producing these matrices was time-consuming, but they were very helpful in displaying the strengths and weaknesses of the argument. Together the coding categories, sorting system, and dual system of case studies and analytic categories gave me a chance to look for other patterns, and increased my confidence in the accuracy of my interpretation of the data.

Mistakes: Lessons from the Field

I made one very serious mistake in the field; I fell behind in writing up my field notes. Writing up field notes immediately is one of the sacred obligations of field work. Yet workers I have known well all confessed that they fell behind in their field notes at one time or another. Researchers are human: — we get sick; we have an extra glass of wine; we get into fights with our spouses; we have papers to grade, due the next day; or we simply don't feel like writing up field notes immediately after an interview or a participant-observation session. On top of that, at least for me, writing field notes is both boring and painful: boring, because it repeats a lot of what you just did and it takes a long time to write a detailed description of a fifteen-minute encounter/observation; painful, because it forces you to confront unpleasant things, including lack of acceptance, foolish mistakes in the field, ambiguity about the intellectual question, missed opportunities in the field, and gaping holes in the data. To be sure, there is a tremendous sense of satisfaction in having placed on paper the experiences of the day and then adding these to the top of a neat and growing pile. But the time! Initially, one hour in the field would take me three hours to write up. Missing sessions of writing field notes can, like skipping piano practice, get quickly out of hand . . . exponentially, in fact.

If I wrote up my interviews two or three days later, I put 'retrospective notes' (or retro for short) at the top of the first page. In many cases I believe that I could have recreated, even several weeks later, a good account of what happened in the classroom, but I imposed on myself a certain 'code of honor'. If I missed my deadline and didn't write the event up within a few days of its occurrence, I wouldn't allow myself to write it up a week or two later and use my recollections as field notes I was sure that the information would be distorted. So there were notes that, I never wrote up despite my best intentions. My delinquencies multiplied because I didn't stop going into the field; gaining acceptance in the field is dependant on being there and being part of things. The more I went the more interesting things I saw, and the more people told me about up-coming events that they encouraged me to attend (i.e., the Easter Hat parade, a play coming to school). Like a greedy child on Christmas Day who keeps opening package after package without stopping to play with them and then asks for more, I kept going to the field, didn't write it up, but went back to the field anyway for fear of missing something really important. I usually went to the field three times per week (alternating schools), or about a dozen times per month. I don't know exactly how many transgressions I committed. My best estimate is that I completed about 100 hours of observation, with more hours at Prescott than at Colton, and I failed to write notes on about one eighth of my field work. Today I faithfully record in my calendar when I go into the field, where I go, and how long I stay. In my current and future work I want to be able, to state, as Lubeck (1984; 1985) did, how many hours of field work the study is based on. This record of visits to the field also helps me keep track of sets of field notes and interviews.

In spite of these omissions I had, of course, quite a large amount of data. I was in the classrooms for several months and had stacks of carefully written notes of routine activities. Many studies (Lightfoot 1983) have been based on far less, but it was a serious breach of field methods and, although I cannot prove it, one that I am convinced is more common than is noted in the literature. In hindsight, the writing up of field notes was linked to the renowned problem of 'going native'. I liked being in the classrooms; I liked the teachers, the children, and the activities — making pictures of clovers for St Patrick's Day, eggs for Easter, and flower baskets for May. I liked being there the most when I felt accepted by the teachers and children. Thinking about taking notes reminded *me* that I was a stranger, forced me to observe the situation as an outsider, and prevented me from feeling accepted and integrated into the classroom. Writing up my field notes was a constant reminder of my outsider status. It was also a reminder of the ambiguous status of my intellectual goals; I knew only vaguely where I was going with the project. I also worried I might be making the wrong decisions, such as when I began to take a more active role in the class at Prescott or spent most of the time at Prescott during independent time (when Mrs Walters needed help) rather than visiting the classroom regularly at other points in the day. There was a lurking anxiety about the field work: Was it going right? What was I doing? How did people feel about me? Was I stepping on people's toes? What should I do next? — and this anxiety was tiring.

The few times when I forgot about note-taking and observing and just enjoyed being there, I felt a tremendous sense of relief. I liked the feeling of giving up being a researcher and simply being a teacher's aide. The seduction of participation sometimes overshadowed the goal of participation; and the cost was a lack of carefully collected information. If I could do it over, I would arrange things so that I had a different set of choices. I would change my schedule and slow down the project. Although it was advantageous to be in both schools at once, in the interest of completeness I would now probably do one school at a time. I was also in a hurry to get through graduate school, a goal that now seems short-sighted. As a result I have developed what I call the Lareau Iron Law of Scheduling:

> Never (and I mean never) go into the field unless you have time that
> night, or in the next twenty-four hours, to write up the notes.

Such rigidity may seem hard to enforce because presence in the field is critical to sustaining access and rapport. There is also the 'somewhere else' problem (Walford 1987) that something critically important will take place and you will miss it. But whatever happens will often happen again, particularly if it is part of the routine social interaction that qualitative workers are usually trying to study.

This iron law of scheduling can be carried out, it just takes self-restraint. And it is crucial: field work without notes is useless and destructive. It is useless without documentation the observations cannot and should not be incorporated into the study; it is destructive because worrying about missing notes takes away valuable time and energy from the project, creates new problems, undermines competence, and turns a potentially rewarding process into a burdensome one. In my experience at least, it is not worth it.

A Hybrid Pattern

In most of the classic studies, the researchers were sustained by grants and field work was all that they did. Today such full-time devotion to field work is uncommon because difficulty securing full-time funding means that researchers are balancing other economic commitments while in the field. For graduate students, making ends meet often means working as a research assistant on someone else's project. For faculty, it means continuing to meet teaching obligations while doing field work. Although researchers would love to face only a computer when they leave the field, many in fact must go to committee meetings, write lectures, go to work, pick up children, fix dinner, etc. For many researchers, a hybrid pattern of commitments has replaced the single commitment model of fieldwork that characterized the community studies of the past.

This new hybrid pattern affects the character of field work in many ways. In my case other obligations severely curtailed the amount of time I could spend in the field. I was working twenty hours per week, I had many school obligations, I had to run my own household, and I was living in an area with family and friends in the immediate vicinity. It was often hard to find six to ten hours a week to go to the schools. In addition I felt the strain of straddling two different worlds. I would leave Prescott school and, with my head swimming with thoughts about how I should have handled Allen poking Jonathan, drive to the university, try to find a parking place in the middle of the day, and go to work as a sociology teaching assistant. It was disorienting. Because being in the field required more formal attire than was the norm among students at the university, I found myself constantly explaining to people I met in the hallway why I was so dressed up. I felt on stage and out of place when I was visiting the classroom, but I also felt myself a misfit at the university. I had trouble getting used to this; it seemed as if I could never establish a routine.

I think that researchers need to take seriously this hybrid pattern of research and analyze the differences it makes in access, entrance, rapport, data collection, and data analysis. It seems to me, for example, that access must be negotiated over longer periods of time, and more often, when the worker is moving in and out of the field than when she/he is living there (see Bosk 1979). Data collection is slower when the researcher is in the field less often, and moving in and out of the field is a strain, though possibly less of a strain than living in an unfamiliar environment for months at a time (Powdermaker 1966). Although data collection takes longer, data analysis and the clarification of the research question may move along more quickly under this hybrid pattern. Being in a university environment as well as in a field setting provides more people with whom to discuss the research question. This ready availability of sounding boards may help the researcher move ahead more rapidly with the data analysis.

Whether a commitment pattern is hybrid or single, all qualitative researchers inevitably experience errors and confusion in their research. In the course of defining the problem, negotiating access, beginning observations, and conducting interviews, many decisions must be made, some of which — in retrospect — are regrettable. This is true in all research, but in qualitative methods the mistakes are usually carried out and observed by the researcher first hand (rather than being committed by others and reported — or not reported — to the principal investigator by subordinates). Qualitative researchers also work in naturalistic settings and they lack opportunities to 'rerun' the data. Moreover, overwhelmed by the immediacy of the field setting, the sheer amount of data collected, and the many possibilities which the project offers, some researchers — temporarily or permanently — lose sight of their intellectual question(s). I turn now to a discussion of this problem.

Part II: Problems with the Research Question

Blinded by Data

Two months into my field work, a graduate seminar on participant–observation was offered by Michael Burawoy. Thinking that it might be useful to have others to talk to about the project I enrolled in the course.[1] As I soon discovered, Burawoy (1979) viewed qualitative data as data that tried to help answer a question. He allowed that the mode of inquiry might be very different than the mode of presentation in the final report, but he was interested in having us — all of us — answer sociological questions. 'So what?' was the question of the quarter.

As Burawoy soon discovered, I resisted this approach. More precisely, I was ambivalent and confused about how to write up the data I was collecting, which grew, literally, by the hour. Data collection is an absorbing process and it pleased me to add more and more field notes to the pile and make arrangements to complete interviews. Still, the sheer amount of data sometimes seemed overwhelming and I did not feel prepared to analyze it. I had unconsciously accepted the methodology of survey research which consists of four steps: a) formulate a problem; b) collect data; c) analyze it; and d) write it up. I was overextended simply trying to get to both schools, take notes, write up the notes, work as a teaching assistant, and keep up with Burawoy's class. As far as I was concerned, the analysis could wait.

My ambivalence, however, centered less on the problem of not having time to do it and more on the proper strategy for analyzing and writing up qualitative research — a problem which ultimately haunts almost all qualitative researchers. I wanted to describe social reality, to supply the details and the vivid descriptions that would draw my readers in and carry them along; I hoped to produce the holistic and seamless feeling of many of the ethnographies that I had read. Some of the many works in this genre are analytical. *Tally's Corner* (Liebow 1968), *Worlds of Pain* (Rubin 1976), and *Everything in Its Path* (Erikson 1976) all have arguments — but the analysis seems subordinate to the data. They certainly aren't written in the 'now-I-am-going-to-discuss-three-ideas' style which characterized everything I had written during graduate school. Captivated by some of the ethnomethodology and anthropology I had read, I was eager to abandon explicit intellectual questions and 'simply' describe social reality. More to the point, I believed that was what good ethnographers did. Describing reality provided intrinsically interesting information. The intellectual ideas, tucked away in a concluding chapter or footnotes, did not spoil or constrain the novelistic portrayal of reality. I had hoped to use my own data to draw compelling pictures which would not — to use a favorite expression of mine at the time — violate the complexity of social reality. But I was also interested in ideas. I had waded through Bourdieu and found his approach useful. I was genuinely interested in the way in which social stratification was reproduced, and in the contribution made to children's life chances, by the interactions between parents and teachers.

As my field work progressed I struggled to determine the 'proper' relationship between theory and qualitative data. I had framed a question before I began my field work, but once I got caught up in the drama of actually being in the field my original question became hazy. I had trouble linking the data back to the original question or modifying the original question. Instead, I was preoccupied by the characters — Mrs Walters, Mrs Thompson, the children, and even my own role in the research process.

This intellectual confusion is reflected clearly in my field notes. My notes — and I know that I am not alone in this — had some sensitive concepts (Glaser and Strauss 1967) but then were all over the map. They were a hodgepodge of observations made on the basis of shifting priorities. One day I recorded the curriculum and how children interacted with the materials, their skills and how they displayed them. Another day I looked at how the teacher controlled the classroom and her methods of authority. Another day I looked at my role in interacting with the children, how I responded when children started breaking classroom rules in front of me, and my relationships to the teacher and the aide. Observations on the relationships between the aide and the children, the aide and the teacher, the parents and the children, all flow indiscriminately through my field notes. I wrote detailed descriptions of special events (e.g., a school play, a description of an easter egg dyeing project). I also watched for and noted hallmarks of social class: labels on clothing, vacation plans, parents' appearances in the classroom, and different relationships between parents and teachers. Anything and everything that went on in the classroom I tried to record. In my efforts to capture social reality as comprehensively as possible, I forgot about the need for a focus.

Burawoy had no such memory lapse. He read a sample of my field notes and promptly advised me to narrow my interests. He also asked me (as well as the other members of the class) to spend a paragraph or two at the end of each set of field notes analyzing what was going on in the notes. After each session of observation, we were to write out our notes and then evaluate them in light of our question. We were expected to assess what we had learned, what new questions had been raised by our observations, and how we planned to proceed. Burawoy's advice was excellent. Today I make my graduate students do the same thing, but, as with much, if not most, good advice (i.e., to lose weight or stop smoking) it was easier to give than to follow. I found the required analyses extremely difficult to do. I hated them. Worse yet, I did them only when I had to — the ten times I was required to give them to Burawoy.

Part of the reason that I avoided these analyses was that they highlighted the murkiness of my intellectual purpose. Methodologically I was clearer; I wanted to provide a rich description of social reality. The problem was that my romance with ethnomethodology didn't help me frame my research question in a way that would allow an answer that made a theoretical contribution. I was asking, '*How* does social class influence children's schooling?' The answer was supposed to be a description of social reality. What I lacked was another, more conceptual, question: 'Do these data support one interpretation and suggest that another interpretation is not as useful?' or to be more specific, 'Can we understand parents' involvement in schooling as being linked to their values? Does cultural capital provide a better explanation for why parents are involved in school?' These questions have 'yes' or 'no' answers which can be defended using data from the study. By framing a 'how' question I could not provide a similarly defensible answer. I could not show that one explanation was superior; I could not demonstrate that these data helped to address an important issue. In short, I could not answer the 'So what?' question.

At the time I did not really understand the implications of posing the 'wrong' question. I analyzed my notes as rarely as possible and I didn't really notice that my goals changed hourly. I was more focused on building rapport with the teachers, taking comprehensive notes, trying to get the notes typed up, and getting permission to interview parents and teachers so I could complete the next stage of the project.

Burawoy, however, *was* concerned about the way I framed my study. He expressed this in all of our meetings. From our first discussion (following his review of my field notes), he repeatedly cautioned me to think the study through 'in greater analytical detail'. This advice sailed right by me or more accurately I ignored it. In the sixth week of the quarter I wrote a paper on what I had learned from my observations. It was long and my first effort to assess what I had learned from almost five months of research. It was all description: how teachers at Prescott and Colton looked, how they interacted with the children, how much math the children knew, where the children took their vacations, and a little about children's feelings about their academic ranking in the class. I discussed parents, noting that Colton parents were rarely there, seemed more deferential, and didn't seem to know as much as Prescott parents. The paper was vivid in parts and dull in others but it didn't define a question. It was an unfocused description of classroom life in two schools.

Burawoy's reaction to the paper, strongly worded and highly critical, proved to be the turning point in the conceptual development of the project. His comments made it clear that I could not continue to conduct a study that posed no problem and articulated no argument. He noted:

> . . . One's reaction to what you have written has to be, so what? What is so surprising? At no point do you attempt to present plausible alternatives to your findings . . . I would like to see you produce a theoretical beginning to this paper. I want you to use the literature to highlight the significance of the data you have collected . . . I really think you have to develop an argument, particularly as I presume this will be part of your thesis.

The chair of my dissertation, Troy Duster, gave me the same feedback although in a different way. Slowly I began to realize that quotes and field notes (which I found fascinating of course) would have to be applied to an intellectual problem. An unfocused 'thick description' would not do.

Using my original formulation of the problem and my conversations with others in my department, I began to try to link up the data with the intellectual problem. I wrote another, much shorter, paper noting the significant correlation between social class and educational achievement and arguing that this correlation was linked to parent involvement in schooling. This attempt was, as Burawoy commented, 'a major advance' over my earlier paper, but I still had a long way to go.

In retrospect, part of my problem was that the question I was framing was too heavily embedded in quantitative models. I was trying to unravel the way in which class difference in family life influenced schooling *and shaped achievement*. I seriously thought I could provide some kind of causal model using qualitative data. Today, that goal strikes me as outlandish. The strength of qualitative data is that it can illuminate the *meaning* of events. It cannot demonstrate that parent behavior 'a' has a stronger effect on achievement than parent behavior 'b' in a sample of two classrooms.

This preoccupation with achievement as a dependent variable and steady immersion in the quantitative literature made me overlook qualitative socio-logical studies that could provide a suitable framework for my project. I had not read many of the socio-linguistic studies that had been done in the United States, nor was I familiar with the work of cultural anthropologists. I unwittingly ignored the work of potential role models — people who had used similar methods successfully and whose studies could provide valuable examples.

I also failed to realize that just as an individual develops a personal identity most researchers develop an intellectual identity, one that often includes a theoretical as well as a methodological orientation. This identity does not usually change significantly over a single research project, although it might be modified in some ways. I began my project admiring radically different types of qualitative research; my own intellectual identity was in flux. I failed to realize that my multiple admirations were prompting me to strive for mutually incompatible goals. This was not, I have come to realize, an idiosyncratic pattern for I have observed many novice researchers do the same.

For example I admired many ethnomethodological and phenomeno-logical studies in which the flesh and blood of real life is portrayed in vivid detail. Yet most of these studies emphasize that it is critical that the researcher's description remains true to the actor's subjective experience. I do not embrace this view. I believe my respondents should be able to agree that I have portrayed their lives accurately, but I do not want to restrict myself to 'folk explanations'. It does not trouble me if my interpretation of the factors influencing their behavior is different from their interpretation of their lives. Parents at Prescott and Colton schools cannot be expected to be aware of the class structure of which they are a part, nor of the influence of class on behavior. I want to be able to make my own assessment, based on the evidence I have gathered and my understanding of social structural factors. It is difficult, if not impossible, to provide a detailed, comprehensive portrayal of social reality (particularly using the actor's subjective experience) which also selects out elements of that experience to build a focused, coherent argument. A comprehensive portrait and a focused argument are different goals. As with many things in life, you cannot do everything. You have to choose.

This is why it is very helpful for a researcher to know her/his intellectual identity at the beginning of a research project. If you know what you believe in, what type of work you are trying to do, what you would consider acceptable and what you would consider unacceptable, you have a framework and general parameters for your research. You are also better prepared to make com-promises: what kinds of weaknesses in your research are you willing to live with and what are completely unacceptable? Being clear about matters such as these can improve both the quality and the quantity of data collection. Well-defined, mutually compatible goals make it easier to focus in the field and also contributes to better organized data.

The Lone Ranger Problem

Even with a clear intellectual identity and a general theoretical question, almost all research questions undergo modification in the light of the data. A favorite description for this in qualitative methods courses is that the research 'evolves'. Many researchers adopt the myth of individualism here. The lone researcher collects the data and, aided by her/his powers of sensitive observation and skill in writing up field notes, the researcher's initial question 'evolves' an becomes more focused. After having collected the data, the researcher retreats into her/his study to write it up and then emerges with a coherent work.

This is a mistaken view of the research process. Research, like everything else, is social. Ironically, this is more obvious in the physical sciences, where researchers must share expensive laboratory equipment, than it is in the social sciences. In the physical sciences, faculty, post-doctoral fellows, graduate students, technicians, and (occasionally) undergraduate assistants all share the same work space — and equipment. Lab interactions and lab politics are a routine part of the work process. Social scientists, even those collaborating on large research projects, rarely work together in such a way. Usually the research team meets periodically for a couple of hours and co-workers may share a computer or an office, but they spend much more of their work time alone than do their colleagues in the physical sciences. Still, the research process in sociology is social. Researchers do not get ideas from vacuums; they arise from a social context. The impact of historical factors on academic agendas is testimony to that fact (Karabel and Halsey 1977). And the ideology of individualism notwithstanding, advances in conceptual models also depend crucially upon an exchange of ideas.

In my own case, my argument (and the relationship between the conceptual model and the data) went through four or five stages, becoming narrower and less sweeping at each point. As the question became clearer my data collection became more focused as well. I began to collect information about parents and I looked closely at the differences between the two schools. I ultimately dropped my effort to explain achievement, and developed an interest in the debates on cultural capital and, to a lesser extent, parent involvement in schooling. To say that my research question 'evolved' is true, but this is far too passive a description. Just as reproduction of the social structure does not happen automatically, so the narrowing and refining of a research project is not an automatic process. Qualitative researchers take steps to *produce* a more focused research question. Participant–observation, writing up field notes, and reflecting on field notes are the steps which are normally emphasized in the literature but there are others. Talking to colleagues is critical to the development of a question. Writing up the results and having the work critically reviewed is another important step. Comparing your findings to the literature and seeing how your conclusions modify the literature is also useful.

Today my rule of thumb is that every third visit to the field should be followed by some kind of effort to push the question forward. This can be a one hour conversation with a colleague (by telephone if necessary), a comparison with other studies, or a long memo which is then reviewed and criticized by others. Such efforts must include reflections on the overall goals of the project, the theoretical question, the data, and the remaining gaps. The analysis at the end of field notes and this 'state of the question push' are similar but not identical. The former is focused around a particular event or dynamic in the field setting; the latter is broader, more reflective, and — most importantly — more social. It is an effort to reach out and place the study in a social context, to get others' feedback, to evaluate the study in terms of its contribution to the field. It is not usually very difficult to arrange this social interaction, but it must be solicited by the researcher; it will not happen automatically.

Thus, all of the conceptual advances in this project were linked to the production and criticism of written work. Writing was helpful because it required that I organize, systematize, and condense volumes of information. It helped me struggle to build the argument and it allowed me to assess the evidence in a new way. The criticism of others, particularly the comments of colleagues around the country, challenged me to rethink some of my ideas. Although I had many enjoyable sessions talking about the project and bouncing ideas around, I learned less from talking and listening than I did from writing. One consequence of this is that every few months or so (depending on the pace of data collection) I write a paper about my current project. (A deadline, such as giving a talk about the research, is helpful here.) These working papers are not polished and in most cases are not publishable.

Overall it was the social interaction (especially the criticism from others) that helped advance my work. While the lone scholar image has its appeal, it does not accurately portray the actual process in qualitative — or quantitative — research.

Writing It Up

After I signed a book contract and was committed to finishing this project, I began to ask colleagues who did qualitative research what books they considered exemplary models of writing up a qualitative project. I was shocked at how much trouble people had thinking of exemplary books. Moreover, when they did recommend books they were not usually within the field of the sociology of education. Several people recommended *Tally's Corner* (Liebow 1967). One colleague recommended Charles Bosk's book *Forgive and Remember* (Bosk 1979), a study of the socialization of medical residents into surgery. It is a compelling book and, I believe, a useful model. Another suggested *Everything in Its Path* (Erikson 1976), an award winning book which portrays the destruction of a community by the failure of traditional support systems following a dam burst.

When I began to reflect on the books that didn't make the list (only 99 per cent of the available literature), it became clear that there were many ways that qualitative researchers could end up producing mediocre books — even those beginning with interesting ideas and good evidence. Many studies represent good solid work but they have a plodding tone and analysis; they lack lively writing. Others seem as though the author(s) had not accurately represented the community under investigation and/or had missed important things in field research. Some books had good ideas and an interesting argument but seemed to be unsystematic in the analysis and portrayal of evidence. Others were long on ideas and short on data, while some lacked an argument all together.

The downfall of many of these books lies in their failure to integrate theory and data. In my own case, as I began to try to write up the results of this study, I would careen rather abruptly from discussions of theory and the research problem to presentation of the data. I also presented very few quotes. Detailed — and negative — comments from reviewers helped me see the error of my ways. Mary Metz, a guest editor for *Sociology of Education*, summarized the complaints of reviewers, complaints that I have echoed in my own reviews of other manuscripts using qualitative methods:

> You need to work with your data and decide what can be learned from
> it and then present your theory tersely as it will help us understand those
> findings and put them in context.

The reviewers also complained that I made sweeping generalizations without enough evidence to back them up, another common problem in manuscripts based on qualitative research.

I used the reviewers' and the guest editor's criticisms to improve my dissertation. I cited and used more qualitative research and I worked to change the focus from a heavily theoretical piece to a more empirically grounded one, but problems remained. I over-shortened the literature review and the quoted material was not integrated with the text. Following Aaron Cicourel's advice, I labored to integrate the data with the analysis, supply more data and be more 'aggressive' in showing 'what is missing empirically and conceptually' from other studies.

Cicourel's advice was useful again as I prepared to write this book; it reminded me to use the data to build an argument. Nevertheless, while I knew that adding more data would strengthen my argument, I wasn't clear how much additional data to include. I had an urge to add almost everything. Finally, in a move of some desperation, I turned to books and articles that I admired and counted the number of quotes per chapter or page; most averaged one quote per printed page. The quotes were not evenly spread throughout the chapters; there would be pages without any quotes and then three or four quotes per page. Most of these studies also provided examples in the text. Of course the right number of quotes depends on many factors, but the count gave me a ball park figure for my own writing which I have found useful. The problem of linking theory and data is an ongoing struggle. I made a rule that every chapter had to have an argument. I also remembered, although I did not always follow, the advice that someone passed on to me that every paragraph should be linked to the argument. I tried to show that my interpretation was a more compelling way of looking at the data than other interpretations. In other words I tried to answer the question, 'So what?'

It will be for others to judge how well I have done in connecting the theoretical argument and the research data. I know that I have done a better job of integration with this book than I did with the written work that preceded it, notably drafts of papers and the dissertation. I used almost none of my dissertation in preparing this book. Instead I began again, adding probably three to four times as many quotes and streamlining and increasing the aggressiveness of the thesis. This pattern of modest improvement in linking theory and data gives me hope: maybe experience will help. In fact a comparison of first and second books does suggest that some people get much better at this as they go along; others however do not, and a few seem to get worse.

Reflections on the Making of Home Advantage

This project had its share of mistakes but it also had its successes. The design, which included interviews with both parents and teachers, is unusual as most studies do one or the other. This yielded insights that would not have been possible if I had studied families or schools. It was also helpful to follow children over time and clarify that parents adopted similar modes of interaction regardless of the teacher. It was very important to supplement the interviews with classroom observation which improved the interviews and enabled me to 'triangulate' in a way that would have been impossible with interviews alone.

In the end I did have a good rapport with the staff, particularly the classroom teachers I worked with most closely. On her last day of school Mrs Walters gave me a hug goodbye; Mrs Thompson thanked me warmly for being in her classroom. In both schools children ran up and gave me a goodbye hug on the last day of school. By the end of the interviews I felt I had genuinely come to know and enjoy many of the mothers and fathers, and I was also certain that in several cases the feelings were mutual. This was a reward. There are plenty of awkward moments in field work, even among the best researchers, but there are also rewards and signs, little and big, of acceptance. These are important to notice and remember. This is harder to do than one would think. Moments of foolishness and the damage they have wrought are easy to worry about. I spent a lot of time fretting about the mistakes I made in this study. They scared me so I wanted to try to hide them; I worried about each and every one of them, and they overshadowed my assessment of the project. This kind of self-criticism, in which the impact of each criticism is five times that of each compliment, is not productive.

It was productive, however, to spend time thinking about the strengths and weaknesses of the study and the confidence which I have in the results. As this appendix and the format of the book make clear, I have confidence in the validity of the interviews. I feel that I was helped by my previous experience as an interviewer. Although it is difficult to prove, I am confident in the quality of the data — that I did not lead, badger, or trap respondents in interviews, that I listened to them carefully and was able to get them to talk in an honest and revealing way. The field notes were also carefully recorded. When I went into the field I thought I would find evidence of institutional discrimination. I thought, as Bowles and Gintis, Cicourel and Kitsuse, and others had suggested, that the teachers were going to differ significantly in their interactions with parents of different social class. I did not find evidence to support this position. When I did not find it I looked for other explanations rather than trying to force the evidence into that intellectual frame. The project did not have as many field notes focused directly on the intellectual problem as I would have liked, but the ones that were there were carefully done.

Can we learn anything from a study of two first grade classes, twelve families, four teachers, and two principals? Yes, I think we can use a small, non-random sample to improve conceptual models. This study shows that a very high proportion of parents would agree that they want to be 'supportive' of their children's schooling but that they would mean very different things by this. It suggests that family–school models are inadequate. Researchers do not spend enough time addressing the differences in objective skills which social class gives to parents. Independent of parents' desires for their children, class gives parents an edge in helping their children in schooling. My confidence in the validity of the findings is bolstered by the fact that they elaborate a pattern that has been noted by many researchers, although often only in passing. They also mesh with the conclusions of other recent works (Baker and Stevenson 1986; Stevenson and Baker 1987; Epstein 1987).

Although not a form of systematic evidence, I must add, that just as after you learn a new word you see it everywhere, after I finished this study I began to notice that social class differences in family–school relationships are as evident in the Midwestern city where I now live and work as it was in the West Coast communities I studied. I see working-class neighbors and friends take a 'hands-off' attitude toward their children's schooling, emphasizing their own inadequacies and turning over responsibility to the school. I see upper-middle-class families, particularly academic couples, trying to monitor and control their children's schooling. I think that while there may be aspects of the argument that need modification, the overall pattern, that class gives people resources which help them comply with the demands of institutions, is really there. Other research, using multiple methodologies, is necessary to establish that and to illuminate the interactive effects of class and parent involvement; for example, working-class parents are much less likely to make requests of the school staff, and when they do make such requests are more likely to have them honored than upper-middle-class parents.

What this study cannot do is provide an assessment of how important individuals' competencies are relative to other factors influencing parent involvement (i.e., values, teachers' roles), nor can it evaluate how common parents' actions are, including parents' supervising teachers and compensating for weaknesses in the classroom. A small sample imposes restrictions that cannot be surmounted with felicitous phrases such as 'one half of the sample believed ...' Large-scale, representative studies are much better for describing the proportion of people who share certain beliefs, and internal variations, while addressed here, can be better elaborated with a larger group. What qualitative methods can do is illuminate the meanings people attach to their words and actions in a way not possible with other methodologies. Although I admire many quantitative studies, they are in some ways 'unnaturally' straightforward. Data analysis and computer analysis have a much smaller range of options and there is less of a domino effect than occurs in qualitative work. Quantitative research does not have the ambiguity and uncertainty of field work.

In my view qualitative work is more cumbersome and more difficult than survey research at almost every stage: formulation of the problem, access, data collection, data analysis, and writing up the results. It is more time consuming; it is harder to spin off several publications; and, to add insult to injury, it is considered lower status by many members of the profession. But it adds to our knowledge in a critical and important way. It is that pay-off that draws me back, despite all I have learned about the enormous commitment of time and energy that qualitative research demands. If it were not one of the only ways of gaining insights into the routine events of daily life and the meaning that makes social reality, qualitative methods would not have a lot going for it. It is too much work. But it is one of the only ways, and possibly the only way, to achieve such insights. The usefulness of these insights rests, however, on the character of our research. Exchanging notes on our disappointments and successes in field research is an important step in increasing the quality of our work.

Notes

1. I am indebted to William F. Whyte's work not only for the idea of writing an appendix but also for providing a model of how to write one. I have shamelessly adopted elements of his organizational structure, including this one, in my appendix. Readers will note, however, a difference in the content and goals of the two appendices. Whyte's appendix elaborates issues of access, entry, and the formulation of the intellectual problem. He also provides a very good discussion of ethics and holding the line between researcher and native. My goals are somewhat different. Although I briefly review the issues of access and entry, my focus is on the practical considerations of data collection, data analysis, and the writing up of the results. I do, however, also discuss the task of formulating an intellectual problem in qualitative research.

2. My job was to help determine if recently arrested defendants were qualified to be released on their own recognizance. To help indigent defendants save bail money, the Own Recognizance Project (OR Project) would prepare cases by providing a summary of the social ties a defendant had to the area, including her/his correct address, contact with

relatives, and employment history. Unlike bail, which was simply a matter of producing the money and the collateral, OR cases required judges' signatures. Primarily because of negative publicity, many judges were very reluctant to exercise the OR option. Although the San Francisco City Prison was not as bad as some prisons, most people found prison so uncomfortable that they wanted to get out as soon as possible. For them OR was too slow and too chancy so they bailed out instead.

3. Unfortunately for those of us not trained in shorthand, it is not possible to write down every single word and idea in an interview, particularly if you are trying to maintain eye contact and build a rapport with the subject. Without a tape recorder researchers must do some editing while taking notes. For most of us this means that some particularly interesting passages are written in more detail than others. Yet what is considered interesting changes as the project and the research question develop, thus note-taking is inevitably altered by these intellectual questions.

4. Whyte (1981) has a good discussion of the problems of access, but almost all books on qualitative research methods discuss the problems. The writing on qualitative methods has increased radically in recent years and there are many good pieces around. Bogdan and Biklen (1982), while directed at research in education is a useful overview. Other works include Silverman (1985), Agar (1986), and from a somewhat different perspective Glaser and Strauss (1967). Although older, Schatzman and Strauss (1973) provide a succint discussion of key issues. In more specialized discussions, Gorden (1987) focuses on interviewing, Kirk and Miller (1986) the problems of reliability and validity in qualitative work, Macrorie (1985) the task of writing up one's results, and Punch (1986) on the politics of fieldwork. Erickson (1986) also has a useful overview of the steps in a qualitative research project using studies of teaching as an example. Finally, for reflections on the research process, see Rabinow (1977), Georges and Jones (1980), Van Mannen (1988), Simon and Dippo (1986), and Schon (1987).

5. As part of the human subjects approval process at the university, I wrote consent forms for all of the parents, children, teachers, and others I interviewed. [Since I was not disrupting the classroom activities, I was not required to gain consent forms from all of the children in the classes.] These forms briefly described the goals of the project and the methodology, including that parents and teachers would be interviewed. Before I gave parents and teachers the forms I stressed that these forms were routine and added that they were developed after serious abuses by researchers, such as prisoners being given drugs without being told. Although I agonized over the content of the form almost no one read it. Only two parents — a lawyer and his wife — read the form carefully before signing; the remaining parents and educators signed it with only a glance.

6. My letter to Prescott was as follows:

Dear Mrs Finnegan:

This letter is in regard to our recent telephone conversation regarding my request to conduct a small research project in your district. As I mentioned, I am a graduate student in a doctoral program at University of California, Berkeley, in the sociology department. As part of my dissertation research, I am conducting a study on social class variations in the family–school relationship for young children. As you probably know, the social standing of a child's family is a key predictor of educational outcome. The purpose of the research is to examine the process through which social position affects the educational process. In particular, the research will focus on the impact which the social position of professional-middle-class and working-class families has on day to day experience of school life.

I would like to conduct a very small pilot study on these issues in Prescott School District. The research would involve one first grade classroom in your district. The study would include interviews with the teacher, principal, school secretary, and five families of the children in the classroom. In addition, I would like to observe the children in the classroom for a short time, perhaps amounting to six or eight visits. All of the interviews would be 'semi-structured' interviews with open-ended questions. The interviews would last a little more than one hour and would be tape recorded. All of the persons in the study would be assured of confidentiality.

The interviews will cover a number of issues in family life and school life. The study will ask both parents and the child questions about the family's approach towards schooling. The parents' view of schooling, the way in which the parents convey this view to the child and the behavior of the parents will be explored. In addition, the conflicts between parents regarding education and the proper type of educational experience will be studied. The purpose of this study is to *compare* differences between working-class and professional-middle-class families in their view of the ideal family–school relationship. The interviews in your district will provide a basic description of the family–school relationship for a small number of families of relatively high socio-economic status.

A slightly different set of issues will be taken up with the teacher, principal, and school secretary (the secretary is included as the front office often is the first point of contact between families and schools). First, it is important to note that I would like to request that the school send a letter to the families indicating that the researcher has the permission of the district to conduct the interviews. I would be happy to contribute in any way possible to the writing and mailing of such a letter.

Secondly, the interviews with the teacher, principal, and school secretary will focus on the amount of information which school personnel have about family life. Questions will focus on the types of information which school staff learn about families, and the informal ways in which this information is gathered. In addition, the research will solicit the perceptions of school staff regarding the way in which family life shapes the day to day educational experience for young children. It is important to emphasize that the purpose of the study is *not* to evaluate teachers, schools, or parents. Indeed, the specific teaching style of a teacher is really of very limited interest as the study seeks to understand social class patterns of family–school interaction.

These brief comments are intended to provide you and your colleagues with better insight into the concerns of the research project. If you or anyone else in the district has further questions, I would be happy to provide additional information. I appreciate your consideration of this request and look forward to hearing from you in the future.
Sincerely,
Annette Lareau

7. With hindsight, this is the letter I would write today:
Dear Mrs Finnegan:
Thank you for taking the time to speak with me the other day. As we agreed, I am writing to request permission to conduct a study in your school district.

In this project, I am interested in learning more about how families help children in school. I would like to visit one first grade classroom in the district on a regular basis this school year (e.g., two times a week). My visits would be scheduled to be at a convenient time. Having worked in classrooms, I know how important it is to take an unobtrusive role in the classroom. I would be happy to work as a classroom volunteer if the teacher would like.

In addition, at a convenient time, I hope to interview the parents of five children in this classroom, as well as the teacher, principal, and school secretary. The interviews will last an hour or so. All information collected would be kept confidential; neither the identity of Prescott school district, nor that of any parents or teachers, would ever be revealed.

I am requesting permission to observe in the classroom and for you, or the school staff, to supply names and addresses of parents, with the understanding that parents may refuse to cooperate in the study. For your information, I have attached a sample copy of the letter which I would mail to parents.

I know that you, and the teachers, lead busy lives. Teachers have reported that the experience of working on this research project was interesting and pleasant. If it would be helpful, I would be happy to make a brief presentation about the project to school staff. If you would like any other information, please feel free to contact me at (618) 453–2494.

Again, I appreciate your consideration of my request. I look forward to hearing from you in the future.

Sincerely,

Annette Lareau

8. I always told people that there was another school involved and that the school was of a different level of affluence. In the beginning I used the term 'socio-economic status'; that really raised eyebrows. I now realize that it is much too long a term and much too academic to be useful.

9. Having come from Berkeley I found this 'Miss Lareau' title to be astounding in the 1980s, but it happened in all of my interactions in the school. No one called me Ms Lareau, and many people asked me: 'Is it Miss or Mrs?' Unmarried teachers, including Miss Chaplan, used the term Miss in all of their interactions. It didn't really bother me, however, and I never asked to be called Ms. I didn't really care what they called me. I was just glad to be in a school doing field work.

10. I met several mothers, including Allen's and Emily's, during these periods. As children's work got underway the mothers would often chat with me and ask me questions about my study. They also observed me in the classroom and my interactions with the children. Mrs Walters often complained about mothers visiting during volunteering saying, 'You get more work out of one parent than two.' In my own case it meant that mothers were watching me just as they watched Mrs Walters. There were also indications that mothers discussed me and my study in their conversations with one another. Thus my role with parents paralleled that of the teachers; Prescott mothers knew more about me, scrutinized, and questioned me much more closely than Colton parents.

11. If there was a statement which I thought was important I would repeat it to myself over and over again while in the classroom and write it down immediately after I left — usually in my car before I drove away. Most of the field notes from Prescott do not have direct quotes; if there are quotes, however, I am quite confident of their accuracy.

12. While interviewing defendants in City Prison for the OR Project I found that by two or three minutes into the interview I needed to have the defendant calmed down, no longer trying to tell me the story of his or her arrest, and concentrating on the names of three persons (with telephone numbers) who could act as references, otherwise I felt the interview was in trouble. This 'transition point', therefore, varies from study to study, depending on both the length and the substance of the interviews.

13. Although I believe I was almost always genuine in my admiration for aspects of the respondents' lives, the content of my compliments and 'fishing expeditions' varied according to social class. In Colton I found myself discussing television programs, admiring respondents' house plants and, to a lesser extent, their clothes. In Prescott I talked about classical music preferences, houses, and house decorations.

14. In these summaries I wrote a description of the respondents, the house, and key parts of the interview. I also listed critical quotes and their location on the tape (i.e., 'good quote about criticisms of school, end of side one').

15. These categories had been the analytic structure of my dissertation which had seven chapters: 1) a literature review and statement of the problem, 2) a description of the research methods, 3) a description of the two schools and the amount of parent involvement in each school, 4) parents' attitudes towards their role in schooling and the degree to which they complied with teachers' requests, 5) family life (i.e., lessons, gender roles, kinship ties) and the influence on family–school relationships, 6) teachers' wishes for parent involvement, and 7) the importance of cultural capital in shaping family–school relationships.

16. The class had a distinct (and very effective) structure. We were divided into groups of four, in roughly similar intellectual areas. We were to meet twice a week outside class to compare and discuss each other's field notes and problems in the field. Twice during the

quarter we made presentations in class and shared our field notes with the entire class. Burawoy also read our field notes and commented on them. Course requirements included a critical literature review to help formulate a problem, a paper based on the field work, and ten sets of field notes.

References

AGAR, M.H. (1986) *Speaking of Ethnography*, Beverly Hills, CA, Sage.

AGGLETON, P.J. and WHITTY, G. (1985) 'Rebels Without a Cause? Socialization and Subcultural Style Among the Children of the New Middle Class', *Sociology of Education*, 58, pp. 60–72.

ALEXANDER, K.L., FENNESSEY, J., McDILL, E. L., and D'AMICO, R.J. (1979) 'School SES Influences' Composition or Context? *Sociology of Education, 52*, October, pp. 222–37.

ALEXANDER, K.L., ENTWISLE, D.R., CADIGAN, D. and PALLAS, A. (1987a) 'Getting Ready for First Grade: Standards of Deportment in Home and School', *Social Forces, 66*' 1, pp. 57–84.

ALEXANDER, K.L., ENTWISLE, D.R. and THOMPSON, M.S. (1987b) 'School Performance, Status Relations, and the Structure of Sentiment: Bringing the Teacher Back In', *American Sociological Review 52*, October, pp. 665–82.

ALWIN, D.F. (forthcoming) 'Historical Changes in Parental Orientation to Children', *Sociological Studies of Child Development, 3*, Greenwich, CT, JAI Press.

AMATO, J.A. (1980) 'Social Class Discrimination in the Schooling Process: Myth and Reality', *Urban Review, 12*, 3, pp. 121–30.

ANYON, J. (1980) 'Social Class and the Hidden Cirriculum of Work', *Journal of Education*, 162, pp. 67–92.

ANYON, J. (1981) 'Social Class and School Knowledge', *Curriculum Inquiry* 11, pp. 1–42.

ANYON, J. (1984) 'Intersections of Gender and Class: Accommodation and Resistance by Working-Class and Affluent Females to Contradictory Sex Role Ideologies', *Journal of Education*, 166, 1 pp. 25–48.

ANYON, J. (1985) 'Social Class and School Knowledge Revisited: A Reply to Ramsay', *Curriculum Inquiry*, 15, pp. 207–387.

APPLE, M.W. (1979) *Ideology and Curriculum*, London, Routledge and Kegan Paul.

APPLE, M.W., and WEIS, L. (1985) 'Ideology and Schooling: The Relationship Between Class and Culture, *Education and Society*, 3, pp. 45–63.

ARANDELL, T. (1986) *Mothers and Divorce*, Berkeley, CA University of California Press.

ARIES, P. (1962) *Centuries of Childhood*, New York, Vintage Books.

ARNOT, M. (1984) 'A Feminist Perspective on the Relationship between Family Life and School Life', *Journal of Education*, 166, 1, pp. 5–48.

ARNOVE, R.F. and GRAFF, H.J. (Eds) (1987) *National Literacy Campaigns: Historical and Comparative Perspectives*, New York, Plenum Press.

ATKIN, J., BASTIANI, J. and GOODE, J. (1988) *Listening to Parents*, New York, Croom Helm.

ATKINSON, P. (1985) *Language, Structure, and Reproduction*, New York, Methuen.

AVERCH, H., CARROLL, S.J., DONALDSON, T., KIESLING, H. and PINCUS, J. (1972) *How Effective is Schooling?* Santa Monica, CA, Rand Corporation.

BAKER, D. and STEVENSON D. (1986) 'Mothers' Strategies for School Achievement: Managing the Transition to High School', *Sociology of Education*, 59, pp. 156–67.

BANE, M.J. (1976) *Here to Stay*, New York, Harper Colophon.

BARON, R.M., TOM, D.Y.H. and COOPER, H.M. (1985) 'Social Class, Race, and Teacher Expectations', in DUSEK J.B. (Ed.) *Teacher Expectancies*, New York, Lawrence Erlbaum, pp. 251–70.

BARR, R. and DREEBEN, R. (1983) *How Schools Work*, Chicago, University of Chicago Press.

BACKER, H.J. and EPSTEIN J.L. (1982) 'Parent Involvement: A Survey of Teacher Practices', *The Elementary School Journal*, 83, 2, pp. 85–102.

BECKER, H.S. (1952) 'Social Class Variations in the Teacher–Pupil Relationship', *Journal of Educational Sociology*, 25, 8, 451–65.

BENIN, M.H. and AGOSTINELLI, J. (1988) 'Husbands' and Wives' Satisfaction with the Division of Labor', *Journal of Marriage and the Family*, 50, May, pp. 349–61.

BENSON, C.S. (1980) 'Time and How It is Spent', in *Education Finance and Organization Research Perspectives for the Future*, Washington, DC, US Government Printing Office. pp. 163–90.

BERGER, E.H. (1983) *Beyond the Classroom: Parents as Partners in Education*, St. Louis, MO, CV Mosby.

BERK, S.F. (1985) *The Gender Factory*, New York, Plenum.

BERNARD, J. (1982) *The Future of Marriage*, New Haven, CT, Yale University Press.

BERNARD, J. (1989) 'The Good-Provider Role: Its Rise and Fall', in SKOLNICK, A.S. and SKOLNICK, J.H. (Eds) *Family in Transition*, 6th ed., Glenview, IL, Scott, Foresman, pp. 143–62.

BERNSTEIN, B. (1972) 'A Sociolinguistic Approach to Socialization; with some Reference to Educability', in GUMPEREZ, J.J. and HYMES, D. (Eds) *Direction in Sociolinguistics*, New York, Holt, Rinehart and Winston, pp. 465–97.

BERNSTEIN, B. (1975) *Class, Codes and Control*, New York, Schocken Books.

BERNSTEIN, B. (1982) 'Codes, Modalities and the Process of Cultural Reproduction: A Model', in APPLE, M.W. (Ed.) *Cultural and Economic Reproduction in Education*, London, Routledge and Kegan Paul, pp. 304–55.

BIELBY, W.T. (1981) 'Models of Status Attainment', *Research in Social Stratification and Mobility*, 1, pp. 3–26.

BILLS, D.B. (1988) 'Educational Credentials and Promotion', *Sociology of Education*, 61, 1, pp. 52–60.

BISSERET, N. (1979) *Education, Class Language and Ideology*, Boston, Routledge and Kegan Paul.

BLAU, F.D. (1984) 'Women in the Labor Force: An Overview', in FREEMAN, J. (Ed.) *Women: A Feminist Perspective*, Palo Alto, CA, Mayfield, pp. 297–315.

BLAU, J. (1986) 'High Culture as Mass Culture', *Society*, 23, 4, pp. 65–9.

BLAU, P. and DUNCAN, O.D. (1967) *The American Occupational Structure*, New York, Wiley.

BLOOD, R. Jr. and WOLFE, D.M. (1960) *Husbands and Wives*, New York, The Free Press.

BLUMBERG, P. (1982) *Inequality in an Age of Decline*, New York, Oxford University Press.

BOGDAN, R.C., and BIKLEN, S.K. (1982) *Qualitative Research for Education: An Introduction to Theory and Methods*, Boston, Allyn and Bacon.

BOSK, C.L. (1979) *Forgive and Remember*, Chicago, University of Chicago.

BOTT, E. (1971) *Family and Social Networks*, New York, Free Press.

BOURDIEU, P. (1976) 'Marriage Strategies as Strategies of Social Reproduction', in *Family and Society*, FORSTER, R. and RANUM, O. (Eds) Baltimore, MD, John Hopkins University Press, pp. 117–44.

BOURDIEU, P. (1977a) 'Cultural Reproduction and Social Reproduction', in KARABEL, J. and HALSEY, A.H. (Eds) *Power and Ideology in Education*, New York, Oxford., pp. 487–511.

BOURDIEU, P. (1977b) *Outline of a Theory of Practice*, NICE, R. (trans.), London, Cambridge University Press.

BOURDIEU, P. (1981a) 'The Specificity of the Scientific Field', in *French Sociology: Rupture and*

Renewal Since 1968, LEMERT, C.C. (Ed.) New York, Columbia University Press, pp. 257–92.

BOURDIEU, P. (1981b) Men and Machines. in KNORR-CETINA, K. and CICOUREL, A.V. (Eds) *Advances in Social Theory: Toward an Integration of Micro- and Macro- Sociologies*, Boston, Routledge and Kegan Paul, pp. 304–17.

BOURDIEU, P. (1984) *Distinction: A Social Critique of the Judgment of Taste*, NICE, R. (trans.), (Ed.) Cambridge, Harvard University Press.

BOURDIEU, P. (1985) 'The Social Space and the Genesis of Groups', *Theory and Society*, 14, 6, pp. 241–60.

BOURDIEU, P. (1987a) 'Forms of Capital' in RICHARDSON, J. G. *Handbook of Theory and Research for Sociology of Education*, (Ed.) New York, Greenwood Press.

BOURDIEU, P. (1987b) 'What Makes a Social Class? On the Theoretical and Practical Existence of Groups', *Berkeley Journal of Sociology*, 32, pp. 1–17.

BOURDIEU, P. and PASSERON, J.C. (1977) *Reproduction in Education, Society and Culture*, Beverly Hills, CA, Sage.

BOWERS, C.A. (1980) 'Curriculum as Cultural Reproduction: An Examination of Metaphor as a Carrier of Ideology,' *Teachers College Record*, 82, pp. 267–89.

BOWLES, S. and GINTIS, H. (1976) *Schooling in Capitalist America*, New York, Basic Books.

BRONFENBRENNER, U. (1966) 'Socialization and Social Class through Time and Space', in *Class, Status, and Power*, BENDIX, R. and LIPSET, S.M. (Eds) New York, The Free Press, pp. 362–77.

BRONFENBRENNER, U. (1979) 'Who Needs Parent Education? in LEICHTER, H.J. (Ed.) *Families and Communities as Educators*, New York, Teachers College Press, pp. 203–23.

BRONFENBRENNER, U. and CROUTER, A.C. (1982) 'Work and Family through Time and Space', in KAMERMAN, S.B. and HAYES, C.D. (Eds) *Families that Work*. Washington, DC, National Academy Press, pp. 39–83.

BROPHY, J.E. and GOOD, T.L. (1974) *Teacher — Student Relationships: Causes and Consequences*. New York, Holt, Rinehart, and Winston.

BRUBAKER, R. (1985) 'Rethinking Classical Theory: The Sociological Vision of P. Bourdieu', *Theory and Society*, 14, 6, pp. 745–77.

BUCHMANN, M. (1989) *The Script of Life*, Chicago, University of Chicago Press.

BULLIVANT, B.M. (1983) 'Cultural Production in Fiji: Who Controls Knowledge/Power?' *Comparative Education Review*, 27, pp. 227–45.

BURAWOY, M. (1979) *Manufacturing Consent*, Chicago, University of Chicago Press.

BUTTERWORTH, E. (1928) *The Parent–Teacher Association and Its Work*, New York, Macmillan.

CAMPBELL, A., CONVERSE, P.L. and RODGERS, W.L. (1976) *The Quality of American Life: Perceptions, Evaluations, and Satisfactions*, New York, Russell Sage.

CAMPBELL, R.T. (1983) 'Status Attainment Research: End of the Beginning or Beginning of the End?' *Sociology of Education*, 56, January, pp. 47–62.

CAPLOW, T., BAHR, H.M., CHADWICK, B.A., HILL, R. and WILLIAMSON, M.H. (1983) *Middletown Families: Fifty Years of Change and Continuity*, Minneapolis, MN, Bantam.

CARNOY, M. and LEVIN, H.M. (1985) *Schooling and Work in the Democratic State*, Stanford, Stanford University Press.

CHERLIN, A. (1978) 'Remarriage as an Incomplete Institution', *American Journal of Sociology*, 84, 3, pp. 634–50.

CHERLIN, A. (1981) *Marriage, Divorce, and Remarriage*, Cambridge, Harvard University Press.

CICOUREL, A.V. (1981) 'The Role of Cognitive-Linguistic Concepts in Understanding Everyday Social Interactions,' *American Review of Sociology*, 7, pp. 87–106.

CICOUREL, A.V. (1987) 'The Interpenetration of Communicative Contents: Examples from Medical Encounters', *Social Psychology Quarterly*, 50, 2, pp. 217–26.

CICOUREL, A.V. and KITSUSE, J.T. (1963) *The Educational Decision-Makers*, Indianapolis, Bobbs-Merrill.

CICOUREL, A.V., JENNINGS, K.H., JENNINGS, J.S., LEITER, K., MACKAY, R., MEHAN, H. and ROTH, D. (1974) *Language Use and School Performance*, New York, Academic.

CICOUREL, A.V. and MEHAN, H. (1985) 'Universal Development, Stratifying Practices, and Status Attainment', *Research in Social Stratification and Mobility*, 4, pp. 3–27.

CLARK, R.M. (1983) *Family Life and School Achievement*, Chicago, University of Chicago Press.

COHEN, D.K. (1978) 'Reforming School Politics,' *Harvard Educational Review*, 48, pp. 429–47.

COHEN, D.K. and LAZERSON, M. (1977) 'Education and the Corporate Order', in KARABLE, J. and HALSEY, A.H. (Eds) *Power and Ideology in Education*, New York, Oxford University Press, pp. 373–85.

COHEN, G. (1981) 'Culture and Educational Achievement', *Harvard Educational Review*, 51, pp. 270–85.

COLEMAN, J.S. (1985) 'Schools and the Communities They Serve', *Phi Kappan Delta*, 66, 8, pp. 527–32.

COLEMAN, J.S. (1987) 'Microfoundations and Macrosocial Behavior', in Alexander, J.C. (Ed.) *The Micro-Macro Link*, Berkeley, CA, University of California Press, pp. 153–76.

COLEMAN, J.S. (1987) 'Families and Schools,' *Educational Researcher*, 16, 6, pp. 32–8.

COLEMAN, J.S. (1988) 'Social Capital in the Creation of Human Capital,' *American Journal of Sociology*, 94, (Supplement), pp. 94–120.

COLEMAN, J.S. and HOFFER, T. (1987) *Public and Private High Schools: The Impact of Communities*, New York, Basic Books.

COLEMAN, J.S., CAMPBELL, E.Q., HOBSON, C.J., MACPARTLAND, J., MOOD, A.M., WEINFELD, F. and YORK, R. (1966) *Equality and Educational Opportunity*, Washington, DC, Office of Education, US Government Printing Office.

COLEMAN, R.P., RAINWATER, L. and MCCLELLAND, K.A. (1978) *Social Standing in America: New Dimension of Class*, New York, Basic Books.

COLLINS, R. (1971) 'Functional and Conflict Theories of Educational Stratification', *American Sociological Review*, 36, pp. 1002–19.

COLLINS, R. (1975) *Conflict Sociology*, New York, Academic Press.

COLLINS, R. (1979) *The Credential Society*, New York, Academic Press.

COLLINS, R. (1981a) *Sociology Since Midcentury*, New York, Academic Press.

COLLINS, R. (1981b) 'The Microfoundations of Macrosociology', *American Journal of Sociology*, 84, 6, pp. 1460–74.

COLLINS, R. (1987) 'Interaction Ritual Chains, Power and Property: The Micro-Macro Connection as an Empirically Based Theoretical Problem', in ALEXANDER, J.C. (Ed.) *The Micro-Macro Link*, Berkeley, CA, University of California Press, pp. 193–206.

COLLINS, R. (1988) 'The Micro Contribution to Macro Sociology', *Sociological Theory*, 6, 2, pp. 242–53.

COMER, J.P. (1980) *School Power*, New York, Free Press.

CONNELL, R.W., ASHENDEN, D.J., KESSLER, S. and DOWSETT, G.W. (1982) *Making the Difference*, Sydney, London, Boston, George Allen and Unwin.

COOK-GUMPEREZ, J. (1986) 'Caught in a Web of Words: Some Considerations on Language Socialization and Language Acquisition', in COOK-GUMPEREZ, J., CORSARO, W.A. and STREECK J., (Eds.) *Children's Worlds and Children's Languages*, pp. 37–64.

COOKSON, P.W. Jr., and PERSELL, C. (1985) 'English and American Residential Secondary Schools: A Comparative Study of the Reproduction of Social Elites', *Comparative Education Review*, 29, pp. 283–98.

COOKSON, P.W. Jr. and PERSELL, C. (1985) *Preparing for Power: America's Elite Boarding Schools*, New York, Basic Books.

COONS, J.E. and SUGARMAN, S.D. (1978) *Education by Choice: The Case for Family Control*, Berkeley, CA, University of California Press.

COOPER, H.M. and GOOD, T.L. (1983) *Pygmalion Grows Up*, New York, Longman.

CORSARO, W.A. (1985) *Friendship and Peer Culture in the Early Years*, Norwood, NJ, Ablex.

CORSARO, W.A. (1988) 'Routines in the Peer Culture of American and Italian Nursery School

Children', *Sociology of Education*, 61, 1, pp. 1–14.

CORWIN, R.G. and WAGANAAR, T.C. (1976) 'Boundary Interaction Between Service Organizations and Their Publics: A Study of Teacher–Parent Relationships,' *Social Forces*, 55, 2, pp. 471–91.

COVERMAN, S. (1985) 'Explaining Husbands' Participation in Domestic Labor', *Sociological Quarterly*, 26, 1, pp. 81–97.

COVERMAN, S. and SHELEY, J.F. (1986) 'Change in Men's Housework and Child-Care Time, 1965–1975', *Journal of Marriage and the Family*, 48, May, pp. 413–22.

CREMIN, L.A. (1964) *The Transformation of the School*, New York, Vintage Books.

DALE, R. (1982) 'Education and the Capitalist State: Contributions and Contradictions', in APPLE, M.W. (Ed.) *Cultural and Economic Reproduction in Education*, Boston, Routledge and Kegan Paul.

DAVIES, D. (Ed.) (1981) *Communities and Their Schools*, New York, McGraw Hill.

DAVIS, A. (1948) *Social-Class Influences Upon Learning*, Cambridge, Harvard University Press.

DAVIS, J.A. (1982) 'Achievement Variables and Class Cultures: Family, Schooling, Job, and Forty-Nine Dependent Variables in the Cumulative GSS', *American Sociological Review*, 47, October, pp. 569–86.

DAVIS, K. and MOORE, W.E. (1966), 'Some Principles of Stratification', in BENDIX, R. and LIPSET S.M. (Eds), *Class, Status, and Power*, 2nd ed., New York The Free Press, pp. 47–52.

DE GRAAF, P.M. (1986), 'The Impact of Financial and Cultural Resources on Educational Attainment in the Netherlands', *Sociology of Education*, 59, October, pp. 237–46.

DEMOS, J. (1970) *A Little Commonwealth*, New York, Oxford University Press.

DEUTSCH, M. (1967a) 'The Disadvantaged Child and the Learning Process', in DEUTSCH, M. (Ed.) *The Disadvantaged Child*, New York, Basic Books, pp. 39–58.

DEUTSCH, M. (1967b) 'The Role of Social Class in Language Development and Cognition', in PASSOW, A.H., GOLDBERG, M. and TANNENBAUM, A.J. (Eds) *Education of the Disadvantaged*, New York, Holt, Rinehart and Winston. pp. 214–24.

DIMAGGIO, P. (1979) 'Review Essay: On Pierre Bourdieu', *American Journal of Sociology*, 84, pp. 1460–74.

DIMAGGIO, P. (1982) 'Cultural Capital and School Success: The Impact of Status Culture Participation on the Grades of US High School Students', *American Sociological Review*, 47, pp. 189–201.

DIMAGGIO, P. and MOHR, J. (1985) 'Cultural Capital, Educational Attainment, and Marital Selection', *American Journal of Sociology*, 90, pp. 1231–61.

DIMAGGIO, P. and USEEM, M. (1982) 'The Arts in Class Reproduction', in APPLE, M.W. (Ed.) *Cultural and Economic Reproduction in Education*, Boston, Routledge and Kegan Paul, pp. 181–201.

DORNBUSCH, S.M., RITTER, P.L., LEIDERMAN, P.H., ROBERTS, D.F. and FRALEIGH, M.J. (1987) 'The Relation of Parenting Style to Adolescent School Performance,' *Child Development*, 58, pp. 1244–57.

DREEBEN, R. (1968) *On What is Learned in School*, Reading, MA, Addison-Wesley.

DREEBEN, R. and GAMORAN, A. (1986) 'Race, Instruction, and Learning,' *American Sociological Review*, 51, pp. 660–69.

DUSEK, J.B. (Ed.) (1985) *Teacher Expectancies*, Hillsdale, NJ, Lawrence Erlbaum.

DUSTER, T. (1981) 'Intermediate Steps Between Micro and Macro Integration: The Case for Screening for Inherited Disorders', in KNORR-CETINA, K. and CICOUREL, A.V. (Eds) *Advances in Social Theory: Toward an Integration of Micro- and Macro- Sociologists*, Boston, Routledge and Kegan Paul. pp. 109–36.

DYE, N. and D.B. SMITH (1986) 'Mother Love and Infant Death, 1750–1920', *Journal of American History*, 73, 2, pp. 329–53.

EDER, D. (1981) 'Ability Grouping as a Self-fulfilling Prophecy: A Micro-Analysis of Teacher–Student Interaction', *Sociology of Education*, 54, July, pp. 151–62.

EDER, D. and PARKER, S. (1987) 'The Cultural Production and Reproduction of Gender: The Effect of Extracurricular Activities on Peer-Group Culture', *Sociology of Education*, 60, July, pp. 200–13.

EDER, D. and SANFORD, S. (1986) 'The Development and Maintenance of Interactional Norms Among Early Adolescents', in ADLER, P. and ADLER, P. (Eds) *Sociological Studies of Child Development*, Greenwich, CT, JAI Press. pp. 283–300.

Education Week (1986) 'Here They Come, Ready or Not', *Education Week*, May 14 1986, 5, 34, pp. 14–32.

ELKIND, D. (1981) *The Hurried Child*, Reading, MA, Addison-Wesley.

ENGLAND, P. and FARKAS, G. (1986) *Household, Employment, and Gender: A Social, Economic, and Demographic View*, New York, Aldine.

ENTWISLE, D.R., ALEXANDER K.L., CADIGAN, D. and PALLAS, A. (1986) 'The Schooling Process in First Grade: Two Samples a Decade Apart', *American Educational Research Journal*, 23, 4, pp. 587–613.

ENTWISLE, D.R. and HAYDUK, L.A. (1978) *Too Great Expectations*, Baltimore, MD, John Hopkins University Press.

ENTWISLE, D.R. and HAYDUK, L.A. (1982) *Early Schooling*, Baltimore, MD, John Hopkins University Press.

ENTWISLE, D.R. and HAYDUK, L.A. (1988) 'Lasting Effects of Elementary School', *Sociology of Education*, 61, July, pp. 147–59.

ENTWISLE, D.R., and STEVENSON, H.W. (1987) 'Schools and Development', *Child Development*, 58, pp. 1149–50.

ENTWISLE, D.R., ALEXANDER, K.L., PALLAS, A.M. and CADIGAN, D. (1987) 'The Emergent Academic Self-Image of First Graders: Its Response to Social Structure', *Child Development*, 58, pp. 1190–1206.

EPSTEIN, J.L. (1986) 'Parents' Reactions to Teacher Practices of Parent Involvement', *The Elementary School Journal*, 86, 3, pp. 277–94.

EPSTEIN, J.L. (1987) 'Parent Involvement: What Research Says to Administrators', *Education and Urban Society*, 19, 2, pp. 119–36.

EPSTEIN, J.L. (forthcoming) 'Effects on Student Achievement of Teachers' Practices of Parent Involvement', in SILVERN, S. (Ed.) *Literacy Through Family, Community, and School Interaction*, Greenwich, CT, JAI Press.

EPSTEIN, J.L. and BECKER, H. J. (1982) 'Teachers' Reported, Practices of Parent Involvement: Problems and Possibilities', *The Elementary School Journal*, 83, 2, pp. 103–14.

EPSTEIN, J.L. and DUABER, S. L. (1988) 'Teacher Attitudes and Practices of Parent Involvement in Inner-City Elementary and Middle Schools,' Paper presented at the annual meetings of the American Sociological Association, Atlanta, GA.

ERICKSON, F. (1986) 'Qualitative Methods in Research on Teaching', *Handbook of Research on Teaching*, M.C. WITTROCK (Ed) New York, Macmillan, pp. 119–62.

ERICKSON, F. and MOHATT, G. (1982) 'Cultural Organization of Participation Structures in Two Classrooms of Indian Students', in SPINDLER, G. (Ed.) *Doing the Ethnography of Schooling*, New York, Holt, Rinehart and Winston, pp. 133–74.

ERIKSON, K.T. (1976) *Everything in its Path*, New York, Simon and Schuster.

ETZIONI, A. (1969) Preface in ETZIONI, A. (Ed.) *The Semi-Professions and Their Organizations*, New York, Free Press, pp. v–xviii.

EVERHART, R.B. (1983) *Reading, Writing, and Resistance*, Boston, Routledge and Kegan Paul.

FARKAS, G., GROBE, R.P. and SHEEHAN, D. (1987) 'Test and Nontest Performance, Work Habits, and Demeanor as Sources of School Achievement Outcomes for Gender, Ethnicity, and Poverty Groups.' Paper presented at the the annual meetings of the American Sociological Association, Chicago, IL.

FIELDING, N.G. and FIELDING, J.L. (1986) *Linking Data*, Beverly Hills, CA, Sage.

FILLION, B. (1987) 'School Influences on the Language of Children', in FILLION, B., HEDLEY, C.N. and DiMARTINO, E.C. (Eds) *Home and School: Early Language and Reading*, Norwood, NJ, Ablex, pp. 155–68.

FINELY, M. (1984) 'Teachers and Tracking in a Comprehensive High School', *Sociology of Education*, 57, October, pp. 233–43.

FISCHER, C.S. (1982a) *To Dwell Among Friends*, Chicago, University of Chicago Press.

FISCHER, C.S. (1982b) 'The Dispersion of Kinship Ties in Modern Society: Contemporary Data and Historical Speculation', *Journal of Family History*, 7, 4, pp. 353–65.

FLORIO-RUANE, S. (1987) 'Sociolinguistics for Educational Researchers', *American Educational Research Journal*, 24, 2, pp. 185–98.

FREIDSON, E. (1986) *Professional Powers*, Chicago, University of Chicago Press.

FRITZELL, C. (1987) 'On the Concept of Relative Autonomy in Educational Theory', *British Journal of Sociology of Education*, 8, 1, pp. 23–35.

FURSTENBERG, F.F. Jr. and SELTZER, J.A. (1986) 'Divorce and Child Development', in ADLER, P. and ADLER, P. (Eds) *Sociological Studies of Child Development*, Greenwich, CT, JAI Press. pp. 137–60.

FURSTENBERG, F.F. Jr. Morgan, S.P. and ALLISON, P.D. (1987) 'Paternal Participation and Children's Well-Being after Marital Dissolution', *American Sociological Review*, 52, 5, pp. 695–701.

GALLUP, G. (1985) 'Special Survey of Teacher's Attitudes Toward the Public Schools', *Phi Delta Kappan*, Princeton, NJ, 66, 5, pp. 323–30.

GAMORAN, A. (1986) 'Instructional and Institutional Effects of Ability Grouping', *Sociology of Education*, 59, October, pp. 185–98.

GAMORAN, A. (1987) 'The Stratification of High School Learning Opportunities', *Sociology of Education*, 60, July, pp. 135–55.

GARET, M.S. and DELANY, B. (1988) 'Students, Courses, and Stratification', *Sociology of Education*, 61, 2, pp. 61–77.

GASKELL, J. (1985) 'Course Enrollment in the High School: The Perspective of Working-Class Females', *Sociology of Education*, 58, January, pp. 48–59.

GECAS, V. (1979) 'The Influence of Social Class on Socialization', in BURR, W.R., HILL, R., NYE, F.I. and REISS, I.L. (Eds) *Contemporary Theories About the Family*, New York, Free Press, pp. 365–404.

GECAS, V. and NYE, F.I. (1974) 'Sex and Class Differences in Parent–Child Interaction: A Test of Kohn's Hypothesis', *Journal of Marriage and the Family*, 36, November, pp. 742–9.

GEERTZ, C. (1979) 'Deep Play: Notes on the Balinese Cockfight', in RABINOW, P. and SULLIVAN, W.M. (Eds) 1st ed. *Interpretive Social Science: A Reader*, Berkeley, CA, University of California Press, pp. 181–224.

GEORGES, R.A. and JONES, M.O. (1980) *People Studying People*, Berkeley, CA, University of California Press.

GILBERT, D. and KAHL, J.A. (1987) *The American Class Structure: A New Synthesis*, Chicago, Dorsey Press.

GIROUX, H.A. (1983) *Theory and Resistance in Education*, South Hadley, MA, Bergin and Garvey.

GLASER, B.G. and STRAUSS, A.L. (1967) *The Discovery of Grounded Theory: Strategies for Qualitative Research*, New York, Aldine.

GLICK, P.C. and LIN, S. (1986) 'Recent Changes in Divorce and Remarriage', *Journal of Marriage and Family*, 48, November, pp. 737–45.

GOODE, W.J. (1969) 'The Theoretical Limits of Professionalization', in ETZIONI, A. (Ed.) *The Semi-Professions and Their Organizations*, New York, Free Press, pp. 266–313.

GORDEN, R.L. (1987) *Interviewing: Strategy, Techniques, and Tactics*, Chicago, Dorsey Press.

GOTTS, E.E. and PURNELL, R.F. (1986) 'Communication: Key to School–Home Relations', in GRIFFORE, R.J. and BOGER, R.P. (Eds) *Child Rearing in the Home and School*, New York, Plenum, pp. 157–200.

GRACEY, H.L. (1972) *Curriculum and Craftsmanship*, Chicago, University of Chicago Press.

GRANOVETTER, M. (1973) 'The Strength of Weak Ties', *American Journal of Sociology*, 78, pp. 1360–80.

GRANT, C.A. and SLEETER, C.E. (1986) *After the School Bell Rings*, Phildelphia, Falmer Press.

GRANT, W.V. and SNYDER, T.D. (1985) *Digest of Education Statistics, 1985–1986*, Washington, DC, US Government Printing Office.

GRAY, S.T. (1984) 'How to Create a Successful School/Community Partnership', *Phi Kappan Delta*, 64, 4, pp. 405–9.

GRIFFITH, A. and SMITH, D. (forthcoming) 'What Did You Do in School Today? Mothering, Schooling, and Social Class', *Perspectives on Social Problems*.

GRIFFORE, R.J. and BOGER, R.P. (Eds) (1986) *Child Rearing in the Home and School*, New York, Plenum.

HAKKEN, D. (1980) 'Workers' Education and the Reproduction of Working Class Culture in Sheffield, England', *Anthropology and Education Quarterly*, 11, pp. 211–34.

HALLER, E.J. and DAVIS, S.A. (1980) 'Does SES Bias the Assignment of Elementary School Students to Reading Groups?' *American Educational Research Journal*, 17, pp. 410–18.

HALLER, E.J. and DAVIS, S.A. (1981) 'Teacher Perceptions, Parental Social Status and Grouping for Reading Instruction', *Sociology of Education*, 54, July, pp. 162–74.

HAREVEN, T.K. (1982) *Family Time and Industrial Time*, Cambridge, Cambridge University Press.

HARKER, R.K. (1984) 'On Reproduction, Habitus and Education', *British Journal of Sociology of Education*, 5, pp. 117–28.

HARRIS, L. (1985a) *The Metropolitan Life Survey of The American Teacher*, New York, Metropolitan Insurance Company.

HARRIS, L. (1985b) *The Metropolitan Life Survey of Former Teachers in America*, New York, Metropolitan Insurance Company.

HAUSER, R.M. and FEATHERMAN, D. (1977) *The Process of Stratification*. New York, Academic Press.

HAVEMAN, R.H. (1977) 'Poverty and Social Policy in the 1960s and 1970s — An Overview and Some Speculations', in HAVEMAN, R.H. (Ed.) *A Decade of Federal Antipoverty Programs*, New York, Academic Press.

HAVIGHURST, R.S. and DAVIS, A. (1969) 'A Comparison of the Chicago and Harvard Studies of Social Class Differences in Child Rearing', *American Sociological Review*, 20, pp. 438–42.

HEATH, S.B. (1982a) 'What No Bedtime Story Means: Narrative Skills at Home and School', *Language in Society*, 11, 2, pp. 49–76.

HEATH, S.B. (1982b) 'Questioning at Home and at School: A Comparative Study', in SPINDLER, G. (Ed.) *Doing the Ethnography of Schooling*, New York, Holt, Rinehart and Winston. pp. 102–31.

HEATH, S.B. (1983) *Ways with Words*, New York, Cambridge University Press.

HENDERSON, A. (1981) *Parent Participation–Student Achievement: The Evidence Grows*, An Annotated Bibliography, Columbia, MD, National Committee for Citizens in Education.

HERMAN, J.L. and YEH, J.P. (1983) 'Some Effects of Parents Involvement in Schools', *The Urban Review*, 15, 1, pp. 11–17.

HESS, R.D., MCDEVITT, T.M. and CHANG CHIH-MEI. (1987) 'Cultural Variations in Family Beliefs About Children's Performance in Mathematics: Comparisons Among People's Republic of China, Chinese–American, and Caucasian–American Families', *Journal of Educational Psychology*, 79, 2, pp. 179–88.

HEYNS, B. (1974) 'Social Selection and Stratification Within Schools', *American Journal of Sociology*, 79, 6, pp. 89–102.

HEYNS, B. (1978) *Summer Learning and the Effects of Schooling*, New York, Academic Press.

HEYNS, B. (1982) 'The Influence of Parents' Work on Children's School Achievement', in KAMERMAN, S.B. and HAYES, C.D. (Eds) *Families that Work: Children in a Changing World*, Washington, DC, National Academy Press, pp. 229–67.

HEYNS, B. (1987) 'Schooling and Cognitive Development: Is There a Season for Learning?' *Child Development*, 58, pp. 1151–60.

HEYNS, B. and CATSAMBIS, S. (1986) 'Mother's Employment and Children's Achievement: A Critique', *Sociology of Education*, 59, pp. 140–51.

HOCHSCHILD, A.R. (1985) *The Managed Heart*, Berkeley, CA, University of California Press.

HODGE, R.W., TREIMAN, D.J. and ROSSI, P. (1966) 'A Comparative Study of Occupational Prestige', in BENDIX, R. and LIPSET, S.M. (Eds) *Class, Status, and Power*, New York, The Free Press, pp. 309–21.

HOGGART, R. (1957) *The Uses of Literacy*, Boston, Beacon Press.

HOOVER-DEMPSEY, V., BASSLER, O.C. and BRISSIE, J.S. (1987) 'Parent Involvement: Contributions of Teacher Efficacy, School Socio-economic Status, and the Other School Characteristics', *American Educational Research Journal*, 24, 3, pp. 417–35.

HOUT, M. (1988) 'More Universalism, Less Structural Mobility: The American Occupational Structure in the 1980s', *American Journal of Sociology*, 93, 3, pp. 1358–1400.

HOWELL, F.M. and McBROOM, L.W. (1982) 'Social Relations at Home and School: An Analysis of the Correspondence Principle', *Sociology of Education*, 55, January, pp. 40–52.

HUBER, J. and SPITZE, G. (1983) *Sex Stratification*, New York, Academic Press.

HUGHES, E.C. (1963) 'Professions', *Daedalus*, 92, 4, pp. 655–68.

HYMAN, H. (1966) 'The Value System of Different Classes', in BENDIX, R. and LIPSET, S.M. (Eds) *Class, Status and Power*, New York, Free Press, pp. 488–99.

HYMES, J.L. (1953) *Effective Home–School Relations*, New York, Prentice-Hall.

HYNES, E. (1985) 'Socialization Values and Punishment Behavior', *Sociological Perspectives'*, 28, April, pp. 217–39.

ITOH, F. and TAYLOR, C.M. (1986) 'A Comparison of Child-Rearing Expectations of Parents in Japan and the United States', in KURIAN, G. (Ed.) *Parent-Child Interaction in Transition*, New York, Greenwood, pp. 137–48.

JENCKS, C., SMITH, M., ACLAND, H., BANE, M.J., COHEN, D., GINTIS, H., HEYNS, B. and MICHELSON, S. (1972) *Inequality*, New York, Harper and Row.

JOFFEE, C. (1977) *Friendly Intruders*, Berkeley, CA, University of California Press.

JONES, J.H. (1982) *Bad Blood*, New York, Free Press.

KAESTLE, C.F. (1978) 'Social Change, Discipline, and the Common School in Early Nineteenth Century America', *Journal of Interdisciplinary History*, 9, 1, pp. 1–17.

KAESTLE, C.F. (1983) *Pillars of the Republic*, New York, Hill and Wang.

KAESTLE, C.F. and VINOVSKIS, M.A. (1978a) 'From Apron Strings to ABCs: Parents, Children, and Schooling in Nineteenth Century Massachusetts', in DENOS, J. and BOOCOCK, S.S. (Eds) *Turning Points*, Chicago, University of Chicago Press. pp. 539–80.

KAESTLE, C.F., and VINOVSKIS, M.A. (1978b) 'From Fireside to Factory: School Entry and School Leaving in Nineteenth Century Massachusetts', in HAREVEN, T.K. (Ed.) *Transitions: The Family and the Life Course in Historical Perspective*, New York, Academic Press, pp. 135–86.

KAGAN, S.L. and ZIGLER, E.F. (Eds) (1987) *Early Schooling: The National Debate*, New Haven, CN, Yale University Press.

KANTER, R.M. (1977) *Men and Women of the Corporation*, New York, Basic Books.

KARABEL, J. (1977) 'Community Colleges and Social Stratification: Submerged Class Conflict in American Higher Education', in KARABEL, J. and HALSEY, A.H. (Eds) *Power and Ideology in Education*, New York, Oxford University Press, pp. 232–54.

KARABEL, J. and HALSEY, A.H. (1977) 'Educational Research: A Review and Interpretation', in KARABEL, J. and HALSEY, A.H. (Eds) *Power and Ideology in Education*, New York, Oxford University Press, pp. 1–86.

KATZ, I. (1967) 'Socialization of Achievement Motivation in Minority Group Children', in LEVINE, D. (Ed.) *Nebraska Symposium in Motivation*, Lincoln, NE, University of Nebraska Press.

KATZ, M. (1967) *Class, Bureaucracy and Schools*, New York, Praegers.

KATZ, M. (1968) *The Irony of Early School Reform*, Cambridge, MA, Harvard University Press.

KELLY, G.P. and NIHLEN, A.S. (1982) 'Schooling and the Reproduction of Patriarchy:

Unequal Workloads, Unequal Rewards', in APPLE, M.W. (Ed.) *Cultural and Economic Reproduction in Education*, Boston, Routledge and Kegan Paul, pp. 162–80.

KELLY, J.B. and WALLERSTEIN, J.S. (1976) 'The Effects of Parental Divorce: Experiences of the Child in Early Latency', *American Journal of Orthopsychiatry*, 46, pp. 20–31.

KERCKHOFF, A.C. (1972) *Socialization and Social Class*, Englewood Cliffs, NJ, Prentice-Hall.

KERCKHOFF, A.C. (1976) 'The Status Attainment Process: Socialization or Allocation', *Social Forces*, 55, 2, pp. 368–81.

KERCKHOFF, A.C. (1986) 'Effects of Ability Grouping in British Secondary Schools', *Sociology of Education*, 51, 6, pp. 842–58.

KIRK, J. and MILLER, M.L. (1986) *Reliability and Validity in Qualitative Research*, Beverly Hills, CA, Sage.

KNOTTNERUS, J.D. (1987) 'Status Attainment Research and Its Image of Society', *American Sociological Review*, 52, February, pp. 113–21.

KOHN, M.L. (1959) 'Social Class and Parental Values', *American Journal of Sociology*, 64, pp. 337–51.

KOHN, M.L. (1963) 'Social Class and Parent-Child: An Interpretation', *American Journal of Sociology*, 68, pp. 471–80.

KOHN, M.L. (1977) *Class and Conformity: A Study of Values*, 2nd ed. Chicago, University of Chicago Press.

KOHN, M.L. (1983a) 'Bureaucratic Man: A Portrait and an Interpretation', in KOHN, M.L. and SCHOOLER, C. (Eds) *Work and Personality*, Norwood, NJ, Ablex. pp. 34–52.

KOHN, M.L. (1983b) 'Occupational Structure and Alienation', in KOHN, M.L. and SCHOOLER, C. (Eds) *Work and Personality*, Norwood, NJ, Ablex. pp. 82–98.

KOHN, M.L. (1983c) 'Unresolved Interpretive Issues', in KOHN, M.L. and SCHOOLER, C. (Eds) *Work and Personality*, Norwood, NJ, Ablex. pp. 296–314.

KOHN, M.L. and SCHOOLER, C. (Eds) (1983a) *Work and Personality*, Norwood, NJ, Ablex.

KOHN, M.L. and SCHOOLER, C. (1983b) 'Stratification, Occupation, and Orientation', in KOHN, M.L. and SCHOOLER, C. (Eds) *Work and Personality*, Norwood, NJ, Ablex. pp. 5–33.

KOHN, M.L. and SCHOOLER, C. (1983c) 'Occupational Experience and Psychological Functioning: An Assessment of Reciprocal Effects', in KOHN M.L. and SCHOOLER, C. (Eds) *Work and Personality*, Norwood, NJ, Ablex. pp. 55–81.

KOHN, M.L. and SCHOOLER, C. (1983c) 'The Reciprocal Effects of the Substantive Complexity of Work and Intellectual Flexibility: A Longitudinal Assessment', in KOHN, M.L. and SCHOOLER, C. (Eds) *Work and Personality*, Norwood, NJ, Ablex. pp. 103–24.

KOHN, M.L. and SCHOOLER, C. (1983d) 'Job Conditions and Personality: A Longitudinal Assessment of Their Reciprocal Effects', in KOHN, M.L. and SCHOOLER, C. (Eds) *Work and Personality*, Norwood, NJ, Ablex. pp. 125–53.

KOHN, M.L. and SCHOOLER, C. (1983e) 'Class, Stratification, and Psychological Functioning', in KOHN, M.L. and SCHOOLER, C. (Eds) *Work and Personality*, Norwood, NJ, Ablex. pp. 154–90.

KOHN, M.L. and SCHOOLER, C. (1983f) 'The Cross-National Universality of the Interpretive Model', in KOHN M.L. and SCHOOLER, C. (Eds) *Work and Personality*, Norwood, NJ, Ablex. pp. 281–95.

KOHN, M., SLOMCZYNSKI, K.M. and SCHOENBACH, C. (1986) 'Social Stratification and the Transmission of Values in the Family: A Cross-National Assessment', *Sociological Forum*, 1, 1, pp. 73–102.

KROEBER, A.L., and PARSONS, T. (1958) 'The Profession: Reports and Opinion', *American Sociological Review*, 23, pp. 582–83.

KUHN, A.L. (1947) *The Mother's Role in Childhood Education: New England Concepts 1830–1860*, New Haven, Yale University Press.

KUHN, T.S. (1979) 'The Relations Between History and the History of Science', in RABINOW, P. and SULLIVAN, W.M. (Eds) *Interpretive Social Science: A Reader*, Berkeley, CA, University of California Press. pp. 267–300.

KURDEK, L.A., BLISK, D. and SIESKY, A.E. Jr. (1981) 'Correlates of Children's Long-Term Adjustment to Their Parents' Divorce', *Developmental Psychology*, 17, 5, pp. 565–79.

LAMONT, M. and LAREAU, A. (1988) 'Cultural Capital: Allusions, Gaps, and Glissandos in Recent Theoretical Developments', *Sociological Theory*, 6, Fall, pp. 153–68.

LAREAU, A. (1987) 'Social Class and Family–School relationships: The Importance of Cultural Capital', *Sociology of Education*, 56, April, pp. 73–85.

LAREAU, A. (forthcoming) 'Family-School Relationships; A View From the Classroom', *Educational Policy*.

LARSON, M.S. (1979) *The Rise of Professionalism: A Sociological Analysis*, Berkeley, CA, University of California Press.

LASCH, C. (1977) *Haven in a Heartless World*, New York, Basic Books.

LEACOCK, E.B. (1969) *Teaching and Learning in City Schools*, New York, Basic Books.

LEE, G.R. (1979) 'Effects of Social Networks on the Family', in BURR, W.R., HILL, R., NYE, F.I. and REISS, I.L. (Eds) *Contemporary Theories About the Family*, New York, Free Press. pp. 27–56.

LEE, G.R. and PETERSEN, L.R. (1983) 'Conjugal Power and Spousal Resources in Patriarchal Cultures', *Journal of Comparative Family Studies*, 14, pp. 23–38.

LEE, V.E. and BRYK, A.S. (1988) 'Curriculum Tracking as Mediating the Social Distribution of High School Achievement',-*Sociology of Education*, 61, April, pp. 78–94.

LEIBONWITZ, A. (1977) 'Parental Inputs and Children's Achievement', *The Journal of Human Resources*, 12, Spring, pp. 242–88.

LEICHTER, H.J. (1974) 'Some Perspectives on the Family as Educator', *Teachers College Record*, 76, December, pp. 175–217.

LEICHTER, H.J. (1979) 'Families and Communities as Educators: Some Concepts of Relationships', in LEICHTER, H.J. (Ed.) *Families and Communities as Educators*, New York, Teachers College Program, pp. 3–94.

LESKO, N. (1988) *Symbolizing Society: Stories, Rites and Structure in a Catholic High School*, Lewes, Falmer Press.

LEVY, F., MELTSNER, A.J. and WILDAVSKY, A. (1975) *Urban Outcomes: Schools, Streets, and Libraries*. Berkeley, CA, University of California Press.

LIEBOW, E. (1967) *Tally's Corner*, Boston, Little, Brown and Co.

LIGHTFOOT, S.L. (1978) *Worlds Apart* New York, Basic Books.

LIGHTFOOT, S.L. (1983) *The Good High School*, New York, Basic Books.

LIPMAN-BLUMEN (1984) *Gender Roles and Power*, Englewood Cliffs, NJ, Prentice-Hall.

LITWACK, E. (1971) 'Kinship and Other Primary Groups', in ANDERSON, M. (Ed.) *Sociology of the Family*, Middlesex, England, Penguin Books, pp. 149–63.

LITWACK, E. and MEYER, H.A. (1966) 'A Balance Theory of Coordination Between Bureaucratic Organizations and Community Primary Groups', *Administrative Science Quarterly*, 11, June, pp. 31–58.

LITWACK, E. and MEYER, II.J. (1973) 'The School and the Family: Linking Organizations and External Primary Groups' in SIEBIR, D. AND WILDER, D.E. (Eds) *The School in Society*, New York, Free Press, pp. 425–35.

LITWAK, E. and MEYER, H.J. (1974) *School, Family, and Neighborhood: The Theory and Practice of School-Community Relations*, New York, Columbia University Press.

LORTIE, D.C. (1977) *School-Teacher: A Sociological Study*, Chicago, University of Chicago Press.

LUBECK, S. (1984) 'Kinship and Classrooms: An Ethnographic Perspective on Education as Cultural Transmission', *Sociology of Education*, 57, pp. 219–32.

LUBECK, S. (1985) *Sandbox Society*, Lewes, Falmer Press.

LYND, R.S. and LYND, H.M. (1929) *Middletown*, New York, Harcourt, Brace and Co.

McCLELLAND, D.C., ATKINSON, J.W., CLARK, R.A. and LOWELL, E.A. (1953) *The Achievement Motive*, New York, Appleton-Century-Croft.

McDERMOTT, R.P. (1977) 'Social Relations as Contexts for Learning in School', *Harvard Educational Review*, 45, 1, pp. 311–38.

McPherson, G.H. (1972) *Small Town Teacher*, Cambridge, MA, Harvard University Press.

Macrorie, K. (1985) *Telling Writing*, Upper Montclair, NJ, Boynton/Cook.

Margolis, D.R. (1979) *The Managers: Corporate Life in American*, New York, W. Morrow and Company.

Marjoribands, K. (1987) 'Ability and Attitude Correlates of Academic Achievement: Family-Group Differences', *Journal of Education Psychology*, 79, 2, pp. 171–78.

Mason, K.O. and Lu, Y. (1988) 'Attitudes Toward Women's Familial Roles: Changes in the United States 1977–1985', *Gender and Society*, 2, March, pp. 39–57.

Medrich, E.A., Roizen, J.A., Rubin, V. and Buckley, S. (1982) *The Serious Business of Growing Up*, Berkeley, CA, University of California Press.

Mehan, H. (1978) 'Structuring School Structure', *Harvard Educational Review*, 48, pp. 32–64.

Mehan, H. (1979) *Learning Lessons*, Cambridge, MA, Harvard University Press.

Mehan, H., Hertweck, A. and Meihls, J.L. (1986) *Handicapping the Handicapped*, Standford, CA, Standford University Press.

Metz, M.H. (1979) *Classrooms and Corridors*, Berkeley, CA, University of California Press.

Metz, M.H. (1986) *Different by Design*, London, Routledge and Kegan Paul.

Meyer, J. (1977) 'The Effects of Education as an Institution', *American Journal of Sociology*, 73, pp. 55–77.

Mickelson, R.A. (1987) 'The Case of the Missing Brackets: Teachers and Social Reproduction', *Journal of Education*, 169, 2, pp. 78–88.

Miles, M.B. and Huberman, A.M. (1984) *Qualitative Data Analysis: A Source Book of New Methods*, Beverly Hills, CA, Sage.

Miller, D. and Swanson, G. (1958) *The Changing American Parent*, New York, John Wiley.

Miller, J., Schooler, C., Kohn, M.L. and Miller, K.A. (1983) 'Women and Work: The Psychological Effects of Occupational Conditions', in Kohn, M.L. and Schooler, C. (Eds) *Work and Personality*, Norwood, NJ, Ablex, pp. 195–216.

Miller, K.A. and Kohn, M.L. (1983) 'The Reciprocal Effects of Job Conditions and the Intellectuality of Leisure-Time Activities', in Kohn, M.L. and Schooler, C. (Eds) *Work and Personality*, Norwood, NJ, Ablex, pp. 217–41.

Miller, K.A., Kohn, M.L. and Schooler, C. (1986) 'Educational Self-Direction and Personality', *American Sociological Review*, 51, June, pp. 372–90.

Miller, R.M. Jr. (1988) 'How Institutions are Interrelated: Linkages and Processes', Paper presented at the annual meeting of the American Sociological Association, Atlanta, GA.

Miller, S.M., and Reissman, F. (1969) 'The Working Class Subculture: A New View', in Grey A. (Ed.) *Class and Personality in Society*, New York, Atherton Press, pp. 99–117.

Miller, W. (1958) 'Lower Class Culture as a Generating Milieu of Delinquency', *Journal of Social Issues*, 14, 3, pp. 5–19.

Mills, C.W. (1953) *White Collar*, New York, Oxford University Press.

Mills, C.W. (1959) *The Sociological Imagination*, New York, The Free Press.

Milne, A., Myers, D., Rosenthal A., and Ginsburg, A. (1986) 'Single Parents, Working Mothers, and the Educational Achievement of School Children', *Sociology of Education*, 59, 3, pp. 125–39.

Molotch, H. and Boden, D. (1985) 'Talking Social Structure: Discourse, Domination and the Watergate Hearings', *American Sociological Review*, 50, 3, pp. 273–88.

Morrison, G.S. (1978) *Parent Involvement in the Home, School, and Community*, Columbus, OH, Charles E. Merrill.

National Commission on Excellence in Education. (1983) *A Nation at Risk: The Imperative for Educational Reform*, Washington, DC, US Department of Education.

National Committee for Citizens in Education. (1974) *Children, Parents, and School Records*, Columbia, MD, Wilde Lake Village Green.

National Congress of Parents and Teachers. (1944) *The Parent–Teacher Organization, Its Origins and Development*, Chicago, National Congress of Parents and Teachers.

National Congress of Parents and Teachers. (1945) 'How to Organize Parent–Teacher

Associations and Pre-school Section of PTAs', Chicago, National Congress of Parents and Teachers.

NATIONAL CONGRESS OF PARENTS AND TEACHERS. (1953) 'Moral and Spiritual Education in Home, School and Community', Chicago, National Congress of Parents and Teachers.

NATIONAL EDUCATION ASSOCIATION. (1972) *Parent Involvement: A Key to Better Schools*, Washington, DC, NEA Press.

NISBET, R. (1959) 'The Decline and Fall of Social Class', *Pacific Sociological Review*, 2, Spring, pp. 11–18.

NOCK, S. (1979) 'The Family Life Cycle: Empirical or Conceptual Tool', *Journal of Marriage and the Family*, 41, February, pp. 15–26.

OAKES, J. (1982) 'Classroom Social Relationships: Exploring the Bowles and Gintis Hypothesis', *Sociology of Education*, 55, October, pp. 197–212.

OAKES, J. (1985) *Keeping Track*, New Haven, CT, Yale University Press.

OGBU, J. (1974) *The Next Generation*, New York, Washington, DC.

OLIVER, M.L., RODRIGUEZ, C.J. and MICKELSON, R.A. (1985) 'Brown and Black in White: The Social Adjustment and Academic Performance of Chicano and Black Students in a Predominately White University', *The Urban Review*, 17, 1, pp. 3–23.

OLNECK, M.R. and BILLS, D. (1980) 'What Makes Sammy Run? An Empirical Assessment of the Bowles–Gintis Correspondence Theory', *American Journal of Education*, 89, 1, pp. 27–61.

OLNECK, M.R., and LAZERSON, M. (1988) 'The School Achievement of Immigrant Children: 1900–1930', in McCLELLAN, B. and REESE, W.J. (Eds) *The Social History of American Education*, Urbana, IL, University of Illinois Press. pp. 257–86.

OSWALD, H., BAKER, D.P. and STEVENSON, D.L. (1988) 'School Charter and Parental Management in West Germany', *Sociology of Education*, 61, October, pp. 255–65.

OTTO, L.B. (1975) 'Class and Status in Family Research', *Journal of Marriage and the Family*, 37, pp. 315–32.

OVERSTREET, H. and OVERSTREET, B. (1949) *Where Children Come First*, Chicago, National Congress of Parents and Children.

PACKARD, V. (1964) *The Pyramid Climbers*, New York, Fawcett World Library.

PARSONS, T. (1961) 'The School Class and a Social System: Some of Its Functions in American Society', in HALSEY, A.H., FLOUD, J. and ANDERSON, C.A. (Eds) *Education, Economy and Society*, New York, Free Press, pp. 434–55.

PARSONS, T. (1964) *The Social System*, New York, Free Press.

PARSONS, T. and BALES, R.F. (1955) *Family, Socialization and Interaction Process*, Glencoe, Free Press.

PARSONS, T. and SHILS, E.A. (Eds) (1965) *Toward a General Theory of Action*. New York, Harper and Row.

PEARLIN, L. and KOHN, M.L. (1966) 'Social Class, Occupation and Parental Values: A Cross-National Study', *American Sociological Review*, 31, pp. 466–79.

PETERSON, R.A. (1976) *The Production of Culture*, Beverly Hills, CA, Sage.

PETERSON, R.A. (1979) 'Revitalizing the Culture Concept', *Annual Review of Sociology*, 5, pp. 137–66.

PFEFFER, J. and SALANCIK, G.R. (1978) *The External Control of Organizations*. New York, Harper and Row.

PODHORETZ, N. (1967) *Making It*, New York, Random House.

POLLACK, L. (1983) *Forgotten Children*, New York, Cambridge University Press.

POWDERMAKER, H. (1966) *Stranger and Friend*, New York, W.W. Norton.

POWELL, D.R. (1978) 'Correlates of Parent–Teacher Communication Frequency and Diversity', *Journal of Educational Research*, 71, 6, pp. 333–41.

POWER, T.J. (1985) 'Perceptions of Competence: How Parents and Teachers View Each Other', *Psychology in the Schools*, 22, pp. 68–78.

PUNCH, M. (1986) *The Politics and Ethics of Field Work*, Beverly Hills, CA, Sage.

RABINOW, P. (1977) *Reflections on Fieldwork in Morocco*, Berkeley, CA, University of California Press.

RABINOW, P. and SULLIVAN, W.M. (1979) 'The Interpretive Turn: Emergence of an Approach', in RABINOW, P. and SULLIVAN, W.M. (Ed.) *Interpretive Social Science: A Reader*, Berkeley, CA, University of California Press, pp. 1–24.

REISSMAN, F. (1962) *The Culturally Deprived Child*, New York, Harper and Row.

RICH, D. (1986) Focus for Education reform: 'Building the Home–School Synergism', in GRIFFORE, R.J. and BOGER, R.P. (Eds) *Child Rearing in the Home and School*, New York, Plenum, pp. 201–22.

RICH, D. (1987a) *Teachers and Parents: An Adult-to-Adult Approach*, Washington, DC, NEA Press.

RICH, D. (1987b) *Schools and Families: Issues and Actions*, Washington, DC, NEA Press.

RIST, R.C. (1970) 'Student Social Class and Teacher Expectation: The Self-Fulfilling Prophecy in Ghetto Education', *Harvard Educational Review*, 40, pp. 411–50.

RIST, R.C. (1977) 'On Understanding the Processes of Schooling: The Contribution of Labeling Theory', in KARABEL, J. and HALSEY, A.H. (Eds) *Power and Ideology in Education*, New York, Oxford University Press. pp. 292–306.

RIST, R.C. (1978) *The Invisible Children*, Cambridge, MA, Harvard University Press.

ROBINSON, R.V. and GARNIER M.A. (1985) 'Class Reproduction Among Men and Women in France: Reproduction Theory on Its Home Ground', *American Journal of Sociology*, 91, 2, pp. 250–80.

ROSSI, A.S. (1984) 'Gender and Parenthood', *American Sociological Review*, 49, February, pp. 1–19.

ROTTER, J.C., HOBINSON, E.J. FEY, M.A. (1987) *Parent–Teacher Conferencing*, 2nd ed. Washington DC, National Education Association.

RUBIN, L.B. (1976) *Worlds of Pain*, New York, Basic Books.

RYAN, B. JUN (1981) *How to Help Your Child Start School*, New York, Perigee.

SAFILIOS-ROTHSCHILD, C. (1970) 'The Study of Family Power Structure: A Review 1960–1969', *Journal of Marriage and the Family*, 31, November, pp. 539–50.

SAINSAULIEU, R. (1981) 'On Reproduction', in LEMERT, C.C. (Ed.) *French Sociology: Rupture and Renewal Since 1968*, New York, Columbia University Press, pp. 152–70.

SCHATZMAN, L. and STRAUSS, A.L. (1973) *Field Research*, Englewood Cliffs, NJ, Prentice Hall.

SCHEGLOFF, E.A. (1987) 'Between Macro and Micro: Contexts and Other Connections', in ALEXANDER, J.C. (Ed.) *The Micro-Macro Link* Berkeley, CA, University of California Press, pp. 207–36.

SCHLOSSMAN, S. (1976) 'Before Home Start: Notes Towards a History of Parent Education in America 1897–1929', *Harvard Educational Review*, 46, pp. 436–67.

SCHLOSSMAN, S. (1983) 'The Formative Era in American Parent Education: Overview and Interpretation', in HASKINS, R. (Ed.) *Parent Education and Public Policy*, New York, Ablex, pp. 7–39.

SCHLOSSMAN, S. (1986) 'Family as Educator, Parent Education, and the Perennial Family Crisis', in GRIFFORE, R.J. and BOGER, R.P. (Eds) *Child Rearing in the Home and School*, New York, Plenum, pp. 31–46.

SCHON, D.A. (1987) The Art of Managing: 'Reflection-In-Action Within an Organizational Learning System', in RABINOW, P. and SULLIVAN, W.M. (Eds) *The Interpretive Turn: A Second Look*, Berkeley, CA, University of California Press. pp. 302–26.

SCHOOLER, C. (1983) 'Serfdom's Legacy: An Ethnic Continuum', in KOHN, M.L. and SCHOOLER, C. (Eds) in*Work and Personality*, Norwood, NJ, Ablex. pp. 261–78.

SCHOOLER, C., KOHN, M.L., MILLER, K.A. and MILLER, J. (1983) Housework as Work', in KOHN, M.L. and SCHOOLER, C. (Eds) *Work and Personality*, Norwood, NJ, Ablex. pp. 242–60.

SCHWARTZ, D. (1977) 'Pierre Bourdieu: The Cultural Transmission of Social Inequality', *Harvard Educational Review*, 47, pp. 545–55.

SCOTT, W.R. (1981) *Organizations: Rational, Natural, and Open System*, Englewood Cliffs, NJ, Prentice-Hall.

SEELEY, D.S. (1982) 'Education Through Partnership', *Educational Leadership*, 40, 2, pp. 42–7.

SEELEY, D.S. (1984) 'Educational Partnership and the Dilemmas of School Reform', *Phi Kappan Delta*, 65, 6, pp. 383–88.

SENNETT, R. and COBB, J. (1972) *The Hidden Injuries of Class*, New York, Basic Books.

SEWELL, W.H. and HAUSER, R.M. (1980) 'The Wisconsin Longitudinal Study of Social and Psychological Factors in Aspirations and Achievements', in KERCKHOFF, A.C. (Ed.) *Research in Sociology of Education and Socialization*, Vol. 1, Greenwich, CT, JAI Press, (pp. 59–100).

SEWELL, W.H. and SHAH, V.P. (1977) 'Socio-economic Status, Intelligence and the Attainment of Higher Education', in KARABEL, J. and HALSEY, A.H. *Power and Ideology in Education*, New York, Oxford University Press. pp. 197–214.

SHAVIT, Y. and FEATHERMAN, D.L. (1988) 'Schooling, Tracking, and Teenage Intelligence', *Sociology of Education*, 61, 1, pp. 42–51.

SHEPARD, L.A. (1986) 'School Readiness and Kindergarten Retention', Paper presented at the annual meeting of the American Educational Research Association, San Francisco.

SHORTER, E. (1977) *The Making of the Modern Family*, New York, Basic Books.

SIEBER, R.T. (1982) 'The Politics of Middle-Class Success in an Inner-City Public School', *Journal of Education*, 164, 1, pp. 30–47.

SILVERMAN, D. (1985) *Qualitative Methodology and Sociology*, Brookfield, VT, Gower Publishing.

SIMON, R.I. and DIPPO, D. (1986) 'On Critical Ethnographic Work,' *Anthropology and Education Quarterly*, 17, 4, pp. 195–202.

SLAUGHTER, D.T. (1977) 'Relation of Early Parent–Teacher 'Socialization Influences to Achievement Orientation and Self-Esteem in Middle Childhood Among Low Income Black Children', in GLIDEWELL, J.C. (Ed.) *The Social Context of Learning and Development*, New York, Gardner Press. pp. 101–31.

SMITH D. and GRIFFITH, A. (forthcoming) 'Coordinating the Uncoordinated: Mothers' Management of the School Day', *Perspectives on Social Problems*.

SOLTOW, L. and STEVENS, E. (1981) *The Rise of Literacy and the Common School in the United States: A Socio-economic Analysis to 1870*, Chicago, University of Chicago Press.

SPANIER, G., LEWIS, R. and COLE, C.L. (1975) 'Marital Adjustment Over the Family Life Cycle: The Issue of Curvilinearity', *Journal of Marriage and the Family*, 37, May, pp. 263–75.

STACK, C.B. (1975) *All Our Kin*, New York, Harper and Row.

STEIL, J.M. (1984) 'Marital Relationships and Marital Health: The Psychic Costs of Inequality', in FREEMAN, J. (Ed.) *Women: A Feminist Perspective*, Palo Alto, CA, Mayfield, pp. 113–23.

STEIN, P.J. (1984) 'Men in Families', in HESS, B. and SUSSMAN, M. (Eds) *Women and the Family: Two Decades of Change*, New York, Haworth Press, pp. 143–62.

STEINITZ, V.A. and SOLOMON, E.R. (1986) *Starting Out: Class and Community in the Lives of Working-Class Youth*, Philadelphia, Temple University Press.

STEVENSON, D.L. and BAKER, D.P. (1987) 'The Family–School Relation and the Child's School Performance', *Child Development*, 58, pp. 1348–57.

STONE, L. (1977) *The Family, Sex and Marriage in England 1500–1800*, New York, Harper and Row.

STRODBECK, F.L. (1958), 'Family Interaction, Values and Achievement', in MCCLELLAND, D.D. (Ed.) *Talent and Society*, New York, Van Nosrand, pp. 135–212.

STRODBECK, F.L. (1965) 'The Hidden Curriculum of the Middle-Class Home', in KROMBOLTZ, J.D. (Ed.) *Learning and the Educational Process*, Chicago, Rand McNally, pp. 91–112.

SURANSKY, V. (1982) *The Erosion of Childhood*, Chicago, University of Chicago Press.

SWAP, S. MCALLISTER. (1987) *Enhancing Parent Involvement in Schools: A Manual for Parents and*

Teachers. New York, Teachers College Press.

SWIDLER, A. (1979) *Organizations Without Authority*, Cambridge, MA, Harvard University Press.

SWIDLER, A. (1986) 'Culture in Action: Symbols and Strategies', *American Sociological Review*, 51, 2, pp. 273–86.

TEACHMAN, J.D. (1987) 'Family Background, Educational Resources, and Educational Attainment', *American Sociological Review*, 52, pp. 548–57.

TRELEASE, J. (1982) *The Read-Aloud Handbook*, New York, Penguin.

TROEN, S.K. (1988) 'Popular Education in Nineteenth Century St Louis', in MCCLALLAN, B.E. and REESE, W.J. (Eds) *The Social History of American Education*, Urbana, IL, University of Illinois Press, pp. 119–36.

TURNER, R. (1960) 'Sponsored and Contest Mobility and the Social System', *American Sociological Review*, 25, pp. 855–67.

TYACK, D.B. (1974) *The One Best System*, Cambridge, MA, Harvard University Press.

UHLENBERG, P. (1978) 'Changing Configurations of the Life Course', in HAREVEN, T.K. (Ed.) *Transitions: The Family and the Life Course in Historical Perspective*, New York, Academic Press, pp. 65–98.

US Department of Education (1986) *What Works*, Washington DC, United States Department of Education.

US Department of Education (1988) *Youth Indicators 1988*, Washington DC, US Government Printing Office.

USEEM, M. and KARABEL, J. (1986) 'Pathways to Top Corporate Management', *American Sociological Review*, 51, pp. 184–200.

VALENTINE, C.A. (1968) *Culture and Poverty*, Chicago, University of Chicago Press.

VANEK, J. (1983) 'Household Work, Wage Work, and Sexual Equality', in SKOLNICK, A.S. and SKOLNICK, J.H. (Eds) *Family in Transition*, 4th ed. Boston, Little. pp. 176–89.

VAN GALEN, J. (1987) 'Maintaining Control: The Structuring of Parent Involvement', in NOBLIT, G. and PINK, W.T. (Eds) *Schooling in Social Context: Qualitative Studies*, Norwood, NJ, Ablex, pp. 78–90.

VAN MANNEN, J. (1988) *Tales of the Field: On Writing Ethnography*, Chicago, University of Chicago Press.

VANNEMAN, R. (1987) *The American Perception of Class*, Philadelphia, Temple University Press.

VENEZKY, R., KAESTLE, C. and SUM, A.M. (1987) *The Subtle Danger: Reflections on the Literacy Abilities of America's Young Adults*, Princeton, NJ, Educational Testing Service.

VERNBERG, E.M. and MEDWAY, F.J. (1981) 'Teacher and Parent Causal Perceptions of School Problems', *American Educational Research Journal*, 18, 1, pp. 29–37.

WALBERG, H.J. (1986) 'Home Environment and School Learning: Some quantitative Models and Research Synthesis', in GRIFFORE, R.J. and BOGER, R.P. (Eds) *Child Rearing in the Home and School*, New York, Plenum, pp. 105–20.

WALFORD, G. (Ed.) (1987) *Doing Sociology of Education*, Philadelphia, Lewes, Falmer Press.

WALKER, J.C. (1985) 'Rebels with Our Applause? A Critique of Resistance Theory in Paul Willis's Ethnography of Education', *Journal of Education*, 167, 2, pp. 63–83.

WALLER, W. (1932) *The Sociology of Teaching*, New York, John Wiley and Sons, Inc.

WALLERSTEIN, J.S. and KELLY, J.B. (1980) 'Effects of Divorce on the Visiting Father–Child Relationship', *American Journal of Psychiatry*, 137, 12, pp. 1534–39.

WALSH, D. (1988) 'The Two Year Route to First Grade', Paper presented at the annual meetings of the American Educational Research Association, New Orleans.

WEXLER, P. (1982) 'Structure, Text, and Subject: A Critical Sociology of School Knowledge', in APPLE, M.W. (Ed.) *Cultural and Economic Reproduction in Education*, Boston, Routledge and Kegan Paul, pp. 275–303.

WHYTE, W.F. (1981) *Street Corner Society*, 3rd ed. Chicago, University of Chicago Press.

WILCOX, K.A. (1978) 'Schooling and Socialization for Work Roles', Unpublished Doctoral Dissertation, Department of Anthropology, Harvard University.

WILCOX, K.A. (1982) 'Differential Socialization in the Classroom: Implication for Equal Opportunity', in SPINDLER, G. (Ed.) *Doing the Ethnography of Schooling*, New York, Holt, Rinehart and Winston, pp. 269–309.

WILEY, N. (1988) 'The Micro-Macro Problem in Social Theory', *Sociological Theory*, 6, Fall, pp. 254–61.

WILLIS, P.E. (1977) *Learning to Labour*, Westmead, Saxon House.

WOODS, P. (1986) *Inside Schools: Ethnography in Educational Research*. New York Routledge and Kegan Paul.

WRIGHT, E.O. (1976) 'Class Boundaries in Advanced Capitalist Societies', *New Left Review*, 98, pp. 3–41.

WRIGHT, J.D. and WRIGHT, S.R. (1976) 'Social Class and Parent Values for Children: A Partial Replication and Extension of the Kohn Thesis', *American Sociological Review*, 41, pp. 527–37.

WRIGLEY, J. (1989) 'Do Young Children Need Intellectual Stimulation? Experts' Advice to Parents, 1900–1985', *History of Education Quarterly*, 29, pp. 41–75.

YOUNG, M. and WILLMOTT, P. (1957) *Family and Kinship in East London*, Baltimore, MD, Penguin.

YOUNG, M.F. (1971) 'An Approach to the Study of Curricula as Socially Organized Knowledge', in YOUNG M. (Ed.) *Knowledge and Control*, London, Collier Macmillan, pp. 19–46.

ZELIZER, V. (1985) *Pricing the Priceless Child*. New York, Basic Books.

Index